BECOMING NATURE

"Do you often feel rushed and far removed from feeling the peace of delighting in the natural world around you? Tamarack Song gives a way to return to heightened sensory awareness and fulfilling kinship with wildlife. Enriched by his background in environmental education, wilderness survival, and wildlife conservation, the author guides readers with a variety of exercises to an active experience with Nature around and within us. Here are practical steps you can take to better know Nature and yourself."

PENELOPE SMITH, AUTHOR OF
ANIMAL TALK AND *WHEN ANIMALS SPEAK*

"Tamarack Song teaches how Becoming Nature is our natural and innate state of being. *Becoming Nature* is beautifully written and filled with practices to help us reconnect with the natural world. This is an important and powerful book to help us improve our personal health as well as bring back balance and harmony to the planet and all in the web of life."

SANDRA INGERMAN, COAUTHOR OF
SPEAKING WITH NATURE AND
AUTHOR OF *WALKING IN LIGHT:*
THE EVERYDAY EMPOWERMENT OF A SHAMANIC LIFE

ALSO BY TAMARACK SONG

Journey to the Ancestral Self
The Native Lifeway Guide for Living in Harmony
with the Earth Mother

Whispers of the Ancients
Native Tales for Teaching and Healing in Our Time

Song of Trusting the Heart
A Classic Zen Poem for Daily Meditation

Entering the Mind of the Tracker
Native Practices for Developing Intuitive Consciousness
and Discovering Hidden Nature

Tamarack Song contributed the introduction and one chapter to
Forgiveness and Child Abuse, by Lois Einhorn, Ph.D.

BECOMING NATURE

Learning the Language of Wild Animals and Plants

TAMARACK SONG

Bear & Company
Rochester, Vermont • Toronto, Canada

Bear & Company
One Park Street
Rochester, Vermont 05767
www.BearandCompanyBooks.com

Text stock is SFI certified

Bear & Company is a division of Inner Traditions International

Library of Congress Cataloging-in-Publication Data
Names: Song, Tamarack, 1948- , author.
Title: Becoming nature : learning the language of wild animals and plants / Tamarack Song.
Description: Rochester, Vermont : Bear & Company, 2016. | Includes bibliographical references and index.
Identifiers: LCCN 2015043285| ISBN 9781591432111 (pbk.) | ISBN 9781591432128 (e-book)
Subjects: LCSH: Human-animal communication. | Human ecology. | Nature study.
Classification: LCC QL776 .S66 2016 | DDC 577.27—dc23
LC record available at http://lccn.loc.gov/2015043285

Printed and bound in the United States by Lake Book Manufacturing, Inc.
The text stock is SFI certified. The Sustainable Forestry Initiative® program promotes sustainable forest management.

10 9 8 7 6 5 4 3 2 1

Text design by Debbie Glogover and layout by Virginia Scott Bowman

This book was typeset in Garamond Premier Pro with Legacy Sans used as the display typeface

Chapter opening artwork by Jennine Elberth
Instructional illustrations by Kristine Scheiner

To send correspondence to the author of this book, mail a first-class letter to the author c/o Inner Traditions • Bear & Company, One Park Street, Rochester, VT 05767, and we will forward the communication, or visit the author's websites at **www.tamaracksong .org**, **www.teachingdrum.org**, and **www.brotherwolffoundation.org.**

Contents

■ ■ ■

I have grown taller from standing with Trees.*
I have grown smaller from crawling with Snails.
I have grown lighter from soaring with Birds.
And along the way I have grown the wiser
by forgetting all that I thought I knew
and becoming my teachers from forest and pond.

They taught me to speak their wordless tongue
to move like a shadow and think like a lake
to dance to the drum of the wild within.
So now and then when I go back to town
I forget that I need to speak words again.
For out in the woods it's a trill or a twitch
and I feel their feelings and dream their dreams
while at the same time they come to know mine.

So I shed my fur and grab a pen
to tell what it's like to rise with the sun,
to swim with a Turtle and touch a Deer.
For these are the gifts I've come to know
when the teasing wind wakens my soul
to enter the wild and see through their eyes.

TAMARACK SONG[†]

---

*Out of respect for my relationship with animals and plants who have been my family and guides, I have capitalized their names in the text, and I refer to them as *he* and *she* rather than *it*.

[†]Written by the author and first appearing in the preface to Joseph Cornell's *The Sky and Earth Touched Me* (Crystal Clarity, 2014).

All author proceeds from the sale of this book go to support the creation of the Brother Wolf Foundation, a nonprofit sanctuary for Timber Wolves rescued from puppy mills and backyard cages. The sanctuary is being founded to foster a renewed, respectful, and mutually beneficial relationship between Humans and apex predators. Through Wolf's inspiration and example we can relearn animal language so that we can truly come to know them, rather than just knowing *about* them. For more information, go to **www.brotherwolffoundation.org.**

In Honor of My Teachers

Having grown up in an era when Nature field guides and outdoor skills classes were practically unknown, I didn't discover until well into my adulthood that it was possible to learn about Nature by instruction and study. I had assumed that one learned directly from the animals and plants, which I did. Along with those teachings I received guidance from my mother, a woodswoman all her life, and from Native American Elders.

Back around 1980, I attended a primitive-living skills class. I was in my early thirties and excited to finally meet other like-minded people. Prior to that my closest nature-loving companions were the Wolves with whom I lived. That was okay with me, as we were family—they knew me better than did any Human. In addition, the Elders would encourage my relationship with the animals by regularly sending me directly to them with my questions about Nature.

The class, with its diagrams, measurements, and unfamiliar technical terms, confused me at first. Then I remembered the Elders speaking in their ever-gentle way about Nature's way and the new way. Their words are echoed in this childhood memory of New Mexico Acoma Pueblo Elder James Paytiamo. His Elders would say:

Listen! Listen! The gray-eyed people are coming . . . nearer every day. [They] . . . are going to get you to drink hot, black water. . . . Then your teeth will become soft . . . your eyes will run tears on windy days, and your eyesight will be poor. Your joints will crack when you want to move slowly and softly. You will sleep on soft beds and will not like to rise early. When you begin to wear heavy clothes and sleep under heavy covers, then you will grow lazy. Then there will be no more singing heard in the valleys as you walk.[1]

I knew the singing; some of my Elders called it "the song of the track." I would listen to it along with the Wolves of the pack I lived with while we lay in the Grass or silently wove through the woods. Oglala Lakota Elder Standing Bear talked about how his people heard the song when he grew up in the 1800s.

> Kinship with all creatures of the earth, sky, and water was a real and active principle. For the animal and bird world there existed a brotherly feeling that kept the Lakota safe among them. And so close did some of the Lakotas come to their feathered and furred friends that in true brotherhood they spoke a common tongue.[2]

At the same time, I understood why the song had become so hard to hear, as I was one of those raised to have poor eyesight and wear heavy clothes. Yet, no matter what our background, I believe we all feel the ancestral yearning from deep within to join in the song of the track. Whether we learn from animals and Native Americans or from books and instructors, all of the lessons go back to the time when we would sit around the evening hearth and listen to stories of the hunt and the insights of Elders. We learned from the animals as well—we understood what they said.

May all that I share on the coming pages be an honoring of those who gave this knowledge to me. I wish to especially honor my Ancestors, who gave me the memories that made the song of the track my nature.

To Know Nature Is to Become Nature

If you were to come across me out in the woods, you might think you were seeing a Human form. Yet, with my grizzled fur and amber eyes, I would be drifting silent as a shadow over the mossy carpet. I'd see shapes and shadows as my pack mates see them, and I'd respond to every sound and smell as did my pack mates. My hungers and curiosities would be the same as theirs; like them, I would be in constant communication with all the life around me.

If you were to call out to me, your words might not register at first, as I'd be in my Animal Mind. It's a consciousness without pretense or filter. Every thought and movement has its purpose—and its cost. To survive, one must be continually aware of his surroundings and attuned to intent. It is the only way to move invisibly and understand the wordless language of animals. It's the only way to know their fears and desires, to know where they are coming from and where they are going.

Sometimes when I melt into the woods I Become a Deer. At other times I Become a Bird or a Frog. All the time I Become Nature; for if I don't, I remain only an observer. An outsider.

A DIFFERENT APPROACH
TO CONNECTING
WITH NATURE

This book has the power to strip away everything that separates us from Nature and show us how to know the soul of an animal. Our jaunts will no longer be a spectator sport; we will *Become* Nature. No longer will we have to settle for catching the occasional glimpses of animals, bringing them closer with binoculars or capturing them on camera. We'll be able to look into their eyes as we connect with them face-to-face. We'll crawl into their skins and feel what it's like to live their lives.

By following the exercises outlined in the 12 steps, we'll be able to learn the ways of an animal's mind and the skills of animal communication that are found in the stories of my previous book *Entering the Mind of the Tracker.* Through these exercises and the resulting changes in our perspectives, we'll learn to Become invisible and move as silently as a shadow. Unlike classes or field guides, we are going to learn as Natives do: through story and direct experience. We will awaken our intuitive abilities, the same ones that our hunter-gatherer Ancestors relied upon for their sustenance and safety. You'll have the opportunity to learn what the Native Americans taught me—a complete communication system that is largely unknown to modern Humans.

We know Nature for her beauty and mystery and as a place to go for solace and inspiration, yet do we know her as ourselves? We came from Nature, and to Nature we shall return when we die; yet something happened between those two events: we left Nature and pursued lives that often ran in contradiction to her. This book is for those of us who don't want to wait until death to return. We want to drink in the essence of life; we want to feel in our marrow what it's like to be at-one with everything. We want to be participants in the drama rather than observers in the bleachers.

Here we will discover that there is nothing magical or clairvoyant about being able to understand what animals say. We will find that touching an animal is just as possible—and maybe as amazing—as reaching out to touch our lover. Each of us is a child of Nature, the same as any Native, with the same intrinsic skills and abilities, and we are every bit as capable of Becoming Nature as they are.

RELEARNING THE OLD WAY

To know Nature, observation and study are not enough. We might be able to score well on a test, or even successfully track an animal, yet that is only a beginning. In a 2012 study biological physicist Gabor Horvath and his colleagues at Eotvos University in Hungary analyzed a thousand pieces of prehistoric and modern artwork to see who most accurately portrayed animal gaits. Most of the time anatomy textbooks and modern artists depicted animals executing impossible gaits. Even Leonardo da Vinci, renowned for his anatomical sketches, got it wrong. Taxidermists fared better, but not as well as the hunter-gatherers of the Upper Paleolithic (10,000 to 50,000 years ago), whose cave art showed accurate gaits most of the time.[1]

Why the difference? I believe it is because when we approach Nature through study and research we become technical naturalists. Rather than our intrinsic way of connecting from the heart and using our intuitive sense, we rely on technology and intellect. In other words, we are out of touch.

Albert Einstein said, "Imagination is more important than knowledge. For knowledge is limited to all we now know and understand, while imagination embraces the entire world."[2] This is just as true for the naturalist as for the physicist, as imagining is a vital skill that we will be using to Become Nature—which includes *our* nature.

When we are children we develop our imagination by playing pretend games so that we can imagine effectively as adults. The skill of imagining, which we will meet in this book as *Becoming,* is fortunately innate. Our Ancestors used it to track animals, to find their way across unfamiliar terrain, and for many other purposes. By Becoming the animal they hunted, they entered her mind, thus discovering where they could find her.

When we Become an animal we get to know her intrinsically, and in so doing we get to know ourselves. Whether we go on to touch that animal is secondary, even though it is entirely possible. By Becoming an animal we get to know her in an intimate way. You might say we develop a loving relationship with her. This experience could well transform our lives, and that is the ultimate reason I am sharing the ways of relationship found in this book.

TO KNOW NATURE IS TO KNOW YOURSELF

We have abilities that go far beyond mere intelligence. They begin to manifest when we allow ourselves to be the animals we are. The reason we find it so hard to use our primal aptitudes, such as moving quiet as a shadow, finding hidden animals, and speaking their language, is that we have not exercised these aptitudes for so long that they have atrophied. The truth is that our nature *is* Nature: every cell and organ in our bodies has been honed over millennia to function best in the Natural Realm. Genetic memories are imprinted in our DNA—we know how to move and see and speak like a Native in the same way that a Robin knows how to build a nest and a Wolf knows how to howl.

Some people tell me that what affects them most deeply in the process of Becoming Nature is that for the first time they come to know themselves. They say they no longer feel separated from Nature: they feel true kinship with Grouse, Deer, and Rabbit. When we can feel the yearning of a vixen Fox in heat or the fear of a Red Squirrel being chased by a Pine Marten, we will have left our self-image and beliefs behind—we will have Become Nature. We will have reconnected with our own core fears and yearnings, thus becoming our *own* nature.

When we are brother and sister to the Birds and Trees, we see how easy it is to treat them with kindness and respect, just as we do with our Human family. As we take care of our Human family's home, we will want to take care of forest kin's home. We will naturally evolve a sustainable lifestyle, consuming and polluting less as we relearn how to live in harmony with all of life.

Each exercise put forth in the following 12 steps is important to practice regularly. We will not automatically transform ourselves by walking under towering Pines with Eagles soaring overhead. The hard reality is that we take our habits and beliefs with us wherever we go, and the only way to change them and awaken our senses is to do the work. The more we dedicate ourselves to our awakening, the more spontaneously we integrate with Nature and start finding enchantment everywhere.

It's like riding a bicycle. Do you remember when you wobbled all over the place and fell time and again when you were first learning to ride? The more you practiced, the better you were able to use your innate sense of balance. Now no matter where you are or what is going on in your life, you can hop on your bike and take off without even thinking about it. That is where we want to be with the skills we will be reawakening in the coming pages. Our nature will again become second nature to us, and we'll begin to hear the voices of the wild without even trying.

TRANSFORMATION
THROUGH THE ANIMAL MIND

In step 12, I share a couple of stories where I forego the opportunity to touch the animal. Once we have regained the ability to speak Nature's language and Become animals, touching them will likely lose its appeal. When we are in a close and trusting relationship with someone we don't need to reach out and touch her to prove it.

Furthermore, I refrain from touching animals out of respect for them, as I don't want to inflate my ego or make a game out of my relationship with them. Touching would keep me in my rational mind, which would interfere with my ability to enter what my Native Elders call "the Silence." In Zen it would be known as "the Gateless Gate" or "No-Mind." I also know it as the "Animal Mind." In our Animal Minds we feel automatically centered. We can think without thoughts and act without getting caught up in *shoulds, woulds,* and *coulds,* both of which are foundational to Becoming Nature.

When we find our Animal Minds we will discover something so earthshaking that it turns lives upside down: life is a verb. Things become experiences; past, present, and future merge into one continuum, and animals Become their relationships to their surroundings, their kin, and us.

This may not sound so remarkable right now, yet when we have relearned animal language and can again comfortably function in our Animal Mind, the people we know will change. In place of the images we have of them, we will begin to see them as organs in an organism, enmeshed in a Web of relationship. Their identities will meld with the identities of others as they transform from nouns to verbs.

My fondest wish for you is that this journey of rediscovery will transform your life. I've watched people who have struggled with chronic depression and danced with suicide find a reason to reengage and live—a reason that goes beyond words, beyond logic. They describe it as a feeling of radiance, and others can feel the vibrant life energy they project. I see many of them rededicate their lives to serving what really matters—Nature's way.

In essence, this book is a rebirthing experience, a return to our original instructions. It describes the way we are designed to function in relationship with the rest of life. Think of this book as our midwife, assisting us as we emerge from the birth canal and open our eyes to a new world.

Jennine Elberth

STEP 1

Remember Nature Speak, the First Language

Every plant and animal is speaking all the time. They are talking to you, and me, and all we have to do is listen. It's that simple, yet it's not that easy, and I will explain why shortly. First, let's get acquainted with animal language. It goes by many names: *mental telepathy, psychic ability, intuition, extrasensory perception, gut feeling, first impressions, nonverbal communication, animal talk, the primal language, interspecies communication.* Each term describes an aspect of animal language, yet not one of them fully captures what it is. I prefer *Nature Speak,* which refers to what it is, rather than trying to explain it.

Nature Speak is the First Language—it is the mother tongue of all life and the foundation of interspecies communication. It is the root from which our spoken and written languages grew. Yet even more than a way to speak and listen, it is the operating system for our minds and the basic lens through which we perceive our world.

Our ability to communicate in Nature Speak is inherent to being Human. Nature Speak, one of a bundle of core operating skills that includes orienteering, tracking, and Envisioning, is imprinted in our DNA, and our brain is wired for it.

Some people see the ability to talk with animals as women's intuition. Even though many well-known animal communicators are female, my experience shows that gender is not a relevant factor. Children of both genders prove to be equally adept, and the same is true with adults. The apparent gender difference arises from the cultural pressure on men, more than women, to be rational-mind centered (see step 3), so the proclivity for Nature Speak has atrophied more in men than in women. Yet before we get into that, let's get to know our First Language.

The Primary Characteristics of Nature Speak

- **Instantaneous:** Little or no transmission or comprehension time is required.
- **Understandable:** It does not require translating.
- **Universal:** Not only Birds and mammals use it but also Butterflies, Trees, and lakes.
- **Intuitive:** It does not have to make rational sense—and it often doesn't.
- **Simultaneous:** There is spontaneous two-way communication.
- **Communal:** All beings in the area automatically participate.
- **Innate:** There is no need to learn it or train for it.

All that considered, we can still set the stage for Nature Speak by entering our Animal Minds, sharpening our senses, and moving like a shadow; all of which we will achieve in upcoming steps. Here we'll get a visceral feel for Nature Speak by looking at what lies beneath the above-listed characteristics.

THE PERSONALITY OF NATURE SPEAK

1. It's Unexplainable

When someone first tunes in to Nature Speak she might say something like, "I don't know where that came from; I just know what it means." She is clear and resolute, yet when asked to explain why, she has nothing to offer. This is because with Nature Speak the mind functions in a realm that goes beyond rationale.

2. There Are No Words

To say Nature Speak comes from a different world is not an exaggeration, as the language used is not word based but rather comprised of ancient memories, impulses, and imaginings (as explained in step 3).

3. We Use It All the Time

It lies at the base of all communication, conscious and unconscious. Here we will learn how to use Nature Speak intentionally and effectively, as our typical approach to animal communication is to tell animals what to do rather than having a conversation with them. Thus, most of us have no idea what is possible in speaking with animals, much less how to engage in the conversation.

4. There Is No Magic Involved

We don't have to be leprechauns, psychics, or one of the last wild Aborigines to speak with animals. Once we get reconnected with our Animal Mind we'll see that communicating nonverbally with a Squirrel or a Crow is as normal as talking with a friend.

5. There Is No Species Barrier

Elephants talk to Lions, Ravens chat with Eagles, and we can speak with Trees, Snakes, or whoever else is around. Yes, I said Trees. In the Natural Realm, a mountain's memories are no less valid than those etched into the folds of our brains.

6. It Taps In to Universal Wisdom

Hollywood animal handler J. Allen Boone describes how his Native American friends would use Nature Speak.

> Their favorite method of acquiring fresh wisdom . . . especially immediately needed information, was not to seek it vocally from some other Indian, or even from printed words . . . each individually [would] . . . *listen for the good counsel from the silence as it gently speaks to each of us in the infinite language of all life.* This language is eloquent in its boundless expression and helpful in the

fresh and needed facts that are always supplied. It is a language that was never difficult for my Indian friends and me to hear and understand, providing that we were "of one mind" and listening "as one mind."[1]

7. It Is Nature Reclaiming Us

When we start speaking the First Language, it will feel like a homecoming, as though Nature is reaching out to connect with us, her long-lost children.

8. It Speaks to the Deepest Part of Us

When you first picked up this book, I bet you thought you'd be learning how to connect better with Nature. It's much more than that. Your inner sanctum—the deepest aspect of what makes you, you—is going to merge with the soul of Nature. For many of you this could be an awakening, an act of communion with the cosmos.

WHY WE NO LONGER TALK WITH ANIMALS

If Nature Speak comes naturally to us, along with it being our primary form of communication, why don't we use it regularly?

How We Lost Touch with Nature Speak

- **We redefined ourselves as a rational species** early on in the civilized era. Other than body language, our ability to communicate nonverbally has lain largely dormant since.
- **Our perceptive abilities have atrophied,** and they are needed for Nature Speak.
- **Children keep reenacting our abandonment of Nature Speak.** It begins early—sometimes by age three—and it is usually concluded around the time they turn six. A fundamental part of early childhood development is the domestication process, which consists of connecting children with reality—that is, reality according to the rational mind. Through positive and negative reinforcement children learn what to see/not see and what to say/not say.

When they are not taken seriously, they eventually quit listening to the family pet and the Birds outside.

- **Regimentation and linear learning finish the job** if it is not completed by the time children start school. What's left of their conscious connection with the natural world and its language diminishes to the point that only faint memories remain, which surface for fleeting moments in fairy tales and dreams. Nature's way has been largely replaced with a world where nearly everything has to be quantifiable and defined with words.

That hardly means, though, that our Nature-communication skills are nonfunctional. Even when they go unrecognized we continue to rely on them to some degree. Whether or not we give nonverbal cues credence we regularly pick up on them. We gauge a person's emotional state before she ever speaks a word, and we decide how to best broach a topic by impressions from facial expression, demeanor, posture, movement, and dress. Sometimes our cues are not directly related to sensory perception, such as when we feel that we are being watched or when we have a hunch about something.

Free-living animals, on the other hand, are always aware of nonverbal cues. They have to be, as at any moment their very survival could be at stake. It's not only about an individual's welfare, because the whole herd relies on each animal's sensory acuity. Something as basic as where an animal gets his next meal is based on his ability to tune in to Nature Speak. For these reasons we will be turning to the experts—wild animals—to teach us the lost skills that will allow Nature to reclaim us.

Let us remember that we are all born wild. Those of us who spend time around young children know that they talk with animals and communicate with entities that are invisible to us. If we had been left to our own devices in a natural environment, we would have grown up as hunter-gatherers and would naturally be speaking with plants and animals. We'd be able to see and hear things that we can now only imagine.

With the techniques outlined in this book we can soon be seeing, hearing, and speaking these things again.

HOW NATURE SPEAK WORKS

First: It's like a movie in which we play all the roles.
Some people describe communicating with animals as an exchange of mental pictures. This is true to a degree; however, we think of a picture as a static image, and Nature Speak more resembles a movie that we view through each character's eyes rather than from outside (see the section on Envisioning in step 11, starting on p. 232). [x-ref]

Second: What we perceive runs through the animal's mind.
If I believed that Deer were less evolved and intelligent than me, it would color my perception of a Deer's thoughts and actions. However, in Nature Speak my attitudes fade away, and I come to know the Deer and her life through her mind.

Third: We experience the animal as an integral part of ourselves.
The Wolf experiences the Deer as a functioning part of herself, in much the same way that I am connected to my arm. It's a deeply organic relationship that I can barely dance words around. My description of the feelings, impressions, and gut connections that constitute animal communication would give you such a woefully inadequate feel for it that it would be like me expecting you to know the depths of a stranger's heart by handing you one of his socks.

Fourth: It gives meaning to everything.
Yet the depths of that stranger's heart are not that far away. Even though I'm now using verbal language, you would only hear incoherent noise if it were not for the underpinning of Nature Speak. A word is nothing in and of itself: it's just a symbol for a memory or a feeling that we must connect with for the word to make sense. I can say *gwumpki,* and if you haven't had a meal of traditional Polish cabbage rolls you might not have a clue as to what the term means. Still, you would probably pick up nonverbally some of what I wanted to communicate, thanks to Nature Speak.

WHERE WE GET STUCK

One reason we get mired in word-based communication is that we have learned to equate communication with words. There is nothing intrinsically Human about word-based communication—it is a learned skill, which we acquire in the same way that a Dog learns to sit or shake hands. Behind every word is a learned association that gives it meaning. *Even though it appears that people are communicating consciously via words, the actual communication process is occurring nonverbally, via Nature Speak.*

Think of word-based language as symbols collected and organized in a certain fashion. Actual communication occurs only if the symbols connect with an impulse, memory, or feeling—something that takes us into the realm of nonverbal communication.

The Two Major Drawbacks to Word-based Communication

1. **It is inefficient and imprecise.** The inaccuracy occurs during the translation from the word to what it symbolizes. If I say "fly" you immediately go through a process of association to figure out what I mean. "Is he referring to the Insect?" you wonder, "or is he going to fly somewhere, or is he telling me to go fly a kite?"

   I have to attach a number of qualifiers to *fly* in order to steer you toward what I am attempting to express, and you will then have to go through the same associative process with each of those qualifiers as you did with *fly*.

   If instead I looked up and you knew I watched Birds, you'd know exactly what grabbed my attention without either of us having to say or associate anything. It is this impreciseness of verbal language that keeps us in our rational minds, continually chattering away in an effort to connect.

2. **Whenever we talk, we are not listening,** at least not very efficiently. Not only are we creating something that has to be heard over, but our minds are preoccupied with selecting, arranging, and associating words, which keeps us from being fully present to listen.

With Nature Speak it is impossible to *just* talk to animals, and it is impossible to *just* listen to what they say. *Nature Speak is spontaneous, with listening and speaking occurring simultaneously and indistinguishably from each other.* We are so accustomed to the back-and-forth of speak/listen, listen/speak that we have work to do before we can begin to communicate effectively with the Natural Realm. In essence, we need to return to our lost childhoods: to that time of naïveté and spontaneity when we had undying curiosity and everything was fair game. We had no beliefs or prejudices, so we could not discriminate. Let us begin the journey back.

RELEARNING NATURE SPEAK

Remember that Nature Speak is not a language that has to be learned— all we need to do is to start listening. The process involves two phases, which we will explore in the next step.

Our Approach to Re-Attuning to Nature Speak

- **Awaken our innate abilities,** which we will do in steps 3 to 7.
- **Develop the following five awarenesses,** which we need to progress through, in order to keep from filtering out Nature Speak.

The most effective approach is to engage in these two phases concurrently. Bookmark pages 16–24 and come back periodically to review the five awarenesses while practicing the exercises in steps 3 to 7, as the combination of exercises and awarenesses is very helpful in restoring Nature Speak as our First Language.

Awareness One: Being Beats Thinking
Thinking Like a Fish

One day an Elder and his student were walking along a riverbank. The Elder commented, "Look at how the Fish swim around in the pond weeds, going wherever they please. What a pleasurable afternoon they are having!"

"How would you know?" said the student. "You are not a Fish."

*"And you are not me," replied the Elder, "so how can you tell me that
I do or don't know what Fish enjoy?"*

*"That is true," mused the student. "I could not know what you know.
Yet does that not apply to you as well? For you are definitely not a Fish."*

*"That is a riddle of the mind," said the Elder, "and feelings are a
matter of the heart. Let's go back to your question, which is how I would
know what gives Fish pleasure. You already know the answer—and you
know that I know it—only you can't find it because you are looking in your
mind. We know what gives Fish pleasure this afternoon because we are
here, walking along the riverbank."*

The Benefits of Being versus Thinking

- **We set aside our preconceived notions and agendas.** The above
  story illustrates how Nature Speak is more about getting our conscious selves out of the way than literally talking with animals.
- **We become more dispassionate and empathetic** members of
  Nature's family. By getting our minds out of the way, we grow in
  kinship, as did the Elder.
- **We come to know ourselves and others** in ways that words can
  barely begin to convey, as seen through the story.
- **Being breeds contentment:** a state of not only accepting but
  also cherishing whatever the moment brings. We cease existing
  and begin living; we quit *thinking about* Nature and start *being*
  Nature.

I've found that the greatest enemies of *being* are reactive feelings
such as anger and envy. Let's take anger: When I look at someone with
fury in my heart, she can usually feel it, even if I try to disguise it. She'll
pick up on subtle cues, or she may perceive it intuitively or psychically.
Whatever the case, it is real, and as in the story above, it does not have
to be rationally understood or verbally expressed.

The same holds in the Natural Realm. If we harbor reactive feelings
or aggressive thoughts, the animals around us will pick up on them and
respond quickly.

Disappearing Turtles

I remember one sunny day when I was wading through the shallows of a lake catching Turtles by hand. I was relaxed and didn't have any expectations other than what was happening right then. For some reason I tabulated how many Turtles I had already caught, and then I figured how many more I could potentially catch. Making a game of it, I focused on the goal, and the Turtles largely disappeared. (To be clear, this wasn't typical hunting, in which projecting one's self through a weapon creates a unique dynamic. I was catching those Turtles by hand and making eye contact with most of them.)

I did the same thing many times over with fishing, trapping, catching Birds, and even Counting Coup on animals. It took awhile for me to realize that if I wasn't in Animal-Mind consciousness, I wasn't going to enjoy any kind of meaningful relationship with wild animals.

Awareness Two: Fear Isolates

Fear is the greatest impediment to speaking with animals. It can be fear of anything: failure, the dark, and even the animals themselves. When we hang on to fear we create a fear-based world that is disconnected from the realm in which the animals live. From our illusory world we then try to bridge the gap, and we inevitably fail.

The reason is that fear constricts, and Nature is a realm of expansiveness. Animals are ever alert, and at the same time they remain relaxed. Staying calm and centered is the best strategy animals can take to be ready for anything. When we are possessed by fear, our state of being is quite the opposite of theirs.

How Fear Isolates Us

- **We become mistrustful and edgy,** which is caused by adrenaline coursing through our veins.
- **We tense up,** and our eyes dart around, trying to find the cause of our fear.
- **We lose perspective.** Our fight-or-flight response has been triggered, and nothing matters other than keeping safe.
- **We become deaf to the subtleties of Nature Speak** from losing our capacity for openness and empathy.

At the same time, I want to state that fear does not have to exile us from the world of Nature. When we embrace our fear it ceases to be our nemesis and instead becomes our guide. Fear is nothing more than a lack of knowing: We fear the night because we do not know what lurks in the shadows or who is making those strange noises. Once we realize that the ghostly voice is just an Owl calling, and that the footsteps behind us are only Mice shuffling in the leaves, our fear subsides, and we're able to open to the experience of the night. Now fear can help protect us by keeping us safe while we venture forth to satisfy our curiosities.

Awareness Three: Nature Is Family

When we immerse ourselves in Nature on Nature's terms we enter into relationship with the animals and plants. This is a true cause-and-effect relationship, as we have become a functional part of Nature's family. What we do affects our family, and what our family does affects us, just as we experience with our Human family.

To Foster Family Ties

1. **Realize that whatever we think and feel affects the animals.** Personal responsibility for our actions is intrinsic to functional relationship, and this is especially true in Nature.
2. **Become humble and respectful.** When we hold animals in the same regard as our Human family members, they respond in kind. When we recognize that each and every plant and animal, each and every stream and mountain, has a unique and incomparable intelligence, we cross the spangled threshold into Nature's family.

And what an awesome family it is. I can't stand as tall as the eighty-foot White Pine I'm sitting under while writing this, I'll never see as well as the Eagle soaring overhead, and my reflexes aren't as acute as those of the perfectly synchronized trio of Fish swimming by in the pond before me.

Hybrid Prejudice

A big lesson in Nature-relationship responsibility came to me around forty-five years ago. I had a fondness for Wolves, and at the same time I harbored negative feelings toward Wolf-Dog and Wolf-Coyote hybrids. I wanted to connect only with Wolves—real Wolves—not mongrels.

Wouldn't you know that I ended up caretaking a Wolf-Coyote pup. I extended myself to her as well as my prejudice allowed. I knew her mixed parentage wasn't her fault, and I wanted her to have a free and fulfilling life. Still, she wouldn't have anything to do with me.

At her first opportunity, she escaped and disappeared. Several friends and I combed the surroundings, yet we couldn't find a trace of her. The shame of it was that I had just made arrangements to partner her with someone who appreciated her for who she was.

I felt guilty and responsible, even though I wasn't surprised at her leaving. I could read the mistrust in her eyes, right along with her conflicting yearning for companionship. She was bottle raised and accustomed to Humans, yet she would rather sulk alone in the back corner of her cage than give me the time of day.

Awareness Four: Comparisons Kill
Looking through Their Eyes

When first attempting to listen to Nature Speak, many of us struggle because we try to apply our sense of perspective and proportion to other animals. This morning I watched a Grasshopper chew through a blade of Grass. To me, the Grass was no big deal; it was just something to walk over before I sat down in a sunny spot to write. Yet to that Grasshopper it was both breakfast and a place to perch. This was brought to my attention— and to hers as well—when she took the final bite that severed the perch, causing her to descend quickly with it.

Earlier this morning I walked by a meadow that lay along the trail I took to gather Blueberries. To me the meadow was just one of several I passed. However, to the family of Ground Squirrels living there it was their entire world.

I then passed a pond where a Painted Turtle was sunning himself on a floating log. On a hot day I seek shade, while the Turtle (like most

Reptiles) finds a place to bake in the sun. Being cold-blooded, he needs the warmth to rev up his metabolism and help digest his food.

My intent here is not to compare for the sake of inherent worth but rather to show how important it is to keep away from any form of ranking.

 ## How to Avoid Comparisons

- **Take whatever we hear from the perspective of the speaker.** Otherwise we are likely to misinterpret it, if not render it entirely meaningless.
- **Be careful about discounting what doesn't fit our reality.** The creature speaking is a sentient being just like us, living on the same planet and having the same essential wants and needs. We are all born of the same mother, so we are bound to have some resonance.
- **Avoid making the animals' reality more special than ours.** It's understandable that one would be so tempted, as life in the farther places can appear unique and fascinating, especially when we first discover it.
- **Listen without preference or prejudice,** which is essential to clearly understanding what an animal is saying. If we remember that his life is of no more or less importance than anyone else's—it just is—we'll be able to join him in his world and hear his story without the spin our subjectivity puts on it.

Awareness Five: It's Their World

The expanded state of awareness where we Become part of Nature Speak is our natural state of being.

What It's Like to Be in the Nature Speak World

- **We become conscious of ourselves in real space and time,** rather than in some artificially based construct.
- **The world shrinks** to what we can connect with directly.
- **At the same time, the world expands** into everything that we

are indirectly connected to and that lies beyond our conscious grasp.

- **It's a realm of richness and substance,** of instant gratification and instant consequence.
- **We feel fulfilled and connected,** whether we are happy or sad, well-fed or hungry, relaxed or anxious.

Some of us believe that animals in the wild dwell in a peaceful state of being and that we need to enter that state in order to find resonance with them. I know people who strive to tune in to the same serene wavelength to which they imagine the animals are attuned. The trouble is that in the natural world peace doesn't exist—it is merely an ideal-based Human construct. A natural-living animal may be relaxed, as mentioned earlier, but he is never at peace. He can't afford to be, as he needs to be ever alert and ready to spring in to action.

"But look at how peaceful my Dog (Cat/Horse/Goat) is," some people will reply. Yes, many domestic animals dwell in what could be called a state of peace. A Horse needs to be broken to remain peaceful enough for another animal to climb upon her back. She has to be trained to remain peaceful around loud noises and sudden movements that would normally alert her to danger. She must learn to not rear up and kick when she feels restrained. I see that the "state of peace," which allows the rapport between our domesticated animal friends and us, is more a state of submission, which we share with them, because we too are domesticated. We can only experience a state of peace with animals on this side of the wall that separates us from Nature.

On the other side of the wall, natural-living creatures dwell in a state of dynamic tension, where there is neither peace nor war but simply a community of fully present, fully engaged plants and animals immersed in whatever the moment brings. It is this state that we want to enter.

When instead we go off looking for that wilderness Shangri-la where we believe all creatures live in harmony, Nature will spit us out and tell us to come back when we have regained some of the savvy with which we were born. As young children we were naturally attuned to shifting weather, changing seasons, eyes focused on our backs, and shadows that move against the wind. Nature Speak is heard when we tune in to that tension, and even more so when we Become one with it.

When we are immersed in Nature's dynamic, our thoughts and feelings are no longer just ours. Nor are the thoughts and feelings of the animals just theirs. Together we become synchronously functioning organs in a great organism, which my Native Elders refer to as the "Hoop of Life." Now much of what we think and feel is what the animals think and feel, and vice versa. It's like the heart pumping blood to the liver, which cleanses the blood on its way to the lungs to pick up oxygen for the other organs, and so on. All of the organs affect each other as they work for the whole. This is the type of relatedness we hear voiced in Nature Speak.

NATURE SPEAK AND DOMESTIC ANIMALS

When I was in college I had a Dalmatian Dog named Shane. As with nearly all Dogs, he was domesticated—he learned my family's way of life, along with the protocols of urban existence.

At the same time, he was a Wolf. He had all the traits of a Wolf, albeit diminished or magnified by selective breeding. Yet the manipulation of his traits didn't seem to matter when his innate Wolf surfaced, as we were then able to communicate in Nature Speak.

Most of the time, though, our intuitive connection was either short-circuited or suppressed by the conflicts and contradictions of our domestic overlays, which meant, "I have an urge to do this, yet I'm supposed to do that," or "I see and hear things that I would naturally respond to, yet I am conditioned not to."

The following comic strip does a great job of illustrating—with a tad of overstatement—Wolf (wild) consciousness and Dog (domestic) consciousness. Where a Wolf is centered in himself and intrinsically connected with Nature's rhythm, a Dog's centeredness and attunement is reflective of his master's.

By permission of John L. Hart FLP and Creators Syndicate, Inc.

We have to be careful about drawing the same parallel between hunter-gatherers and urbanized Humans as between Wolves and Dogs. Unlike Dogs, all Humans are still genetically hunter-gatherers. No one has bred us to be more suited to domestic life than wild life, and our species has not yet lived domestically long enough for natural selection to do the job. Stone Age and modern Humans, then, are genetically and functionally the same.

This means that communicating in Nature Speak will come more naturally between Humans and wild animals than between Humans and domestic animals.

WHAT TO EXPECT FROM NATURE SPEAK

Something we need to get used to right away with Nature Speak is that animals walk their talk—they say what they mean, and they do what they say. There is no need to read between the lines or wonder whether they are telling the truth. Nature is an arena of instant action and reaction, where first impressions mean everything. There is no time to mull something over and relate it to the past or to look for hidden meaning. An animal who dwells in the past quickly becomes a part of another animal's future.

It has to be that way, as those who are unable to get it right then and there cannot be allowed to pass the trait on to their offspring. Wild animals live so close to the means and ends of their existence that every thought, communication, and action counts. Imagine how difficult their lives would be if they were not able to trust in what they saw or heard.

The same is true for us regarding Nature Speak. So that we may be on the same communication wavelength as the animals and have the same sense of trust and immediacy, we'll learn the following, in the order given.

To Communicate in Nature Speak, We Must

1. **Understand instantly what is being said.**
2. **Take it at face value.**
3. **Act accordingly.**

I wouldn't blame anyone for being excited about talking with animals and wanting to run out in the woods right now and try it out—he'd hardly be the first. I need to give warning, though, that most of us will end up standing out there asking, "Where's the action—where are all the voices I'm supposed to be hearing?" It'll seem as though the animals are hiding from us, and we won't have the foggiest as to where to look for them. If we did happen to find one or two, they'd probably flee anyway.

It might be hard to believe right now, but once we're again a fully functional Nature Speaker (I say "again," because we were as young children) we will experience the opposite problem: We'll be inundated with voices from all directions telling us where the animals are and what they're up to. Rather than striving to hear one voice, we'll be struggling to isolate just one voice from the chorus.

What we learn about nonverbal communication in the Natural Realm applies to the Human world as well. We'll be able to hear what people are thinking and feeling, even though they're not outwardly expressing it. We will learn about matters that are not intended for us, which could include things we don't want to know about.

However, it will be different from in the past, when we overheard gossip or saw something in writing that wasn't intended for our eyes. An aspect of Nature Speak is being accepting of whatever comes. The better we get at Nature Speak, the more we will find ourselves able to empathize with another person without taking on their thoughts and feelings. We'll find it easier to remain respectful of another's point of view and not get defensive.

As our skill with Nature Speak progresses, our Human relationships will likely become more functional and fulfilling than in the past. Rather than trying to maneuver through relationships riddled with control, rescuing, or enabling issues, we'll be able to draw upon the deep understanding and empathy that is intrinsic to Nature Speak.

Nature's way is to learn by doing, and right away in the next step we are going to begin communicating in Nature Speak. Anthropologists tell us that a culture is embedded in its language, and the same is true of the Nature's culture. Through the gateway of Nature Speak we are going to reunite with our long-lost animal kin in a way that up until now most of us could only imagine.

Learn the Silent Language of Birds

I am a birdbrain. I grew up watching Red-winged Blackbirds nesting in the meadow behind my house and in the wetlands I romped. My friends and I would bike around the countryside seeking out old barns and feed mills that had resident Pigeons, whom we would catch and habituate to our backyard lofts. When I got a car, my canoe and I would head regularly for the North Country, where we would paddle and camp in the company of Loons on many a lake.

I have endless stories of my early adventures with Birds, and I still have a bad case of Birds on the brain. Keeping Rock Doves (commonly called Pigeons) for thirty years and living in the wilds with Birds for most of my life, I've had great opportunity to develop close relationships with many Birds. Along with that I've conducted avian research, holding a position on the team working to crack the mystery of Birds' homing ability at Cornell University's Lab of Ornithology, and then conducting flight dynamics research at the University of Wisconsin-Madison. I founded the Messenger Pigeon Project, for developing a reliable strain of Homing Pigeons to deliver messages and medical supplies in remote areas of the world. Along with having an extensive collection of wings, skins, and feathers, I offer workshops on Bird physiology, flight dynamics, and camouflage. I teach feather reading, where my students learn how a single feather can tell a Bird's life story.

Entering Susie's World

Birds evolved from a fascination to an obsession when I was eight years of age and visited Dave, a friend who lived on a farm. He held a small cardboard box before me with a nestling Rock Dove snuggled into the straw. Explaining that she fell out of her silo-top nest, my friend asked if I wanted her.

She became so tame from being hand raised that she would fly down to my shoulder, her favorite perch, and sometimes follow me when I went biking. I called her Susie, and in return she taught me how to sex Pigeons—she turned out to be a male. Whenever I hear Johnny Cash's song, "A Boy Named Sue" I can only smile.

Along with Susie and other wild Pigeons, I raised pedigreed flying and show breeds. By learning to speak their cooing language and read their silent vocabulary, I gained the ability to tell at a glance what they were thinking and feeling. It's been a few decades since I've lived with Pigeons, yet what I've learned from them about Nature Speak continues to enrich my relationship with all animals. When I can see, feel, and think the way other living beings do, I come to know their world, along with knowing them in ways that go beyond understanding. The intuitive feel I've gained for animals, thanks to Pigeons and other Birds, has helped me live comfortably with Wolves and successfully track Cougars.

Perhaps my greatest lesson from Birds was that in order to hear Wolf, Cougar, and other animals, I had to Become them and listen with my wild mind.

HOW BIRDS TEACH ABOUT THEMSELVES

I clearly remember the day that I Envisioned I was the Spruce Grouse I was watching, and I came to realize why he seemed so tame. But first, a little background information: We are fortunate to have two species of Grouse here in Lake Superior country, Spruce and Ruffed. The most common is Ruffed, whose prime habitat is mixed deciduous-coniferous forest. They are found throughout Appalachia, the northern tier of states, and up into northern Canada and Alaska. Spruce Grouse, who favor dense stands of Spruce and Tamarack, are creatures of the boreal forest. They are not very common where I live in northern Wisconsin, which is at the southern limit of their range. Contributing to their scarcity is the fact that they show little fear of Humans (which gives them their common name, Fool's Hen), so they need to be protected from hunting in order to survive.

As with many Far North animals, Spruce Grouse seem tame. When I Envisioned I was that Grouse, I didn't feel tame at all—I was employing a sit-tight strategy to help ensure my survival. Much of the North is sparse forest, open bog, and tundra, where a fleeing animal would be highly visible and have nowhere to hide. In habitats of that sort, freezing and hoping not to be seen is often the best survival strategy. The energy-sucking deep cold is another factor encouraging as little movement as possible to conserve calories.

In contrast to the Fool's Hen, Ruffed Grouse are known for their explosive escapes. She'll sit tight until you are just about to step on her, and then she'll take off in such a violent whir of wings that it makes your heart jump. By Envisioning that I was a Ruffed Grouse, I was able to see how sitting tight and trusting in my superb camouflage coloration made sense—why risk being pursued if I could bluff my way through?

In the thick, young forests where Ruffed Grouse like to make their homes, they typically take off and disappear from sight faster than you can catch your breath. So why sit tight and risk being discovered? If I hadn't Envisioned being that Grouse and felt what it was like to have a Goshawk tight on my tail, I might still not know the answer. Sitting snug and camouflaged-in clearly felt more secure—and upped my survival odds—over trying to outfly the feathered equivalent of a heat-seeking missile.

A BRIDGE TO NATURE SPEAK

As birdbrained as I might be, I am hardly alone—all you have to do is look in a mirror to find another one. We Humans (along with all Mammals and Reptiles) have a section of our brains that is the same as a Bird's. In the next step we'll learn how to access this special brain, which we need for Nature Speak.

But first, we need a bridge to take us from theory to practice with Nature Speak, and Birds are prime candidates. They are highly visible and can be found nearly everywhere, in any season, and they are like us in relying to a high degree on vocal communication.

Before we start, I would like to clear up a misconception that could stall our progress. It is commonly believed that song is a Bird's primary language. Ornithologists and laypeople alike typically study birdsongs to identify species and learn their behaviors. This practice can be both productive and personally rewarding, as most songs are clear and unmistakable. The downside is that Birds' vocalizations, like ours, are symbolic: they convey only an approximation of what is going on in their world.

Still, birdsong is an ideal doorway to Nature Speak, as it provides common ground between the Natural Realm and us. Birdsong will be our catalyst to discovering and learning Birds' other language—the precise, lyrically descriptive way they silently communicate between themselves and with other species. Their silent language is an aspect of Nature Speak.

The Two-Step Approach to Learning Birdsong

1. **Choose a Bird and learn his basic vocabulary.** At the same time we will observe the Bird, in order to pick up nonverbal cues, just like we read each other's body language and facial expressions.

2. **Wear earplugs, to help read the Bird's nonverbal language** without the aid of the verbal. Once we are weaned off our dependence on vocal cues—which keeps us locked in our rational brain—we will be able to relax into our Animal Mind and start hearing Nature Speak.

HOW BIRDS TEACH ABOUT OTHER ANIMALS

Robert Wolff, a friend of mine who has a special relationship with Birds, recently told me a story that shows how what we are learning here from Birds can apply to other animals as well. But first, let me introduce Robert: He is the author of *Original Wisdom* (Inner Traditions, 2001), which I encourage you to read for its lucid portrayal of an aboriginal people, the Senoi of Malaysia, who practice Nature Speak. Robert, who is now in his midnineties, grew up in Southeast Asia and the Pacific Islands, where he had the opportunity to live with a number of aboriginal peoples.

Robert told me that he came across his first Tiger in the wild at eight years of age. "I saw the Tiger," he said, "and the Tiger saw me, and the Tiger smiled." Robert likens his close relationship with Tiger to that between a Native American and his animal guide.

Robert has developed a deep understanding of Red Junglefowl (*Gallus gallus*), a wild gallinaceous Bird from Southeast Asia who is the progenitor of the domestic Chicken. Robert now lives in Hawaii, where descendants of the semi-domestic Junglefowl brought to the islands by Polysenian settlers have gone feral.

By reading their silent language, Robert has made some findings that contradict the conventional wisdom.

Busting Chicken Stereotypes

- **Roosters are aggressive.** The reputation comes mainly from staged cockfights. In their natural state, roosters are actually quite placid. When they come into contact with each other they typically butt chests. As with many animals (us included), roosters turn violent when they are forced together into tight spaces.
- **Hens are docile.** It turns out that hens are the fighters—they are very protective of their chicks.
- **Chicks are timid.** They are so protective of each other that even day-old chicks will jump toward a person or other perceived threat that gets too close to one of their siblings.
- **A rooster's crow is a territorial proclamation.** It's actually an "I'm here" announcement (which we'll discuss later in this step).

Robert told me about one rooster who would come up to the house and crow in an alcove, in order to amplify his "I'm here."

According to Robert, Tigers roar for the same reason that roosters crow, and a roar can be heard for up to two miles.

This discussion of Tigers and Junglefowl is relevant to Bird language—and to Nature Speak in general—because it illustrates how vitally important it is to listen with the ears of the animal (steps 6 and 11 show how). Our general tendency is to run what we hear through our assumptions translator, which often does nothing more than reinforce those often-erroneous conjectures.

FROM SYMBOLIC TO DIRECT COMMUNICATION

Whether we speak of Tigers or Junglefowl, it soon becomes apparent that all creatures speak the same language when we listen to what is being communicated beneath each one's distinct vocalizations. If a Dog raises his hackles, a Bull paws the ground, and someone shakes his fist in our face, we understand in no uncertain terms what they're saying—and that they're all saying the same thing—even though they are perfectly silent. In fact, we might have already felt the fist-shaker's "voice" before he raised his fist. That is direct communication.

However, if he were to convey my message verbally—that is, symbolically—we might not understand him if he were speaking German. We'd be even more confused if he suppressed his emotions because he was afraid of upsetting us. Even if he used English he might further confuse us by beating around the bush or speaking in platitudes.

How does that example relate to birdsong? There is a parallel between the direct and symbolic communication examples above and Birds' silent and spoken languages. Birds vary their vocalizations (and mimic other Birds) for many reasons, including competitiveness, dominance, fear, hunting strategy, and the time of day. Yet, like our words, their vocalizations need to be translated, and as is typical with translations, something will be lost.

Seeing, Not Hearing, Is Believing

To understand Bird language we don't necessarily need to hear Birds vocalize. They communicate very well through direct communication—so well, in fact, that a deaf person could better understand what a Bird is expressing visually than what a blind person could grasp from the Bird's accompanying vocalization. I can say "I love you," but if it's coming through gritted teeth, it could mean something entirely different.

When first hearing the deaf-blind person comparison, some people think it's pretty far-fetched. Yet it only takes a bit of practice to discover that it's true.

The Value of the Seeing Language

- **No interpretation is needed.** A Bird's body language, perching position, and even flight pattern, can be read loud and clear, the same as with that fist waved in our face.
- **We can tune in to it nearly any time,** whether or not the Bird is singing.
- **It alone conveys so much, and so precisely,** when we consider that the myriad head bobbings, feather rufflings, wing-tail displays, and other actions have clear meanings.
- **Much of the preciseness comes from the *way* it is executed,** just as the way I wave to a person conveys how well I know her and how glad I am to see her.
- **Gestures reveal aspects of character,** such as level of self-confidence and extrovertedness.
- **Some people don't have an ear for birdsong.** Distinguishing one Bird's characteristic call from another's can be nearly impossible for some, especially with closely related Warblers, Sparrows, Thrushes, or Vireos. Added to this confusion are variations of an individual's song, differences between the songs of two Birds of the same species, and songs that sound similar even though they come from unrelated species.

This discussion is not intended to diminish the value of knowing and understanding birdsong. Rather, it gives us another doorway to the world of Birds—one that takes us right into their minds and hearts. In addition, it gives us a ringside seat to the most intimate of their affairs. Let's keep in mind that our overriding goal for understanding direct communication is for it to help us join in Nature Speak.

How Birds Speak without Singing

Let's not forget the times that Birds are not calling. They use their audible language far less than their silent language, which they speak almost constantly. The wind and other sounds can drown out the sounds of Birds, and at other times we are too far away to hear them. Binoculars can help by bringing their images closer, but not their calls.

I've very much enjoyed the rare opportunities I've had to work with deaf people on birdsong. They've already learned silent communication skills and are not sound reliant, so they can usually pick up on a Bird's nonverbal language quite quickly.

"But what if the Birds are hiding or you just can't see them?" I am asked regularly. Here I find blind people fun to work with. Their highly sensitized hearing gives them a knack for deducing the nonverbal aspects of a birdsong from its verbal nuances.

It's important to know whether a Bird is deliberately lying low, as that can be just as expressive as his visible activities. The answer depends in large part on the species, as the males of some make a point of being conspicuous, while the males of others keep concealed. Yet with the skills you'll be learning in steps 7 and 9, you'll often be able to detect a Bird's discrete movements.

Keep in mind that Birds speak their silent language in unison with their vocal communication. When we know both their silent and vocal methods of communication, one can be used to confirm the other. Or when one is unclear or missing we have the other one to fall back on. I especially appreciate the deep sense of knowing that I gain from reading both languages.

Practical Applications for Birdsong

In addition to renewing our relationship with Nature, there are numerous practical applications for understanding animal communication, such as warning us about danger, improving tracking and hunting skills, and knowing other animals. Bird rescuers, animal control personnel, and researchers can be more effective when they understand the Birds they are working with. I've used my animal communication ability to help catch hundreds of Birds and other animals by hand, for banding and other purposes. In a survival situation, the skill could keep us from starving.

Raven's Gift

Whenever I move to a new location, one of the first things I do is check to see whose home I am moving in to. Once it was a family of Ravens, who kept in touch with each other with an ascending, gurgly, musical gaawaw. *I learned the call, yet when I practiced it on them, they told me bluntly that I was interfering with their ability to keep connected with each other.*

I agreed, realizing that my decision to practice it on them had come from my rational mind rather than my Animal Mind. Either I did it for my own edification or to show others what was possible with animal communication. In neither case was I coming from a place of empathy, so I quit calling to them unless I was directed to do so by my Animal Mind. Yet I continued to learn by listening, but in my Animal Mind, which I found greatly facilitated the process.

After living for ten years with that Raven family, I moved in with another family in the national forest about eighty miles to the west. Neither they nor the surrounding families used gaawaw *as their keep-connected call. Instead, they had a high-pitched, gravely sounding* waah.

What I Learned from Ravens

- **Individuals develop unique calls to distinguish themselves from their companions.** Members of many other species do the same. These calls are sometimes adopted by their comrades and passed on to succeeding generations.

- **View each Bird as an individual.** This was my big teaching, as it's so convenient to generalize.
- **Behaviors, diets, and hunting-foraging styles can vary among individuals,** along with calls.
- **Differences in calls, though sometimes extreme, were insignificant in effect.** Think of it as the difference in warmth between a blue coat and a green coat.
- **There is significantly less variation** in silent language than in verbal language.

The more I learned about Birds' silent language, the more I was drawn to pay attention to it. An unexpected bonus was that my rate of learning in all aspects of Bird biology increased dramatically.

HOW TO LEARN THEIR SILENT LANGUAGE

Even though our focus is on silent language, we will start with vocal language, as it is easiest to learn something new when we can relate it to something familiar. Virtually everyone, even those of us in crowded cities, recognizes the trilling of Robins, the cooing of Pigeons, and the chirping of Sparrows. Once we know a Bird's songs and their meanings we can move on to the correlating mannerisms. At that point, we will no longer need to rely on the songs alone to understand what the Bird is saying. We will then be ready to learn the Bird's silent language vocabulary that is not song related.

 ### The Five Steps to Learning a Bird's Silent Language

1. **Learn the songbook:** Memorize a Bird's repertoire of songs.
2. **Turn off the music:** Once you're able to identify a Bird's calls, wear earplugs while the Bird is calling to learn his accompanying behavior without hearing the call.
3. **Practice:** Drill yourself until you can name the behavior at a glance.
4. **Expand:** Learn the behaviors not related to song. Note perch loca-

tions and time spent on each perch, along with behavioral changes related to habitat and season.

5. **Predict:** Practice foretelling the Bird's calls and nonverbal cues.

This approach is similar to the way we learn a new human language: we start with commonly used phrases to build a basic vocabulary and understanding of grammar, then we gradually become conversational.

Our teachers will be the Rock Dove (*Columba livia*), Red-winged Blackbird (*Agelaius phoeniceus*), and Great Northern Loon (*Gavia immer*). I chose them because they are visible and demonstrative when vocalizing, have easily accessible habitats, and are common where they occur. Following are descriptions of their most-used vocalizations, along with notes on what to watch for regarding their silent language.

Don't shy away from studying more than one species at a time. If you have the energy it will only accelerate the learning process, as much of what we learn from one Bird will apply to others.

How about Learning from Recordings?

At this point, listening to recordings of birdsongs could short-circuit our learning process by keeping us from gaining an intuitive feel for associating a song with its related nonverbal cues. The song descriptions below will give enough information to allow us to go directly to the Birds for the rest of the teaching. It is only they who can give us the holistic experience necessary to know their complete language.

Remember that what we are starting with here is Silent Bird Language 101—the easiest nonverbal phrases—because they occur in conjunction with verbal phrases. Most of a Bird's silent language is truly silent, being spoken while a Bird is quietly going about his daily business. Rather than spelling out what the silent-language phrase looks like for each song, I will give a few postures, under "Nonverbal Cues," to watch for with each species. This will encourage the development of the observational skills necessary for expanding our nonverbal vocabulary beyond its relationship to song.

If you are not familiar with the following species or would like more extensive information than what I provide here (such as physical characteristics, mating behavior, and diet), consult a Bird-identification field guide or online resource.

For European readers, I list comparable species. You will need to familiarize yourself with their vocalizations, which will differ from those of their American counterparts. However, the silent vocabulary will be very similar.

ROCK DOVE

Habitat and Range: Feral populations of the Rock Dove (*Columba livia*) are found in urban and agricultural areas throughout the civilized world. Being granivores and ground foragers, they frequent fields, parks, streets, and sidewalks. They roost and nest on buildings and rock outcrops. Nearly all of us live, work, or play close enough to resident Rock Doves to conveniently spend time with them.

European Equivalent: None needed. The Rock Dove is common to abundant throughout Europe, with the exception of the northern reaches of Scandinavia.

Vocalizations: Who is not familiar with a Pigeon's cooing? We hear it mostly from courting or fighting cocks; yet hens coo as well, only less often, and they are quieter than cocks. Listen for regular and insistent cooing during the spring-summer mating season, with sporadic cooing throughout the rest of the year.

The Four Most-used Rock Dove Vocalizations

- **Call Coo:** A regularly repeated, low *aroo* at the rate of about one per second. Cocks will use it, sometimes plaintively, to lure hens to the nest.
- **Posturing Coo:** The commonly heard *a-coodle-oodle-oo*, rising a note on the *oodle,* is used year-round by cocks in territorial displays. It may be employed defensively or aggressively.

Rock Dove range map

The Rock Dove

- **Courting Coo:** Similar to the posturing coo, only slower and more resonant, with the *oo* dragged out. Used by cocks to attract hens and while driving them to the nest.
- **Distress Grunt:** A deep, quick *ruh!* given by both sexes when in a state of fear or agitation.

Nonverbal Cues

Watch for head bobbing in both sexes, spread-tail dragging and inflated crops in cocks, and wing clapping or snapping in association with certain vocalizations. Every move of a cock's elaborate courtship dance, and every gesture of the hen's response, tell a part of the mating story. Watch for how an individual's vocalizations affect other flock members.

Learn by Living with Them

Wouldn't it be nice to have wildlife carrying on their daily affairs right outside our window? In many urban areas all we need is a nest box on a windowsill, and we'll attract a pair of Pigeons. A double nest box should be around 12" × 28" × 14" high and can be screwed directly to the sill or attached using inexpensive spring-net

Dovecote

◄ Double nest box

tension rods for a no-nick mount. Likewise in an available back-yard, outbuilding, or rooftop, you can construct a small dovecote and stock it with several wild-caught youngsters (see illustration on p. 42). You can build a dovecote in a day from scrap wood or sheet metal, or instead create or purchase a work of art such as the one illustrated on page 42. Plans for a wide variety of cotes can be found online. Once you provide a place for bird's to nest, you'll have the opportunity to learn Bird language in a flock context, along with what could be the Nature-based learning experience of a lifetime.

RED-WINGED BLACKBIRD

Habitat and Range: One of our most abundant and easy-to-identify Birds, the Red-winged Blackbird (*Agelaius phoeniceus*) can be found in marshes, swamps, and wet meadows throughout North America, the only exception being the Far North. Comfortable in a broad range of habitats, she nests nearly anywhere there is water and vegetation—even a roadside patch of Cattails will do. I sometimes find them away from water as well, in upland meadows and Alfalfa fields. During the spring–early summer breeding season, singing males are easy to spot as they perch conspicuously on Cattails, shrubs, fences, and high wires.

European Equivalent: The Common Reed Bunting (*Emberiza schoeniclus*) breeds throughout Europe and most of Asia. Abundant and favoring heavily vegetated wet-soil habitats, she is a worthy counterpart to the Red-winged Blackbird. The Bunting is called *Rohrammer* in Germany, *Bruant* in France, and *Escribano Palustre* in Spain.

Vocalizations: Depending on who you ask, the Red-winged Blackbird repertoire consists of from four to ten types of calls. I say *types* because many vocalizations are intermediate forms that can be hard to categorize—these guys are great at making up what best fits the situation. Yet we need a starting point, so here I list five call types that I hear most frequently, are quite easy to identify, and clearly relate to specific behaviors.

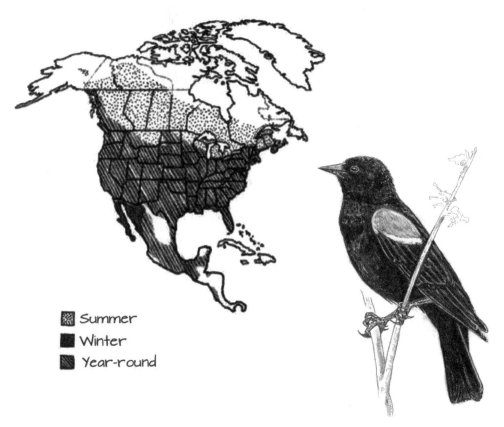

■ Summer
■ Winter
■ Year-round

Red-winged Blackbird range map   *The Red-winged Blackbird*

The Five Red-winged Blackbird Call Types

- **"I'm here" (Male):** The species' signature *conk-a-reee,* executed from a highly visible perch as a territorial marker and to draw predators away from the nest. Also used in subdued form on the ground when courting.
- **"I'm here" (Female):** A short, crackling chatter, to keep her mate informed of her presence. Seldom heard because it is usually given in conjunction with her mate's *conk-a-reee.*
- **Check-in:** A matter-of-fact coarse-sounding *tchek* that males and females make year-round: in flight, while feeding, when confronting rivals, and as a flock alarm. A variation is a quick, squeaked *wht.*
- **Scold:** A fast, intense *chak chak chak,* used as a plaintive alarm call when directly threatened.

- **Alarm Whistle:** Males respond to predators entering their territories with a sharp *teeew,* at the rate of about one per second. Can
be clearly whistled or trilled, in either of two octaves.

Nonverbal Cues

With their jet-black plumage and sharply contrasting yellow-rimmed
red shoulder patches that can be either displayed or hidden, males can
clearly display a range of emotions and motivations. Along with gestures, feelings, and intensity level, note the Bird's choice of location.
Notice how the time of day affects focus and expressiveness.

GREAT NORTHERN LOON

Habitat and Range: Known better as the Common Loon (*Gavia
immer*), breeds in medium- to large-size lakes throughout Canada,
Alaska, and the northern lakes region of the United States. Although
Loons may not nest in your area, the ease of observation—along with
the high entertainment value of their antics—makes them well worth
taking in when you venture into the North Country.

European Equivalent: The Red-throated Diver (*Gavia stellata*), known
as Red-throated Loon in North America, breeds on small lakes and
ponds across northern Eurasia, including Scandinavia and northern
Scotland and Ireland. The Black-throated Diver (*Gavia Arctica*),
called Arctic Loon in North America, breeds on the large lakes of
Scandinavia and Russia.

Vocalizations: As with all other Loons except the Red-throated, the
male is the primary vocalizer. Each male has his own distinct yodel,
and the yodels of mature males can be distinguished from those of
adolescents. As well known and seemingly stereotypical as a Loon's
calls are, their varied intensity, pitch, and duration speak so much
more than a first impression might indicate.

The Four Most Common Loon Calls

- **Hoot:** Can sound like a hoarse yap, though it varies considerably.
It's used as a friendly greeting when in close proximity and to call

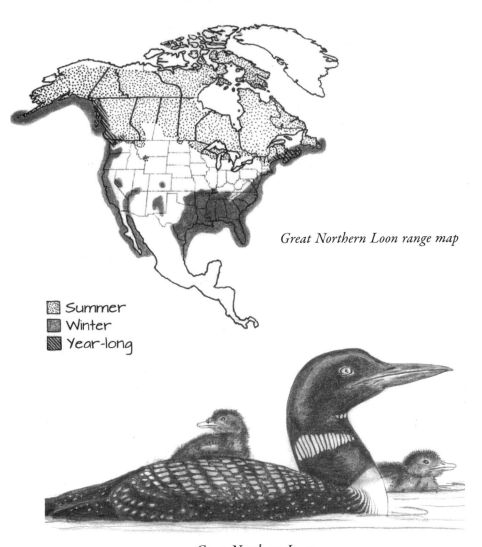

Great Northern Loon range map

Summer
Winter
Year-long

Great Northern Loon

other Loons, whether they are chicks, mates, or unrelated. This call is seldom heard by people.

- **Wail:** Resembles a Wolf howl and can have the same hair-raising effect on Humans. Used to find other Loons, it can echo across a lake on a quiet evening and carry for a mile or more.
- **Tremolo:** Sounds like a nervous, quivering laugh; used when agitated or excited. Males also use it when flying over lakes to look for other Loons. The distinguishing feature between distress and loca-

tor calls is that the latter is performed when the Birds are airborne, so the sound will carry. Sometimes a pair will perform a tremolo duet.

- **Yodel:** Starts with three slow, rising notes, with voice breaking between each (as with a Human yodel), followed by *o-oh waa* repeated numerous times. It's the "I'm here" call, used only by males during breeding season to mark territory and dissuade other Loons.

Nonverbal Cues

Posturing is a Loon specialty. Yodeling males will lay low with neck outstretched and beak just above the water. Tremolos, accompanied by either rearing upright or running over the water, might be followed by a dramatic escape dive or take-off. And then there are the antics that inspire the phrase *crazy as a Loon:* they go seemingly berserk bobbing, splashing, flipping, slapping the water, taking mad dives . . . and all they are doing is taking baths. So as easy as Loons might be to observe, reading their antics can be equally as confusing. Yet only at first, because for the astute, a Loon's message is loud and clear, whether or not any vocalization can be heard.

Remember to Turn Off the Music

Being so verbally oriented, many of us will find it hard to wear earplugs to help in learning the Bird's silent language (see point 2 on p. 32), especially after having just learned what those beautiful songs mean. Yet it is a vitally important step, so I'll give you some motivation: once you learn a Bird's silent language, his songs will sound all the more lovely.

THE ANATOMY OF A BIRDSONG

Now that we have a feel for birdsong and are on track for using it to rekindle our Nature Speaking ability, I'd like to take you on a tour deep into the song of a male during breeding season. The nuances of his song are known by only a few people, yet they are there for everybody to hear. The main reason we miss so much is that we listen through *our* ears rather than through his.

To us, the songs of many Birds sound melodic and joyful. They lift our hearts—we write poetry about the haunting call of the Loon and the flute-like trill of the Thrush. But what is birdsong to the Birds? Do they see themselves as the creators of beautiful melodies, or, as many ornithologists and birders will tell you, are they only carrying out the onerous task of warning other males of their kind that any territorial infringement will be taken as a call to battle?

Those options strike me as mainly anthropomorphizing: projecting onto the Birds what our motivations would be in similar circumstances. When I attune to the Birds' reality, I find that our reasoning might touch on their reality, yet for the most part our rationalizations blind us to what the Birds are actually experiencing.

The most valuable thing I learned from Birds is that there is only one way to truly understand what they are doing and why, and that is to *Become them* (taught in step 11). Research and study can be helpful, yet to get beyond our projections and romantic notions nothing beats becoming birdbrains. Once we do so we'll begin to understand why Birds would get a chuckle out of us calling their vocalizations *songs*.

What I Learned through Becoming Birds

- **A respect that bordered on reverence** was the first and most cherished gift.
- **It gave me a doorway to enter Bird consciousness,** then step back to Human perspective and reflect on what I had gained.
- **I could fly up to the treetop with—or rather, *as*—the Birds** and feel the wind swaying the branch under me, rather than merely observing.
- **I was able to see what they saw** and how they saw it, and I could eat what they ate.
- **In doing so, I felt what they felt:** their motivations and reactions become mine.
- **I learned what male Birds' vocalizations actually were:** a com-

bination of ID card, traffic light, advertisement, word of comfort, matchmaker, referee, and hormonal regulator.

- **I got in-depth perspective on the concurrent intricate panto-mimes** they performed with perch locations, flight patterns, body language, and even time of day.

All of that can come through a single song, which might consist of just a few notes. How could I—or anyone—not be left in awe from such a seemingly simple cornucopia?

A Song's Roles

Let's take a look at the three primary roles played by a typical male Songbird's call during the breeding season.

What Song Accomplishes

1. **It facilitates intraspecies cooperation.** A male Bird calls to give notice to other males, yet not as much for warning as to help the caller be a functioning organ within the greater organism, which is comprised of all the members of his species in the area. They need each other, finding strength in numbers and through functioning in symbiotic relationship. From our perspective they may appear to be defining and defending their territories. However, from their view, they are helping each other to keep focused on their respective nests. Rather than being competitive, they are working together to provide a mutual support network.

2. **It gives predator protection.** One reason they all call at the same time is that the more voices there are, the less a predator is able to focus on one—the same technique used by animals who herd, flock, or school together. Predators have a much more difficult time isolating and capturing an individual from a group than catching a solo animal.

3. **It helps monitor population density.** Some species need a minimum population density in order to nest successfully. When a population falls below that critical number in a particular region, they either abandon the area or die out. Such was the

fate of the Passenger Pigeon. Yet with other species, isolated pairs can and do nest successfully. If you've ever found a solo male calling during nesting season, with no other males in sight or earshot, he is likely a member of one of those species that can nest alone.

This raises the question: If he is the only male in the area, why does he bother singing? Doesn't it contradict what I stated above about symbiotic relationship being the reason for male vocalization?

The Gender Interplay

Occasionally I'll hear someone lament about the plight of the poor female, who does most of the parenting work while the regal male struts and sings. Whenever I can, I take the opportunity to help that person see the vital role played by that pretty little song.

Though relationship with others of his kind is a strong inducement for male singing, it is far from the only reason. The males of many species will vocalize whether or not they are in the proximity of other males. Here are the core reasons the Birds gave me for doing it.

The Five Vital Functions Singing Performs for the Nesting Female

First: It gives her comfort and reassurance. She needs to know that he is taking care of things out there, and his song provides that. It allows her to relax into the job of brooding eggs and feeding young.

Second: It contributes to her psycho-emotional health. One seldom-seen benefit of male singing is the contribution it makes to self-empowerment and stress reduction for both him and his mate.

Third: It gives her eyes to the world. When not nesting or needing shelter, most Birds choose daytime perches that give them the visibility to view oncoming predators and have time to escape. However, when breeding, many species choose their nesting niches for the cover they provide, which contributes to nesting success. The drawback is compromised visual range, so keeping attuned to her mate's song helps her see where she can't look.

Fourth: It protects her. By bedecking himself in boisterous colors and perching out in the open to sing and display, the male sets himself up as a lightning rod. To get a full picture of what it's like to be a fancy-dancy male, we need to Become him and experience the precision and alertness necessary to survive and sing another day.

Fifth: It conserves her energy. Nesting is a tremendously draining task for the female—so much so that if something happens to her mate, she might not be able to continue alone. Most females end up having no choice but to abandon their nests. I've found that the older the young, or the closer the eggs are to hatching, the more likely it is that the female will attempt to parent solo.

Hormones stimulate a Bird to sing, which at the same time encourages hormonal production. Yet it may not be so much the song as the act of singing that leads to this hormonal surge. I've watched mute Birds go through the motions of singing, and *although they couldn't produce audible song, they still fared well at mating and raising young.*

Song Plays Matchmaker

There is an altruistic side to a male's urge to chirp: it helps unmated males find unclaimed territories. When all the paired males sing simultaneously, single males can listen for the sound vacuums, which point to unoccupied areas that might be suitable for nesting. At the same time, the chorus of calls can steer unmated females away from established pairs and toward areas where they are more likely to find eligible males.

Hanky-Panky

What I've shared thus far is not intended to give the impression that all is neighborliness and marital bliss in the Bird burbs. When we listen to the silent language of Birds, we begin to discover juicy secrets. *Pairings and territories can be solidly established, yet the observant person will still find scrapping males and a fair amount of hanky-panky going on.* Genetic testing has shown that with some species up to 60 percent of the offspring can be sired by males other than the female's mate.[1] Although the Common Loon (one of our study species) is not one of them, seventy-five out of a hundred species surveyed in one study showed extra-pair fertilizations (EPFs).[2] Another study showed that male Red-winged Blackbirds (another one of our study species) are successful in 20 percent of their EPFs.[3] The Reed Bunting (one of our European study species) has a 50 percent EPF rate.[4] Over the years I've watched hundreds of both male and female Rock Doves, who mate for life and are ostensibly monogamous, engage in extra-pair copulations. A Bird's song may not be the equivalent of ours, yet when it comes to mating behavior, Birds fit our behavioral model quite well.

Now that we have a basic grasp of Nature Speak, we can venture in to our Animal Mind. There is no entry without Nature Speak, as it is the only language our Animal Mind knows. By going in to our Animal Mind we will be learning how to enter the minds of all animals. From there, Becoming an animal is only a matter of presence.

STEP 3

Awakening the Animal Mind

We cage and leash animals; we remove their claws and reproductive organs; we leave them alone for long periods of time; we isolate them from their own kind; and we turn them into milk, egg, and meat factories. We have our rationalizations for doing so, yet are we sure they are anything more than justifications for our actions? What if we could hear how the animals felt?

Sometimes when kept animals talk with me in Nature Speak about their lives, the only thing that keeps me from flying into a rage is that I realize it wouldn't do anybody any good—animal or Human—if I end up dead or locked away.

MY COMING OUT

Susie Lives On to Revive Our Nature

Some of my most potent childhood memories are of the times I was forced to reckon with the clash of the rational and animal worlds. One experience stands out with Susie, the wild Rock Dove you met in the previous step. She was a part of my family—the one with whom I talked Nature Speak—and

shared nearly every moment that I could get away from the rational world. Susie and I intrinsically knew each other's thoughts and feelings, needs, and desires. We were respectful of each other and stayed fully present and engaged when we were together. Every moment of her life she was free to come and go and do whatever she pleased. Every afternoon when I got home from school I went right out to spend time with Susie and the other members of our Nature family.

One day my dad came home from work and told me I had to get rid of Susie and the other Pigeons, because we didn't have anywhere to keep them over the winter. I wish I had thought to ask him if he would pack my little brothers off because we didn't have a bedroom for them. I wish he and I could have communicated in Nature Speak.

Instead, I rationalized with him the best a nine-year-old could. Dad held logic in high regard and often told me that I needed to value it more. Yet it wasn't logic that told me wild Pigeons don't need special wintertime accommodations. To a large degree my father and I lived in different worlds and spoke different languages.

My dad was seldom swayed, and I soon realized that this was not going to be one of those rare exceptions. I ran out the door and sank into a heap behind the garage, hoping my deep, heaving sobs would somehow bring about a miracle.

A neighbor boy took the Pigeons, and I would go over to see them every once in a while. When they first saw me, they weren't happy, because they remembered our relationship. Yet when I wasn't there, they did alright: they formed new family bonds and adjusted to the new routines.

One Saturday morning when I went over to visit, there were no Pigeons. The boy tried hard to protect my feelings, and maybe his own as well, by keeping tight-lipped about what happened to them.

Several days later, while playing along the fence line bordering the field that ran behind both of our houses, I noticed a disturbance in the snow. I dug around and came up with the headless bodies of several Pigeons. One in particular drew my attention.

"It can't be," I told myself. This deflated carcass with the pale, disheveled feathers just couldn't be my Susie. He's bigger, his feathers glisten in the sunlight, and . . .

> *Reburying him in the snow, I showed no emotion. Suppressing the bitterness and first upwelling of rage that I remembered ever feeling, I decided to go underground from then on with my natural-world relationships—I wasn't going to let anybody get close enough to do that to one of my own ever again.*

It's time to resurface. Susie's story is my motivation to help everyone I can reach awaken to their Animal Minds. There are many, many Susies in this world, and each and every one of them deserves to live as they are intended. And so do each and every one of us.

I, THE ANIMAL

When we immerse ourselves in Nature and remain present without expectation, we connect with the natural world and tune in to Nature Speak. We will understand on a level deeper than words what it means to be part of the whole that surrounds us.

When I Enter My Animal Mind

- **There is just one reality shared by all.** In the rational world there are as many realities as there are people.
- **Animals act differently around me than they had before.** It just took joining with them as a fellow animal in the Hoop of Life.
- **I become fully present and responsive to the energies at play,** where before I was an observer with my own agenda. Like a Rabbit who relaxes when Fox tells him she isn't hungry, I meld into the Web.
- **I see and hear what was once unheard and unseen.** Animals and plants talk to me all the time, both audibly and through the Silence of Nature Speak.
- **Animals tell me their intentions before they act.** Rather than needing to read their actions, I see them as reflections of deeper intent.

- **I see that there is no equality.** Many think we need to treat plants and animals as equals to communicate with them. However, one Tree is bigger than the next and commands more sunlight and nutrients, and one Ant species enslaves another.

When I enter my Animal Mind, I go deeper inside than my civilized, habitual self. There I see that Nature functions within an entirely different and vastly complex system. At the same time, I find it incredibly easy to live within that system, as I don't have to think about it. I just need to listen.

It Takes Listening

When we enter into relationship with Nature on her terms we are joining in a true cause-and-effect association, just as with our Human relationships. This carries with it a responsibility, as in the story I shared in step 1 about the Wolf-Coyote hybrid pup. Even though I met her physical needs, she could feel my prejudice regarding hybrids. She was used to human interaction, yet she wanted nothing to do with me and escaped at the first opportunity.

How we think and feel does affect the animals with whom we are in silent communication, and we sense this through our Animal Mind. Young Chief, the leader of Oregon's Cayuse tribe, would not sign the 1855 Treaty of Walla Walla, which ceded tribal lands to the United States government, because he said he didn't have the right to speak for the Hoop of Life. He was in his Animal Mind, honoring his relationship with his plant and animal kin.[1]

We civilized Humans have made a mess of things. We are pillaging our planet faster than she can mend, and in the process we are methodically killing off nearly everything that does not directly serve us—or merely gets in our way. We have a lot to heal and a lot to make up for. Perhaps the most profound step we can take is to embrace the children of Nature as our kin. When enough of us again consider them worthy of listening to and opening our hearts for, the balance will be restored.

A saying comes to mind: *To know you is to love you.* When we take the time to listen to someone's story, to understand what her life is like, we come to see that her needs and wants are very similar to ours. We develop a fondness for the person, a caring relationship, and we treat her with respect and consideration.

The same is true with the creatures of the Natural Realm. Through spending time talking with Monarch Butterfly caterpillars, I've become very protective of the Prairie Milkweeds that constitute their only food source. During a summer I spent listening to the stories of Mosquitoes, they told me how I could live in harmony with them. I learned that the last thing they wanted was for me to be a passive victim, driven crazy by their need for nourishment. They helped me to see that I needed them just as they needed me, and if they were to drive me out of the woods, we would both lose. From listening to Cougar's instruction I learned how to track her. She showed me only because we had talked, and she knew I wasn't coming to hurt her.

Listening for Life

Why would predators tell prey animals that they aren't hungry, and why would prey listen to that and trust in it? If prey animals lived in a constant state of stress, they'd neither stay in prime shape, nor would they be able to successfully reproduce. Both prey and predator would ultimately suffer. By listening to and respecting each other's immediate needs, both prey and predator thrive.

OUR TWO-TRACK BRAIN

Our brain is comprised of two parts: the limbic system and the neocortex.

The Limbic System

Also known as the *old brain* or *Animal Mind* (my preferred term), the limbic system is our seat of consciousness. It governs social processing, behavior, long-term memory, pain, pleasure, and motivation, including our fight-or-flight mechanism. It is the source of our gut feelings, our attractions and repulsions, and all of those urges that are hard to explain or resist. When my young son said, "If it's good for my mouth, it's good for my stomach," it was his Animal Mind speaking. We have essentially the same Animal Mind as Amphibians, Reptiles, Birds, and Mammals.

The Neocortex

Commonly called the "new brain" or "rational mind" (the term we'll use), the neocortex is the seat of deliberate thought. It governs language and our spatial sense (this is a gross oversimplification, yet it will work for our purposes). The neocortex, which is only found in Mammals, evolved as an adjunct to the Animal Mind to give it additional range and scope for the complexities of survival and the hunt. Here is the source of our shoulds and shouldn'ts, our planning and projecting, and our studied approach to life.

When information enters the brain it gets directed either to the Animal Mind or the rational mind. Verbally based input goes to the rational mind, which unfortunately for us Nature seekers is neither our seat of consciousness nor the location of our primary brain functioning. This is what limits our ability to commune with Nature when we turn to books and other word-based media as our doorway.

Yet we see ourselves as rational, verbally oriented beings, and we consider the rational mind to be predominant.

The Drawbacks of Rational-Mind Dominance

- **The rational mind can handle barely one-twentieth of the amount of input** processed by our Animal Mind.
- **Only 1 to 5 percent of our decisions and actions are consciously made** and controlled.[2]
- **The rational mind evolved to serve the Animal Mind,** rather than the other way around.

WE, THE CONFLICTED SPECIES

Have you ever noticed that when you are lost in feeling or deep thought that it can be difficult to talk about it? The same is true in Nature when something profound is happening, and we are participating. Our mental switchboard directs the input to our Animal Mind, where we can comprehend what is going on in a much deeper sense than we could with the rational, word-based understanding of the rational mind.

It is here in the Animal Mind that we can understand the nonverbal language of animals, and it is from here that we can speak to them. This is where we learn what animals are doing and why. We enter their world, not as odd-minded outsiders speaking an unintelligible language, but as fellow creatures who can understand and be understood. Animals then relax around us, knowing that we belong. Word-based understandings can give us glimpses and short-term satisfaction, though deep and lasting relationship must be fostered nonverbally in the Animal Mind, the dwelling place of our ancestral memories and core motivations.

We function best when the rational and Animal Minds work in sync with each other, which is the norm for hunter-gatherers. In this state we are clear in our decisions and motivated in our actions.

Much of the stress and turmoil in our lives results from this conflict between the rational mind and the Animal Mind. We often receive different messages from each mind, as with, "I'd like to eat this piece of cake, but I know it's made with sugar and hydrogenated oil," or "I'm attracted to that person, but I know it's wrong."

Legends of the original Paradise (Shangri-la, Garden of Eden, Arcadia, Atlantis, Heaven) are metaphors for the never-ending struggle between the Animal Mind and the rational mind. Paradise symbolizes our natural state of being, where our two minds work in sync with each other. The serpent/beautiful woman/pot of gold represents the voice of our Animal Mind, guiding us to keep living according to our nature. The conflict arises when the voice of the rational mind tells us that living in Paradise is unachievable/sinful/animal-like.

How We Live Out the Conflict in Our Daily Lives

When the Animal Mind dominates, we are passionate about what we do, and we are intuitively guided. At the same time, we can procrastinate when there is no immediate need to act, as there is no emotional motivation or gratification.

When the rational mind dominates, we can be focused, unfeeling, highly efficient, and productive. We tend to be self-possessed and anti-social.

When both minds are in balance with each other—which means the rational mind functioning as an adjunct to the Animal Mind—we can simultaneously feel, engage, and be productive.

Over time, our rational minds have largely taken over our lives. This was made possible by the fact that we Humans have what may be the highest rational mind to Animal Mind ratio of all mammals. *Rational-mind dominance sets the stage for isolating us not only from part of ourselves, but also from Nature and our animal kin. This is why we feel like strangers in a strange land when we are out in Nature and why we find it difficult to speak with the animals and frolic with them.*

THINKING WITHOUT THOUGHT

In the rational-linear world we have word-based thoughts. In this step we explore a deeper self who functions by thinking wordlessly, or what I call *thinking without thought.* Modern-day culture has trained us to be goal-oriented, with the expectation that we have something to show for our thoughts. In Animal-Mind consciousness, we think in order to engage in relationship. Whether it is communicating, foraging, tracking, or scouting, it's all about relationship. Animal-mind consciousness involves continual engagement and constant nonrational thinking, as relationship is not a product but a process.

I'll illustrate this point with a traditional Zen story.

The Mind's End

"Some say that Awareness is outside of us," states a seeker. "However, in our culture, we believe that Awareness is inside each of us. So is it not true that Awareness and I are one?"

"Where is inside?" asks the master. "And where is outside?"

The seeker points to himself and says, "Inside is within me." With a broad sweep of his hand he adds, "Outside would be all around me."

"How do you separate the two?" asks the master. "Where do you draw the boundary?"

"It is my skin," replies the seeker. "Inside my skin is me, and outside my skin is everything else."

"And where is your mind's skin?"

"It has no skin," came the reply. "It is inside my head—my head is the boundary."

"I see," replied the master. "Then your mind must be very small."

As the story demonstrates, the mind is capable of only so much. To rely on it for our connection to Nature limits us to its little world and the scant knowledge it holds. Why depend on our own minds when we can have access to the knowledge of all the animals, the Trees, the hills, and the wind? Add to this the wisdom of countless generations of our Ancestors, and one has to wonder why we would want to limit ourselves to just *our* mind.

What Trips Us Up

"Many people are afraid to empty their own minds lest they plunge in to the Void," said ninth-century Zen master Huang-po. "Ha! What they don't realize is that their own mind *is* the Void." What we cling to so tenaciously and call knowledge actually shows our ignorance. What we claim to be intelligence only exposes our arrogance and disconnectedness.

How Thought Interferes with Thinking

- **A word-thought cluttered mind smothers intuitive voices,** where a freed mind easily receives them.
- **Rational thoughts divide and distract the mind,** making it unavailable for intuitive wisdom.
- **Rational thoughts impede the mind's ability to be fully devoted to the present,** which is the doorway through which intuition enters our consciousness.

Some people interpret the no-mind guidance of Zen masters as "to free the mind, do not think." What they are actually saying is clarified in this line from the ancient Zen verse *Song of Trusting the Heart:* "When we hold on to a thought, the truth is hidden."[3]

Letting go of thought, which is the Chinese Zen concept of *wu-nien,* does not necessarily mean letting go of thinking. It is possible to think without thought, which is our pure functioning state. The Chinese Zen term for this practice is *ta yung.*

The Limitations of Thought-based Thinking

- **It is restricted to the knowledge the mind already possesses.**
- **The knowledge is dated—it's history.**
- **Knowledge-based actions often flounder in unconventional circumstances.**
- **Acting on knowledge alone tends to be mechanical, encourage foregone conclusions, and lead down blind alleys.**

Thought-free thinking is the now. It is *ta yung:* pure, functioning Animal Mind–based awareness. This state creates the unbounded sense of presence that invites the intuitive voice. Without the clutter of old information and the well-worn groove of predictable deductions, questions abound and new information floods in. Intuition, combined with fresh and stored knowledge, creates a dynamic that transforms an experience in Nature to a flowing dance with our surroundings.

> *When we stop the mind's drive to know*
> *there is nothing we cannot know.*[4]
>
> *All is vibrant, clear, and spontaneous*
> *with no mental exertion.*
> *Thought, anyway, would be useless*
> *on what thought cannot fathom.*[5]
> FROM *SONG OF TRUSTING THE HEART*

BEWARE OF THE RATIONAL-MIND TRAP

When we are in our thinking-without-thought mind and tuned in to Nature Speak, everything we hear is relevant. However, when we run nonverbal input through our rational mind, it sounds like gibberish. It's like trying to tune in a channel on an old dial radio and getting only static.

When we Become an Animal, it is vitally important to not think about what we see, hear, or intuit, lest we either distort or discount it. The rational mind's job is to interpret things and relate them to what we already know. This is just the thing we want to avoid doing—we want to take things at face value, just as they are given. We are tuning in to another animal's reality, which is quite distinct from ours. Inaccuracies and distortions will follow our attempts to relate their experiences to our own.

Because we are so conditioned to a rational-linear reality, we automatically revert to it as the litmus test for our experiences when we first begin to truly immerse ourselves in Nature. This reversion is no fault of ours. It's just a knee-jerk reaction, as we are creatures of habit and pattern. Old habits die hard, yet when we give ourselves the time and support to change, Nature Speak will become our default program.

The switching over can be frustrating at first, as it often seems to take forever. However, we'll find that it becomes easier as we progress, as we are genetically programmed for Nature Speak. It's like feeling groggy when we get up in the morning: we have to push ourselves at first, it hurts to open our eyes, our muscles are stiff, and we feel irritable. However, once we start moving and get a taste of sunshine and fresh air, the dynamic of the day sweeps us along and we forget all about what it was like when we first opened our eyes.

During this transition from our analytical to our experiential mindset, let's be careful of judging the process. If we can accept something without bias it's only a short step to cherishing it. Following is a simple and effective three-step exercise to enliven the Animal Mind. Practice it regularly, using any experience you feel drawn toward, and the analytical curtain will begin to part before you.

To Revitalize the Animal Mind

1. **Embark** on an experience without a goal in mind.
2. **Accept** all turns in the road.
3. **Cherish** whatever the experience brings.

KNOWING THE EXPERIENTIAL MIND-SET

Our eyes don't really see; they just transmit electronic impulses from reflected light to the brain. It's the brain that sees. It acts like processing software that finds patterns in the impulses and matches them up with symbols, which we then run through our memory to see if they connect with something.

As we exercise our experiential mind, more and more of what now lingers in the darkness will come to light. The exciting part of being in our experiential mind-set is that we have a ringside seat to what is continually flowing in from the darkness. This ringside seat is called "being in the now and tuned in to Nature Speak."

How to Tell When We're in Our Experiential Mind-Set

- **We won't find anything familiar to grab onto,** as this state is spacious and undifferentiated. For virtually all of us, it's a scary place to be—it's Zen master Huang-po's *Void*. This is just as it should be, and it will take most of us awhile to get used to it.
- **It is constantly filling.** All systems work toward equilibrium by filling in their vacuums. A crater in a wetland fills up with water, and air rushes in to our lungs when we expand our chest. The Animal Mind resembles such a system seeking equilibrium.
- **It's a dynamic place to be.** The Animal Mind is anything but the inert void we typically Envision a vacuum to be. It's not the emptiness of the vacuum we experience but rather the vacuum's filling. We Envision a vacuum as a void only when the rational mind compares it to its stable-state surroundings.
- **We engage with our surroundings interactively, rather than reflectively.** Reflective engagement would be the philosopher or mathematician who sits in a room isolated from the means and ends of existence and then uses an intellectual shovel to dig for meaning. Interactive engagement is demonstrated by team game players, who need to be immersed in the moment and attuned to their teammates in order to make split-second decisions and

function as an organism. There is no time to reflect on a past play or bask in the glory of a particularly clever execution. The mind is fully in the now and engaged in the means and ends of existence.

The team player is Nature Speak consciousness: thinking without any thoughts. My Zen tracking buddy Paul Rezendes calls it "thinking without a thinker." With Animal Mind thinking, we open our mental processes completely to whatever thoughts, feelings, and impulses swirl in the ethers around and within us. This is living in the here and now, and this is why it becomes impossible to hold an attachment to any outcome (see "Invisible Meal" on p. 141).

LETTING GO OF GOAL ORIENTATION

"When we are silent and still, the walls that separate us from Nature vanish," says J. Allen Boone.[6] To enter in to the Silence of Nature (which we will learn about in step 6) we must let go of goals and expectations. Without doing that, we might still be able to hear what an animal is saying; however, we will not fully understand it. When animals move, they seldom focus on getting from point A to point B. A stream does not begin with the intent to flow into the sea, yet we go into Nature thinking it does.

Our rational-linear mind-set only seems to work after we isolate ourselves from Nature. Focusing on a goal projects us into the future and takes us out of the moment. To be in our Animal Mind we must be in the same moment as the animals, and that is the present moment. If we are anywhere else, we will miss what they say.

Let's say I go out in the woods with the goal of speaking with a Coyote. I wait, I watch, and I listen. My eyes are focused on the trail that I think a Coyote will come down. My ears are attuned to any sound that might come from a Coyote. The day wanes, and no Coyote, so I go home disappointed.

Little did I know that if I had maintained perspective and stayed immersed in the moment I would have seen a pair of Goshawks flying silently through the Trees above me on their forays to feed their young. I may have noticed the doe and fawn stealing quietly through the Raspberry patch just behind me, along with a Red Fox late in the afternoon carrying a Rabbit she had just caught.

Getting into Animal Mind-Set

Here's a quick way to activate our Animal Mind: instead of saying "turn left" or "it's on my right," give directions using *north, south, east,* and *west*. It automatically switches both members of the conversation from ego-centered analytical mind-set to Nature-centered experiential mind-set.

HOW TO LIVE IN THE NOW

As we come to understand the hidden language of animals, we'll go through a two-step process: learn how animals think, and relearn how to think that way ourselves. What tends to slow down the process for us is that when our kind became sedentary urbanites we also became reflective thinkers. We now like to explore the *hows* and *whys* of things, along with their relationship to other things. In doing so we end up dwelling on them. That is reflective and projective (future- and past-based) thinking, which disconnects us from the now.

How Animals Stay in the Now

- **They accept things as they exist.**
- **Experiences come and go in their lives,** and as soon as they go, they're gone.
- **Events happen for their own sake.** They don't need to be analyzed or categorized.
- **Animals don't need to prove or disprove anything,** nor must they be right or wrong. They just need to be.

The minds of our hunter-gatherer Ancestors functioned in much the same way. They were creatures of spontaneity, as were the animals they lived with and called sister and brother. Sure, it was a matter of survival, as one had to be fully present in a world of constant change, where both gifts and threats often came unexpectedly.

Our minds, like the minds of all animals, are designed to function as fast as lightning, take care of what is right before us, and prepare for the immediate future. Our Ancestors had no need or desire for intellectual delving, and there was little call for long-term planning. They lived in balance with the cyclical way of things: Fish ran upstream every spring to spawn, herd animals and Birds migrated every spring and autumn, berries ripened every summer, and so on.

Short-term adjustments were needed to accommodate poor berry seasons or cold springs that kept the Fish from spawning. Yet on the whole, Nature's rhythms kept all of life connected and immersed in the here and now.

Even though modern-day culture lures us out of the now and into our intellects, we can practice stepping aside from that by engaging in activities that involve quick-wittedness, spontaneity, and coordinated effort. Engaging in these activities will help us easily switch to our animal kin's sense of presence when we go to join them.

Exercises to Develop Now Thinking

- **Play a team sport** or game that requires coordinated effort, quick thinking, and decision making. For the activity to be effective, it's important to play it consistently—once a week at least. Over the weeks you should notice yourself more and more easily sliding into now consciousness when you go out on the field. The longer you play, the easier it will be to switch back and forth from reflective thinking to spontaneous, interactive thinking.
- **Play board games** that require the same unified effort as team sports. Refrain from playing games such as chess, which require a good amount of reflection. They are counterintuitive and develop neural pathways that conflict with the brain's natural proclivity for spontaneous processing.
- **Create Immediate Consequences.** The quicker we experience the effect of our actions, the more we keep in the now. When

we step out in the rain without protection, we're immediately wet.

- **Limit Choices.** In the Natural Realm, choices are minimal to nonexistent: when Raspberries are ripe, Raspberries are eaten, and when Blueberries are ripe, Blueberries are eaten. The more choices we give ourselves, the more we dwell in our rational minds and the less connected we are to the now.

WHAT IT'S LIKE TO BE IN ANIMAL MIND

In the stealth Guardian mission trainings I conduct, we have a saying: "only actions speak." It applies just as well here. We've been discussing the differences between the Animal Mind and the rational mind, and now it's time to take a look at how they each show in real life.

How to Tell that We Are in Animal-Mind Consciousness

- **We are going to feel silly,** especially at first. The supposedly lower, small-brained animals will start to come across as profoundly wise and good at what they do. When we reflect on our experience (a rational-mind process), we're bound consider some of it trite, even foolish.
- **We will encounter internal resistance,** again mainly at first. Our schooling and our cultural experience in general have trained us to resist immediate engagement and instead rationalize in order to arrive at conclusions and increase our chances of winning.
- **We become amoral.** In the realm of impulse, intuition, and visualization, right and wrong make no sense. A mother Bobcat out hunting for something to feed her kittens has no consideration for the morality of what she is doing or how it fits into the greater scheme of things. She hunts to feed her family, period.
- **Everything just is.** We take what we hear at face value, and we interact with no sense of superiority or judgment. There is no proper or improper, smart or stupid.
- **We are spontaneous.** Here is the most reliable clue that we are

in Animal Mind. When we create a story, a calculation, or an idea, we engage in a mental process that takes time. The Animal Mind's deep thinking is instantaneous. We know it as first impressions, gut feelings, inspirations, and premonitions. There is no rumination required. It is just there, and we are just there—in our Animal Minds and in the now.

When we fall out of Animal Mind consciousness, we fall out of sync with the animals and stick out like a Fox in a henhouse (and with about the same effect). We act like a soccer player who is running around aimlessly while his teammates are flowing together in a coordinated effort.

We can fine-tune our state of consciousness by watching the animals around us. They will tell us immediately by their actions whether we are in resonance with them, and we can then make immediate adjustments.

Along with letting go of goals and thought-based thinking, we can help ourselves stay centered in our Animal Minds by reducing the media candy we feed our rational minds. Even something as seemingly innocuous as keeping tabs on time is a rational process that inhibits us from being where the magic happens. We'll be looking at this right after we learn how to have a balanced relationship with clock time, videos, and music in the next step.

STEP 4

The Time-Media Trap

Imagine meeting someone with whom you feel instant resonance. Right away you say, "I want to get to know you, so if you'll excuse me, I'm going to go do a little research and see what I can find out."

To get her name, you call a friend who you think knows her. You then turn to your laptop to see if you can find her on Facebook or LinkedIn. She appears in a couple of YouTube clips, which fascinate you all the more. When you Google her name you find her blog and an article she has written on one of your favorite topics.

Now, imagine that you instead asked to spend the day with her. You'll now get to see how she moves, the sound of her voice, and how she smells. You'll learn what she likes and what she fears. As you look into her eyes and listen to her stories, you'll gain a feel for her emotional makeup and intellectual bent. As you spend more time with her, you'll learn about her life's journey and how she is faring with it.

At the same time, she's getting to know you. And who knows, the two of you may feel some synergy and realize you have the beginnings of a relationship.

The second scenario is this book's approach to developing a relationship with Nature, and in this step we'll explore a number of perspectives and lifestyle-modifying suggestions to help develop that kinship.

Jennine Elberth

This step's intent is not to negate the value of a studied approach to Nature, as much can be learned from afar by utilizing books and videos. However, if we want to develop intimate relationships with the Trees, Flowers, Birds, and Mammals, we must *Become* Nature. This requires that we refrain from studying Nature—at least for a while.

Most of us were not taught that it is possible to develop a relationship with Nature in the same way that we do with our fellow Humans. This is due in part to the fact that *technology and our passion for productivity have rewired our brains to override our Animal Minds and tune out Nature Speak.*

Yet there is good news: Neuroscientific research confirms that we have the ability to remap our neural connections (see step 3). Along with that, we can restore our atrophied sensory and intuitive abilities (see steps 6 and 7), which are so vitally important for feeding our Animal Mind and communicating in Nature Speak.

However, the neural-connection remapping requires that we evaluate our sensory input, along with our relationship to technology and media. The ideas and exercises in this step are specifically crafted to help us develop the sensory aptitude for finally getting to know Nature, instead of just knowing *about* her.

LEAVING TOOLS, ENTERING RELATIONSHIP

In order to have the mystery and magic of the animal world come alive for us, it is important to understand why we have grown content to know *about* an animal rather than truly getting to *know* her.

The Two Reasons We Settle for Knowing *about* Things

- **It has become our way of life.** No longer do we gather the plants and rub shoulders with the animals, so we're not inclined to develop feeling, sensing relationships with them. We are more likely to see them on a screen or read about them than spend actual time with them, so it makes sense that we would do more of the same in our attempt to know them better.

- **We come from a tool culture,** which makes us inclined to take tools with us to help us commune. Along with special clothing and footwear, we might grab binoculars, a camera, a GPS, and a smartphone or tablet.

It makes you wonder how Native people can have their fabled skills of finding and stalking animals with the help of nothing but their innate abilities. The truth is that we have the same intrinsic skills, only our reliance on tools has deadened them. We now feel insecure in the woods and can't trust in ourselves—we have become tool dependent.

However, making a few changes in our daily routines will have us well on our way to becoming tool independent. We'll again be able to see and feel things that no binoculars or data processor could ever give us. If anyone feels content with bringing an Eagle up close with a lens, that's fine. Yet for those of us who would rather feel the *whoosh* of air from her wings as she flies directly overhead, let's leave our binoculars at home and read on. We who prefer watching animals make their tracks over looking at pictures of them, and joining animals while they eat instead of reading about their diets, will leave our gadgets up on the shelf for a while and progress all the faster on our way to relationship.

A FRESH PERSPECTIVE ON CULTIVATING RELATIONSHIP

Every picture tells a story, yet its interpretation depends on how a person views the world. As literate people, we've learned to read images in the same way we read words. An aid society recently showed a film to a group of illiterate African villagers to teach them how to drain standing water to help reduce disease. When asked what they learned from the video, the villagers replied that they saw a Chicken run across a clearing and people walking through. None of the villagers said anything about draining water.

They completely missed the gist of the film. Or did they? Thinking they understood the film quite well, they saw it as they lived their lives: in the moment. When they saw an animal (the Chicken), it meant their next meal; and when they saw people, they watched intently to see what the people were doing. The villagers viewed each character as having his own story, as in real life, rather than the film having a storyline.

How We Differ

- **We have learned to approach a picture, book, or film by future projecting.**
- **We know that single words or actions mean little on their own** and that we need the entire book or movie to get the story. A single character is only one piece of the story puzzle that must be completely assembled.

How This Mind-set Affects Us

- **The more we rely on printed and filmed material to learn about Nature, the more we distance ourselves from Nature.**
- **We miss what each animal and plant is up to.** It is these stories—the events of the now—that form Nature as she exists.
- **Anything other than being in the now with Nature can only be a construct** of who she is.
- **Study and detached observation can give us intellectual knowledge** and observational skills; yet without embracing Nature in the moment and in her way, we will remain the outsider.
- **Even though we might know more, we feel less.** Having actual relationships with the animals will remain an unfulfilled and distant dream.

Yet if we take what this step offers seriously, we could be not only introduced, but welcomed, to a whole new world that we never knew existed.

OUR BRAINS ON MEDIA

It is important to remember that the intent of this step is not to paint a negative picture of popular culture, media, or technology. In moderation, they can be tools for learning and growth—if we use them as occasional adjuncts to experiencing Nature firsthand rather than as substitutes.

At the same time, I would be remiss if I didn't mention the large body of research pointing to the negative effects of too much television, recorded music, computer, and smartphone use on brain functioning. Here in step 4, we will explore the effects of media on the Animal Brain, which, as we learned in the previous step, is the seat of Nature Speak.

Perhaps the most powerful single thing we can do to encourage our connection with Nature is to change our relationship with media.

How Wireless Technology Short-Circuits the Brain-Nature Connection

- **We have instant access to any kind of information** at the touch of an iPad or smartphone.
- **We have unlimited television, movie, and music options.**
- **To know more about a Tree or animal, we no longer need to go outside** and ask the Tree or animal—we can Google it.
- **Our instruments will tell us the weather,** lay out a map before us, and tell us what direction to walk.

We have learned to connect with life in a way that leaves us disconnected. The disconnect is not only from our world but also from ourselves and each other.

Smartphone use in particular has permeated our culture to such a degree that it is now the norm to see people dining in restaurants and engaging with their phones rather than one another. More and more employers are establishing policies to limit cell phone use, and states are passing laws to ban their use while driving. The pervasiveness of smartphones and the way in which we are using them has created a phenomenon some researchers call the "checking habit": the repetitive scanning of online and social media content.[1] In a real sense, we have internalized technology. In doing so, we have diminished our multisensory and intuitive capabilities to fit a culture that emphasizes visual input and feedback.[2]

MEDIA CREATES REALITY

Our relationship with media is merely an extension of our civilized world, where mechanized mega-farms grow our food, multinational corporations prepare it, huge utilities provide our water and energy, and faceless people in faraway lands furnish our clothing. These systems give us cheap necessities and lives of convenience—along with lives of dependence. Along with that, we have become dependent on media to shape our thoughts and paint our world.

How Media Shapes Our Personal Reality

First: Ever-changing popular opinion and cultural whims create media reality, which supplants our Nature connection.

Second: We subscribe to media's version of the world and live in a perpetual cycle of conformity with it, losing touch with a good share of our own authenticity.

Third: We use media as a coping mechanism, to numb ourselves so we can get through—and recuperate from—the day.

Fourth: We have trained ourselves to become passive receptors— observers rather than participants.

Instead of being actively engaged in relationship, we sit on the sidelines fulfilling our relationship needs by watching sitcoms, reality shows, romantic comedies, documentaries, and adventure films while our own life—our potential life, that is—passes us by.

We tend to do the same with Nature: we find a good vantage point to sit and watch. It's the way we've been trained to relate to life: sit at a desk at school or work, sit in front of the TV, sit and watch a game or concert. No matter where, what, or why, it nearly always amounts to watching others live their lives.

But not anymore. The first part of the book awakened us to our potential for becoming active participants, and from this point on we're going to learn exactly how to do it. *Nature requires that we show up as we are: ready to engage with other beings as they are.* We will increasingly find the joy in Becoming Nature as we learn to grow more into our authentic selves, apart from whom media tells us we should be.

Media's Real-time Robbery

Let's take a close look at one form of media to see its effect upon us. Which form we choose doesn't matter any more than which fast-food burger we eat, as they all influence us similarly. We'll go with television, as it's our most common and accessible form of media.

A recent study of nearly thirty thousand adults shows that while watching television may bring us short-term pleasure, it can also cause long-term malaise. Regardless of age, income bracket, educational level, or marital status, those who are happier watch less TV than those who are unhappy.[3]

Further research reveals that for every hour of TV per day we watch, we are 5 percent less content than those of us who watch none. Those who watch a lot of TV generally have up to three times more yearning for material goods than nonwatchers.[4] A third study corroborates the aforementioned two by demonstrating that TV can reduce our life satisfaction up to 50 percent by causing us to form unrealistic views of life. We then draw conclusions and comparisons that can be hurtful to others and ourselves.[5]

It doesn't stop there. Television disconnects us from our reality and in its place creates an artificial life. In order to be a part of it, we feel compelled to keep turning on the TV. As the studies indicate, we then unknowingly get caught up in an endless downward spiral.

What TV Steals

- **Authentic personality:** Yearning for TV reality, we lead TV character–influenced lives.
- **Time:** Every hour plugged in to virtual reality is another hour of disconnect from natural reality.
- **Observational skills:** The more we passively watch and listen, the weaker our sensory skills become.
- **Communication skills:** The less we communicate, the less capable we become of communicating effectively.

- **Relationship:** Our natural world grows foreign as we become increasingly familiar with the world of TV. In Nature, we end up wandering around like strangers in a strange land.
- **Money:** We can't live entirely in TV reality, so we attempt to re-create it by surrounding ourselves with the consumer goods we see on TV.

How TV Stole Athabaskan Culture

In 1980 the Gwich'in, an Athabaskan people who live in northern Alaska, the Yukon, and Canada's Northwest Territories, were introduced to something that they now refer to as an addiction. It was television. Traditional ways were set aside to make more and more room for watching TV. It became their cultural experience, and to participate in their new culture, they had to keep watching. Said one tribal member, "Television made us wish we were something else. It taught us greed and waste, and now everything that we were is gone."[6]

So, what can be done? We don't have to passively accept life according to television. Like many Gwich'in are doing today, we can reclaim our natural culture, which is rooted in the Hoop of Life.

To Reclaim Our Nature-based Culture

- **Don't demonize television.** It's not the tool that is the problem, but how it is used.
- **Be selective with what we watch,** only turning on the TV for programs that complement our life and Nature rather than detract from it.
- **Use our newfound time to get involved** in those Nature-related activities we've dreamed about for so long but just couldn't find the time to begin.

By following these points we can transform our life as we know it. Instead of settling for the life of distraction and passivity offered by TV, we can again become actively engaged in *our* lives. Rather than being entertained, we will be having fun—and there is a world of difference between the two.

RE-ATTUNING
OUR EARS TO NATURE SPEAK

To reenter the Silence of our Animal Mind, we first need to eliminate the noise that our rational-mind life has created. Continual sound, whether it is music or background noise, debilitates us in ways that make it difficult to dwell in our Animal Minds.

What Sustained Sound Costs Us

- **It reduces our sensitivity to unique sounds.**
- **It interferes with cognitive functioning.**
- **It affects mental health** by increasing stress levels, along with worsening the symptoms of depression and anxiety.[7]
- **It clogs the brain** with largely useless information.

Contrary to what many believe, continued exposure to background noise does not lead to adaptation. Several studies show that the stress associated with such noise can result in the release of cortisol, which in excess impairs emotional learning, planning, reasoning, and impulse control.[8]

If our goal is to attune our minds to Nature Speak, we must rethink our relationship with recorded music as well as with background noise. When we play our favorite songs over and over, we inject predictability into a form of communication that was, in prerecorded times, often spontaneous and always different, even if the same song was played repeatedly. Now our minds are lulled into a place of complacency, where we can tune in to the middle of a familiar song and know exactly what's coming next.

Sounds in the Natural Realm are hardly ever so predictable, and it takes an alert and trained ear to pick up on the variances and interpret them. Listening to live—not prerecorded and repeated—natural sounds automatically trains our minds to read them. We have the innate ability; all we have to do is dust it off and exercise it. The fewer recorded sounds and the more natural sounds we listen to, the faster we will readapt to Nature Speak (which, as we learned in steps 1 and 2, is more about listening than speaking).

Natural sounds can help restore both our relationship with Nature and our ability to function from our Animal Mind. Nature Speak and the sense of relationship with all life will once again come naturally for us. The African people mentioned earlier, along with other non-technological, Nature-based peoples, live in a world of sounds that are of personal significance.

One fundamental reason that these people are fully alive and lead dynamic lives is that their actions are based on forces that relate directly to their sustenance and safety.[9] We can take a big step in that direction by turning off our radio, as well as our iTunes and CD player. This suggestion is not meant to overlook the vital healing role that recorded music plays in some people's lives but rather to offer an alternative to the cloud of sound that often envelops our days.

IT'S ALL IN THE MIND

Contrary to what many believe, we are born with a brain that is largely unprogrammed[10] (note that did I did not say *empty*). *Our brains become programmed through exposure to stimuli,* which is why it is important to expose babies and young children to as many varied experiences as possible. Our ability to adapt to changing circumstances is predetermined by our early experiences.

If our caregivers select our exposure based upon their beliefs and priorities, we will imprint on these things. The imprinting is automatic, as our brains are incapable of distinguishing between long-term positive and negative input. No matter what we think or feel about something, it will over time create an associative mental imprint, or *neural connection.*

What Neural Connections
Are and How They Work

- **Neurons that fire together, wire together.** Neurons are specialized cells that transmit nerve impulses. When one set of neurons brings us the image of a Bird and another set of neurons imports the song of the same Bird, these two sets of neurons will link.[11]

- **Repetition does the wiring.** Once the link is formed, we just have to hear the song to associate it with the image, and vice versa.[12]
- **Neurons that fire apart, wire apart.** This prevents us from seeing a Bird one moment, hearing the song of another Bird the next moment, and wiring the two together. This also allows us to reprogram our brain.[13]
- **New experiences add new neural connections,** the potential for which is nearly limitless. Repetition and sameness neurologically reinforce routines, which make us predictable and inadaptable. We must cultivate new learning opportunities and reach outside our comfort zone, or we will develop a lazy, stagnant mind.[14]
- **Unlearning occurs simultaneously with learning.** The brain is designed for novelty, so it has the ability to respond quickly to new stimuli. Old neural connections that limit our abilities are erased automatically during the formation of new links that expand our potential. To keep the mind adaptable, it is important to continually learn and experience new things.[15]
- **Neurons out of sync fail to link.** We can read in a book about a particular Bird singing a particular song, yet this is only an intellectual understanding. When we hear the song, we have to sort through our memory files—an intellectual process— to link it up with the image of the Bird we retained from the book.[16]

On the other hand, if we learn the Bird and her song together, through direct experience with the Bird, the song and the Bird become one in our mind—the auditory and visual neurons link. The song is the Bird and the Bird is the song. Whereas artificial exposure, such as through a book or video, requires repeated exposure to create a neural connection, direct exposure to a new stimulus establishes a connection that is both intuitive and instantaneous.

SEEING IS NOT ALWAYS BELIEVING

Our Animal Mind understands that we cannot trust what we see. Visual input goes first to the rational mind, where it is stored in our short-term memory to be processed. If the input is shown to be of value, it is then transferred to the Animal Mind, the seat of long-term memory.

The reason our mind cannot automatically embrace what it sees is that visual input escapes tactile detection.[17] Plato went so far as to take a moral stand against visual art, saying it was a falsehood.[18] On the other hand, what we smell and relate to emotionally is intrinsically relevant and goes directly to the Animal Mind.

To show how untrustworthy visual input can be, stare at something that is bright red, then look at a piece of white paper. The image you were staring at will appear on the paper, only it will be green.

The Best Ways to Rewire Our Brain

1. **Immersion in Nature** is the ultimate reprogramming experience, as it involves all senses (sight, hearing, taste, touch, and smell) simultaneously. It quickly increases our usable intelligence by replacing outdated or useless data with relevant information.
2. **Neural input that involves as many senses as possible.** Pictures and reading material are only visual, and videos and TV are just audiovisual.

It's not that hard to increase intelligence, because, as already mentioned, unlearning occurs simultaneously with learning. At the same time, we increase our ability to be spontaneous and adaptable.

AUDIOVISUAL MATERIAL MEETS THE ANIMAL MIND

To grasp something visual and communicate about it we need to develop mutually recognizable symbols. Visual comprehension and verbal communication are both intellectual processes seated in the rational mind, which is symbol based. Here is why we tend to rely so heavily on visual, written, and spoken materials when we are seated in our rational minds[19] and why using such materials for connecting with Nature keeps us locked in our rational mind-sets.

The Pros and Cons of Various Audiovisual Aids

- **Controlled visual input, such as pictures and the printed word, has a stronger effect on us than controlled audio input.** Where we can glance back at a page or picture to renew our attention, audio input disappears as soon as it is paused or turned off.[20]
- **Writing and pictures are abstractions that disengage us from the realm of relationship.** The established relationship exists with the material, which exists outside the mind, so we must remain attached to the material.[21]
- **Further abstracting the relationship is the fact that word-symbols are themselves abstractions.** When we read *Bird,* the concept of a Bird comes to mind rather than an actual Bird.[22] Imagine describing a Bird in writing to someone who had never seen anything like it. And then imagine stepping outside and merely pointing to a Bird.[23]
- **Storytelling in the oral tradition encourages us to function from our Animal Minds.** Along with voice, a storyteller uses visual and nonverbal cues, setting, Envisioning, and audience interaction to engage the listeners' total being. The experience draws upon long-term memories and training, both of which are rooted in the Animal Mind. Every time a story is told it is somewhat different, which develops the elasticity of both the storyteller's and listeners' minds.[24]

The bottom line is that writing and speaking have transformed Human consciousness. Without the written word or speech, the abstractions that keep us locked in our rational minds—and keep us separated from Nature—would cease to exist.[25] There is power in merely closing a book, clicking the *off* switch, and stepping outside. Even the songs, programs, and books—including this one—that inspire us to commune with Nature can get in the way if we don't set them aside after they've served their purpose.

Exercises to Improve Our Mental Functioning in Nature

Decategorize

Do you remember the African tribal people we talked about who picked up on the stories of individual characters rather than following the video's storyline? That's what we need to do to bring the animals forward from Nature's backdrop. We can accomplish this by viewing our surroundings without categorizing. A group of people then becomes a gathering of individuals, and a grove of Trees turns into three Birches, an Aspen, and two Maples. The key is to decategorize consistently, and our minds will do the rest.

Look Less, Smell and Feel More

There are two kinds of neural impulses: warm and cold. Visual input is cold—it is sent to the rational mind, where it feeds abstract thought. What we smell and respond to emotionally is warm—it is routed to our Animal Mind. Relationship development requires the warm input of feeling and olfactory cues, and Becoming Nature is all about relationship. Pictures of plants and videos of animals are cold input, which is routed to our rational mind. As we now know, that will only get us so far. On the other hand, when we crush Cedar needles and inhale the essence or nuzzle our faces into a warm pelt, we revel in the feelings and enter into relationship with Nature. The mind knows what to do when we give it what it needs.

To Make It Easier

When we want to commune with Nature, it helps to leave caffeine, nicotine, sugar, THC, and other stimulants behind. Being centered in the Animal Mind takes calm and balance, and stimulants only keep us spinning in our rational minds, like a Hamster on an exercise wheel.

Look less, smell and feel more.

TIME BY DICTATE

We fell out of sync with Nature's time line because of our desire to control what we hear and see. It began when we adopted agriculture as a means of survival. When we were hunter-gatherers we followed the migrations of animals and the turns of the seasons. That changed when we started to use rich river bottomlands for agriculture. To work around the vagaries of flooding and drought required discipline and coordinated effort. Rather than using our intelligence to flow in sync with Nature, as we had done for millennia, we then had to work to maintain control of Nature, which severed our relationship with her.[26]

Controlling Nature for agricultural purposes included controlling time, which was necessary in order to efficiently govern labor, planting, and harvest. We needed to focus continually on the work at hand, so we could no longer respond spontaneously to what we saw and heard in Nature. No longer could everything be in the now; instead each thing had to have its own time.

We carry this legacy with us when we wear a watch or carry a cell phone.

A Watch's Stowaways

- **We pack civilization with us.** When we look at something other than the sun, plants, and animals to suggest what to do and when, we tune out Nature Speak and our own intuition. Even if we keep our watch or phone in a backpack and don't look at it, we are still subconsciously aware of the fact that we could check it any time (remember that 95–99 percent of our mental process is subconscious). This awareness can interfere with us being fully present, along with dulling our senses and putting a spin on our perceptions.

- **It knocks us out of the now.** A glance at a watch is all it takes to switch us to rational-mind consciousness, which is necessary to note the time and assess its significance. It then takes time to transition back to Animal Mind consciousness. Those of us in the early stages of renewing our relationship with Nature will likely find it difficult, if not impossible, to switch back.

- **It disconnects us from ourselves.** Instead of feeling our hunger, we have our wristwatch tell us when we should eat. We check in with it to see how much time it took to walk a section of trail, how much time we've been out, and how much time we have left.

Even when we have no reason to know the time, we tend to glance at our watches out of habit.

To Become one with Nature's rhythm we would serve ourselves much better by glancing at the sun. When we do, we notice changes in cloud cover and wind direction. We might wonder why the Birds are no longer singing, or we could pick up on the movement of an animal. An opening has been catalyzed, rather than the disconnecting and distancing that occurs when we focus on our timepiece.

If an animal looked at a gizmo to organize her day and keep track of her thoughts and feelings, we'd have a good argument for taking a watch into the wilds, as it would help us come to know her. However, coming to know the moods and motivations of an animal is a matter of feeling and sensing. Observing that *at 2:45, the Hawk left her nest, and at 3:17 she returned with a Chipmunk to feed her chicks* helps to know animal behavior, yet not the animal herself. When we assemble data, we simply project our analytical approach to life onto Nature.

It's not too hard to live without a watch, not only off the pavement but also in everyday life. With nearly everyone else having either a watch or a cell phone on them, if not both, all we have to do is say, "Hey, what time do you have?" when there's a need to know. When driving, we have the car clock whenever it's needed.

I haven't carried a timepiece since college, and in the more than forty-five years since, I've had no problem running multiple businesses, raising children, and maintaining a busy schedule of appointments. Best of all, my unscheduled moments, whether at home or in the woods, automatically reflect the rhythm of the now. Yet it doesn't have to be all or nothing. Some of us will not be able to go watch-free right now, and some of us will have periods when we can do it. What's important is to realize that every step we take without a watch is a step closer to Becoming Nature.

It can also be a substantial step toward a life "where every day doesn't start with an alarm clock and end with the television."[27]

A Time Test

To see how often you actually need to note the time, keep track for one full day of how often you check your watch or phone. On another day, go without your time devices and keep track of how often you need to ask someone else for the time. You would be the rare person if those two counts came anywhere near each other.

In these first four steps we have covered all the basics of mental attunement, including what tends to get in the way. From here on, the pace will quicken toward getting close enough to look into the eyes of an animal and even enter her body and mind. There is no more Human-Nature barrier—we can now remember how to see, hear, and move, and the animals will accept us as one of their own.

STEP 5

Be Where the Magic Happens

Dawn Ensemble

One of my most memorable early-morning experiences occurred as I sat out in the backyard to await the dawn. Before I could detect any light, a single White-throated Sparrow broke the silence by singing his species' classic pure-sweet-Canada-Canada-Canada *in an Aspen grove bordering the yard (last year I heard a White-throated repeat* Canada *twenty-seven times in a row—a Guinness record, no doubt). About fifteen minutes later, a distant Robin warmed up with his familiar* cheerio, cheery-up, cheery-up, *and then another joined in. A group of raspy-sounding Crows in the high Pines adjacent to the Aspens seemed to take the Robins' cue, although my impression was that they had things to talk about among themselves and were not taking prompts from any other Birds.*

The Crows flew off, and it quickly grew lighter, with one song after another breaking out in rapid succession. They combined to form such an uplifting chorus that I lost all interest in keeping track of who was singing when and from where. Red-winged Blackbird's *conk-a-ree*

blended with rough-voiced Phoebe calling his own name. In the background the haunting *oh, holy, holy* of Hermit Thrush echoed through the woods, along with Veery's cascading, ethereal trill. Piercing it all was the periodic crescendo of Wood Thrush's flutelike *fri-to-lay.*

As dawn melted into day, the players one by one packed up their instruments and let the chorus dwindle to a loose ensemble. I left too, going to join my family and staff for breakfast. We ate outside, enjoying the occasional trill and warble of the backyard Birds. While we listened, I wondered how many of us realized that the mealtime serenade was just the wind-down of a grand orchestral performance put on to greet the dawn.

As I recall that morning, it occurs to me that many are using this book to learn how to do the inspiring stuff like becoming invisible, speaking with animals, and getting close enough to touch them. To do these things, we need to be where the animals live, and we need to be there when they are there. I heard the morning chorus because I was up with the Birds; my breakfast companions just caught the last notes.

For the time and energy we expend to see animals, the rewards are much greater when the animals are out and showing themselves. Following are guidelines for being where the magic happens.

Where to Find Animals

- **They are the easiest to find when they are moving,** and they generally move most when they first wake up. They shift from bedding to hunting-foraging areas, along with going to get a drink.
- **Dawn and dusk are the inspired times.** Animals are either hungry and searching for food, or they are tired and anxious to get back home and rest. Diurnal (day-active) animals rise at dawn, which is when nocturnal (night-active) animals turn in. At dusk we see the reverse, with diurnal animals calling it a day and the nocturnal crowd waking up to begin their "day."
- **At midday, many animals bed down and nap.** This is quite obvious with Birds, as they are most vociferous at dawn, often

with a minor reprise at dusk. They are relatively quiet during midday. It's infinitely easier to see animals when they are moving around than when they are resting and napping, as then they are either well concealed or well camouflaged.

- **They are most visible when they are most interactive and least cautious.** Breeding season and migration are ideal times, as animals can be active at any time during the day.

HOW WE LIVE CAN HELP US FIND ANIMALS

The overwhelming majority of our activities and involvements are habitual—even our responses to new situations are patterned on previous experiences. These habits become our modus operandi, and we get addicted to some of them because of the comfort and familiarity they provide.

Over time, we start defining ourselves by our habits. We will even defend them, as we have come to see them as who we are. At this point habits become a glitch in our return to Nature's way—which is being ever open and adaptive—as habits are the antithesis of adaptation.

Nature's way is a way of life, and living by habit is a way of life. We can't just set our habits aside when we go out in the woods, because we take them with us wherever we go and they affect everything we do. Returning to Nature consciousness takes consistency, which some of our habits may not allow.

Working on establishing lifestyle patterns that free us of three key habits is crucial before we proceed any further, or else the next steps will not have any lasting effect. When we release ourselves from the grip of certain habits, we allow ourselves to return to Nature. In doing so we simultaneously return to our own nature.

Throughout our lives we've been encouraged to conform to the modern way of living, often at the expense of our true nature. Returning to Nature opens a doorway that reminds us of who we were before we were taught how to be. It gives us the opportunity to be our authentic selves.

Habits That Keep Us
from Being with the Action

- **Sitting still:** Children learn best when they are allowed to explore their environment through touch and by freely moving about, yet we insist that they sit at desks for hours each day. Carrying the habit into our adult lives, we have forgotten the joy—and necessity—of spontaneous movement and play.
- **Sleeping in:** Though we may be content with our sleep-wake patterns, we often have no objective perspective on whether these are learned habits or if they are intrinsically part of us.
- **Ignoring our body's rhythms:** We have a normal daily activity-relaxation cycle, which we tend to override because it doesn't fit into our routines. The fallout is that we lose our edge and end up functioning as though we are only partially present.

We discuss the first habit, *sitting still* (and all its aspects: mental, emotional, and physical) throughout this book. The other two habits, *sleeping in* and *ignoring our body's rhythms,* will be covered thoroughly in this step. It will serve us well to take this process as seriously as we take our relationship with Nature, as they are one and the same.

I've changed my habits: I'm usually up before first light, I don't listen to recorded music (see step 4), I refrain from caffeinated beverages, and I take breaks and naps during the day. Some of my friends think I lead a Spartan life. "Why don't you go for comfort?" they ask. They tell me how they like to sleep in, drink coffee, and listen to tunes while they're driving or working.

"Sounds painful," I tell them in mock seriousness. "If I lived like that, I'd be miserable." I explain to them how getting up with the dawn makes me feel good about the day, because I feel kinship with the stirring animals and singing Birds. Their energy empowers and inspires me. When I lay down at night, I'm genuinely tired from having a full day, and I feel blessed that sleep comes easily.

Yet those friends who haven't lived it have trouble relating to my story. I tell them that I don't consider my lifestyle Spartan at all, but rather liberating. It's the reason I'm slender and in good shape, I add, and why I have few health problems and stamina for extreme physical activities. It's why I can run around lightly dressed in the wintertime while others are tired and shivering.

I find that it's hard for many people to see that a good share of their limitations is a direct result of their habits and lifestyle. Others who are overweight, have health issues, or need stimulants to keep them going view it as a reasonable price to pay for sustaining their lifestyle. I show individuals' research pointing to the high rates of depression, cardiovascular disease, and early death for people who live as they do, yet it seldom makes a difference. The same holds for studies demonstrating that they could be more intelligent, creative, and productive if they lived by their natural rhythms.

At the same time, I know people who have returned to our original design, and who are eternally grateful for having done so. Some switched because of health crises, while others changed because something inspired them. Whatever the case, I am heartened by the way they've turned their lives around and by the example they provide for others.

DAWN: THE PLACE TO BEGIN

Dawn, by Three Otters and a Steamroller Deer

It was the break of day, and I paddled into the open expanse of Scattering Rice Lake from the outgoing stream. The fog parted in front of me, and barely two canoe-lengths ahead three playful Otters were taking turns diving off a floating log and climbing back up to do it again. I was close enough to hear their soft chirps, yet it was dark enough that I could remain undetected in the vapors.

Another morning I woke up before dawn, by first light I was making my way silently down a trail that bordered a pond on one side and a brushy meadow on the other. About midway down the pond's shoreline I heard what sounded like the chug-chug *of a steam locomotive so close that it was about to run me over.*

Instantly my eyes sprang open as wide as they could go, trying to make something out in the dim light. A hot flash of adrenaline had me wanting to fly off to safety. Yet I was petrified—I had no idea as to which way to bolt or what I might run in to if I did.

It's a good thing I stayed put, as right beside me materialized the image of Deer, who was obviously just as confused and panic-stricken as me. First he thrashed into a Hazelnut thicket in the opposite direction from me, then he spun around and came right for me. I jumped more than ran, barely clearing the space in time for him to go thundering through it.

That was one of the most frightful moments of my life, yet I have no doubt that I'd do it again if given the opportunity. Native Elders tell me that it's good to be up with the sun, and had I not been, I'd have missed so many profound experiences with Nature. The sun is our father, the Elders say, bringing gifts of warmth and light for us to wake up and receive. "To me there is a lesson in the fact that [Prairie Chickens] rise early in the morning and dance with the rising sun," says Oglala Lakota Standing Bear. "That is the logical time for creatures of the day to start their activities . . ."[1]

Why Get Up at Dawn?

- **We are genetically programmed to do so.** Were we living immersed in Nature, we would naturally arise at first light.
- **It helps us Become Nature.** For us to develop relationships with animals and plants, it helps to know Nature's day as they know it. Diurnal animals (and we are one) rise with exuberance at dawn, and we can experience them in all their glory when we are up and out with them.
- **We feel most rested when we sleep at night** and more energized when we awake with the dawn.
- **The rising sun and all the awakening energy energizes us**—we get infused with lust for the day. We can't help but be affected by the swirl of life around us.

Dawn is a special time for me, because it's when I am at my peak. The day is at its most serene, vibrant, and pulsating, all at the same time. What an experience to revel in the exuberant energy of the singing Birds and the sun breaking over the horizon, screaming to flood the world with light and warmth! I feel inspired and energized, with my creative juices flowing better than at any other time of the day. When I'm not outdoors, dawn is my special writing time, as the house is quiet and there are no distractions. I prefer dawn's natural light to the harsh lightbulbs of my past late-night life, and I feel good to have accomplished so much before most others' workdays have begun. Yet what I enjoy most is having my day's work done early, so that I have my afternoons and evenings free for other things.

What It Takes to Rise with the Sun

For much of natural life, including Native people, getting up with the dawn is a matter of survival. As the saying goes, the early Bird gets the Worm, which clearly implies what is left for the late Bird. The saying is a metaphor for what nourishes us emotionally and intellectually as well.

If a deep relationship with Nature such as is enjoyed by Native people were as easy as taking a leisurely stroll through field and forest, there would be no need for this book. Rising with the dawn, which may be the single most fruitful change we can make, is especially challenging for virtually everybody who has grown accustomed to sleeping in. I'll give some ideas that have worked for others, and then I'll give special attention to those that need in-depth coverage.

 ## Tips for Getting Up at Dawn

- **Consistently rise at dawn,** whether or not you are still tired.
- **Go to bed early.** After a few days of getting up at dawn, you'll soon be tired enough to fall asleep when you do go to bed.
- **Wind down evening activity** well before bedtime.
- **Create a quiet sleeping environment.**
- **Refrain from reading, watching videos, or listening to music** just before sleep.
- **Have the evening meal early enough** that it will be digested before you go to bed.
- **Dim house lights** after the evening meal.
- **Believe in it.**

Break the Sleep-In Habit

"We must learn to reawaken and keep ourselves awake," says Henry David Thoreau, "by an infinite expectation of the dawn. . . . Cultivate the habit of early rising. It is unwise to keep the head long on a level with the feet."[2] Rumi tantalizes us further with, "The breeze at dawn has secrets to tell you. Don't go back to sleep."[3]

Morning energy is so strong that it even touches those of us who sleep in, as we cannot rest as well as in the night. When we wake up after the Birds have quit singing, we are greeted by the day's doldrums, and it sets the pace for our day. The converse is true as well: we who regularly arise at dawn begin our days infused with an energy that gives us an emotional edge and makes us less prone to depression.

 ## Techniques for Breaking the Sleep-In Habit

- **Immerse in what we'd like to become.** The success rate for changing habits is low when we try to depend entirely on willful effort. Change occurs gradually, and we need continual support through the process. A characteristic of our psyche is that we gradually become what we surround ourselves with, and we can take advantage of that by associating with people who also honor the dawn. This is one of the easier ways to form a new habit and leave the old one behind.

- **Replace the habit:** As we have discussed, sleeping in is nothing more than a habit, and the best way to break a habit is not by trying to fight it but by letting a new practice naturally supplant it. Rather than going to bed earlier in the hope of waking up earlier, we go to bed at our normal time and make sure to get up at dawn. We will then be genuinely tired the coming night and will naturally want to go to bed earlier than usual.

- **Envision who we want to be:** Even though we are clearly aware of the benefits of early rising, some of us are still going to have trouble mustering the motivation. What works for me in such instances is to realize that I create my own reality. If I begin viewing myself as a day person who awakens with the dawn, I will become one. Once I establish this new vision of myself, I will find myself making subtle changes in my life to fit the image.

For most of us it will take only a few days of getting up early before we will want to go to bed early as well, yet for a few of us it will take from a week up to a month. We need to keep faith in the fact that our old sleep habit will eventually wither, and we will no longer need to force ourselves to awaken at dawn. Many of us will be infused with a zest for life that we haven't felt for a long time.

Busting the Night Owl Myth

I am a morning person, and so are you. I realize that I just triggered a potential argument with roughly one in three of us, which surveys show to be the number who believes that they are night people.[4] We're quite certain that we are creatures of the night, as that's when we come alive and are most creative and productive. Because of this, we're not going to be easily convinced that we are genetically wired to rise with the Larks.

Yet for just a moment, let's allow for another possibility, one that could offer a considerable advantage in our relationship with Nature and have a positive impact on both our physical and emotional health. If the night-person concept were an illusion, what would that mean?

Why We Are Not Night Owls

- **Our mental functioning is diminished, because our mind is attempting to switch to sleep mode.** Despite the popular belief that evening people are more alert later in the day, recent research shows that those of us who think we were at the top of our game at night are actually our most creative and efficient in the morning, just like day people.
- **Night people struggle more overall with life than early risers.** One 2012 study of 732 people indicates that morning people feel happier throughout the day and have better dispositions than night owls. Early risers tend to be more motivated, alert, and socially fulfilled than night people, who typically suffer from social jet lag due to their late rising and late-night habit.[5]

- **Our physical health is compromised.** Researchers find that morning people have stronger immune systems and are healthier in general than night people, who are more prone than early risers to diabetes, cancer, obesity, and a number of other ailments.[6]

The bottom line is that if we keep trying to rev up at night when everything else is slowing down, we are bucking not only Nature's tide but also our own tide.

Nourishing Sleep Is Night Sleep

"We were taught to go to bed when the rest of the world went to rest," says Ogallala Lakota Standing Bear. "When darkness came and all the Birds and animals went to sleep, we were sleeping too. That helped us to become strong and healthy, so that we grew up to be strong, stout-hearted men."[7]

Why Night Sleep Is Best

- **Daytime sleep is less restful and regenerative than deep-night sleep,** which is when our bodies grow and heal. During the stage known as "deep sleep," the pituitary gland releases growth hormones that stimulate tissue growth and muscle repair. At the same time, our immune system is activated, to help the body defend itself against infection.[8]
- **The up-late habit is particularly harmful to children,** as both their physical and mental growth occurs during normal night-sleep time.
- **Night-sleep time is the best for dreaming,** which is essential for emotional cleansing and attuning to our inner wisdom. Dreaming is so vital to our psycho-emotional health that if we were consistently shortchanged on dreamtime, we would likely start suffering anything from anxiety, irritability, and difficulty concentrating to memory, coordination, and sense-of-time disturbances.[9]
- **Daytime sleepers are at high risk of heavy overeating and**

psycho-emotional imbalances, including aggressive, masochistic, and paranoid behaviors.[10]

Turn Off the Bright Lights

We didn't evolve with brightly illuminated environments after sunset. We used the subdued light of oil lamps, candles, or fire for cooking, craftwork, and occasionally to help us find our way. For the most part we slept at night, so we had no great need for illumination. A small light within a mantle of darkness still allowed the night to signal our body and mind to quiet itself and to prepare for sleep.

Today's artificially bright night environments stimulate our adrenal glands to continue functioning in order to give us daytime-like energy. We then don't feel tired, which could lead us to conclude either that we are night people or that we don't need as much sleep as the average person.

Along with what we've already discussed about the value of winding down for the night, early evening is the time to prepare for restful sleep by reflecting on the day and quieting the mind. We evolved in environments that provided this transition time. Like athletes who take time to cool down after physical activity, we need to do the same to maintain optimal health and reach our full potential.

When we maintain a bright-light environment after dark, we rob ourselves of that transition time, which may be a reason some of us wake up still tired and stressed, without enthusiasm for the new day.

To Simulate Primitive Night Lighting

- **Use subdued or low-wattage overhead lights.** I have eliminated overhead lighting in all but one room of my house.
- **Utilize task lighting,** which focuses only on the area of activity.
- **Use shades or cowl fixtures** to keep lights from illuminating the entire area.
- **Employ nightlights** for steps, hallways, and bathrooms, especially for guests.
- **In bedrooms especially, use only dim lights.**

Is It True That Dim Light
Is Bad for Our Eyes?

Contrary to popular belief, reading or engaging in other activities in low light does not hurt our eyes. I find that my eyes feel less strained and more relaxed in dim light than in bright light. They burn less and feel more refreshed in the morning.

NEXT, ATTUNE TO OUR BODY'S RHYTHMS

When I was in my late twenties I worked nearly all my waking hours. I was driven by the belief that I had to earn my way back to Nature by buying land and setting aside savings. After a few years I became so depleted that by midday I was hardly able to stand up. Not understanding what was happening to me, I would sometimes just break into tears in the middle of an activity.

Seeing that I needed help, a friend took me to a holistic practitioner. It didn't take him long to read the symptoms of burned-out adrenal glands. He told me straight up that either I had to start listening to my body and following my heart or I was going to die at a young age.

I knew that meant I had to radically change my lifestyle, and I had to do it right then. Making arrangements for others to run my business, I moved to a secluded cabin in the forest. There I engaged in a regenerative process under the practitioner's guidance that included eliminating stress, waking at dawn, taking naps, and adopting a rebuilding diet.

Six months later I felt some semblance of my old self. A year later I felt better than my old self, and I never looked back. I still greet the dawn every morning, I still rest and take naps when my body says it's time, and I'm now in the best shape of my life.

An Argument for Naps

- **Increased sleepiness in the afternoon is common,** and in long-standing, traditional cultures, rest and nap periods are a normal part of daily routine. Spanish-speaking peoples take *siestas,* Italians have scheduled *riposos,* and subsistence farmers and hunter-gatherers typically take naps when needed.

- **Naps improve performance.** Power naps are gaining popularity in industrialized countries, where employers find that even though their employees lose some work time, they are overall more productive and do better quality work than employees who don't nap. Research at Harvard University, which confirms that people in general thrive on naps, showed that where a half-hour nap can stabilize performance, a one-hour nap will improve it.[11]
- **Neither caffeine nor extra night sleep can compare to naps,** according to a 2008 British study. The researchers found a one-hour nap to be the most effective way to restore an afternoon energy slump.[12]

To be fully present and connected with our sensory and intuitive powers, we need to be naturally awake and energized. Stimulants create the appearance of energy, alertness, and presence; however, that appearance is only partially valid. With some internal gears artificially shifted to high and others still in low, we end up out of sync with ourselves.

Tuning in to Nature Speak and being fully observant require us to be fully present in our Animal Minds, while stimulants rev up the rational mind. Our Animal Mind functions at only one speed, so if the rest of our metabolism is not functioning at the same speed, we fall out of Nature consciousness.

The Danger of Night Work

According to an American Psychological Association article on the dangers of night work, "Humans evolved to relax and cool down after dark and to spring back into action come morning," states an American Psychological Association article.[13] Dr. Charmane Eastman, a physiological psychologist at Rush University in Chicago, adds that "People who work the night shift must combat their bodies' natural rest period while trying to remain alert and high functioning. . . . All the sleep in the world won't make up for circadian misalignment."[14]

What Regulates Our Daily Rhythm

The urge to take a nap is a response to our circadian rhythm, the body's biological clock, which regulates our daily activity-rest-sleep cycles. It is made up of clusters of nerve cells in the hypothalamus, a specialized area at the base of the brain that links the nervous system to the glandular system.

Our energy fluctuates according to our circadian rhythm, peaking and ebbing throughout the day. In our natural state we would be active during the peak of our rhythm and relax during its ebb to recharge. However, we live in a society that structures productivity by a mechanical clock rather than a biological one. This often means that productivity comes at the expense of rest, which (other than being counterproductive, as already discussed) does not honor our body's natural energy rhythms.

How we disrupt our circadian rhythm:

First: We—and our bosses—expect our energy to meet expectations imposed on us by the modern workday, so we push ourselves.

Second: Our circadian ebb threatens our productivity, so we either rely on sheer willpower or turn to stimulants (caffeine, sugar, loud music) to see us through.

Third: We grow fatigued, which over time can become chronic and difficult to recover from.

My story, which I just related, is a good example. The ebb of my circadian rhythm comes around once a day, in the early afternoon. If I take a nap, I wake up refreshed and enthusiastic for the rest of the day, with no desire to stimulate myself with energy food or drugs in order to keep going. If I don't nap, I'll usually regain most of my energy after the ebb in my rhythm cycles. However, I now know that pushing through the ebb means I am whipping my adrenal glands to over-perform. If I nap when my cycle is not at its low ebb, I'll often wake up groggy and unmotivated.

Disregarding our circadian rhythm can lead to serious physical and emotional problems. When pushing ourselves beyond our allotted day's energy becomes our norm, we run the risk of burning out our adrenal system, which may result in an under-functioning thyroid gland, as was my case. This can result in chronic tiredness, lost enthusiasm for life, depression, and weight gain. If we drag ourselves to an allopathic practitioner, we will likely be treated symptomatically, with antidepressants, thyroid supplements, or a diagnosis of chronic fatigue syndrome. Some of our symptoms may be alleviated, yet we never really get better.

Now that we have awakened to who we are as natural animals and have reconnected with the ways animals communicate, we are ready to enter the Silence. There we will be greeted by anything but silence, as what we were once deaf to will now rise out of the mists and cast its magical spell upon us. Once barren landscapes will come alive with the chatter of plants and animals telling the most soul-gripping stories there are— the stories of their lives.

Jennie Elbarth

Enter the Silence, Listen, and You Will See

When people go out in the woods with me, I'll sometimes motion for them to be quiet. They might think I'm asking for silence, yet it's actually the reverse. Silence is passive, and I'm encouraging them to enter an *active* state of listening. When we talk and make noise we block out what is going on around us. However, when we remain quiet, it's as though a curtain has been lifted—everything around us comes alive. Of course, it was all already there; we just had to start listening.

Within the Silence,
Wolves Announce Their Return

I remember paddling a wilderness river late one summer afternoon with my teenage son and daughter. It was hot, the breeze had calmed, and I asked them to paddle silently so that we could Become one with the stillness. Hearing the flapping of Birds' wings as they darted across the stream in front of us, along with Fish sucking Insects off the surface of the water, we soon discovered that stillness hardly meant quiet. We could even hear the Dragonflies darting over the water's surface.

Sunset neared, and still not a Bird sang. The silver-tinged sky lay as polished as the river's mirror-smooth surface. We quit paddling and sat as still as the Lily Pads.

Soon we heard a lone howl. It started softly, drifted over the valley, and was immediately echoed by another howl. They seemed to rise from the high bank bordering the river far upstream.

Although muted by the distance, the howls cast a spell over the valley that made everything else disappear. The shyness of the voices, along with their unsteadiness and timbre, took over my consciousness. If I were standing, my knees would have buckled. This wilderness hadn't heard the howl of a Wolf for more than fifty years, when the last Wolf in the state was hunted down. What we heard was not from an adult pair who had wandered in from Canada, nor was the voice from transplants who may or may not survive. And they weren't fragile pups, most of whom don't make it through their first year. No, these were frisky adolescents, born and raised here—true natives! In that moment, my life felt complete.

If my kids and I had been talking and carelessly paddling, we might have gone home with nothing more than a story of a pleasant afternoon's paddle, and the wilderness would have kept her secret. It was only because we entered the Silence that she could speak to us and share the good news.

THE DYNAMIC OF SILENCE

The act of being with an animal in Silence creates trust and rapport. It is a tangible sign of genuine interest and commitment to relationship. The sense of presence conveyed by both beings says more than any verbal exchange ever could. Silence creates the sort of connection that invites us to do more than simply keep our mouths closed while sitting quietly under a Tree. In this dynamic, we Become one with the animals and all other living beings. Here is where there is no separation between Humans and Nature; here is where the magic happens.

No Room for Silence
As discussed in step 4, we now live in a culture that embraces continuous sound in the form of white noise, machinery, idle conversation,

music, and many other forms of media. They can all have a detrimental effect on our mental health and our ability to connect with Nature. It all began when we as a species started living, working, and playing indoors. By isolating ourselves from the natural sounds of the Silence, we lost touch with it. That's the culture we live in today, which is so out of sync with the natural world that most of us have no idea what it's like to live fully connected with it.

Given the hectic nature of our lives, many of us are beginning to understand the need to cultivate quiet time. I notice that more and more ashrams, monasteries, and other religious centers are offering silent retreats. While they are a good place to start, our daily routines must also change.

What Happens When We Become Accustomed to a Full-Scheduled Life

- **We no longer feel comfortable during lulls,** so right away we look around for something to do.
- **We feel ill at ease when nobody is talking,** as we have gotten used to being surrounded by constant chatter.
- **Even when alone, we'll play music or call somebody,** just to fill in the space.
- **We find it difficult to embrace the quiet in Nature,** the same as at home.
- **We miss a great deal of what the animals have to share with us,** as we can no longer find the stillness within the Silence.

One reason many of us live hectic, noisy lives is that we think they will make us more productive. By slowing down and incorporating Silence into my life, I have discovered the opposite.

What Being Silent in a Quiet Environment Has Given Me

- **I learn more.**
- **I get more done** in less time, and I do it better.
- **This reduces stress** and creates openings for other activities.

- **It's much easier to listen** and observe.
- **I can more easily focus** and give people or tasks my undivided attention.
- **Life overall becomes richer** and more relaxed.

Silence Is Wisdom

The real potential for gaining what we want and need lies in Silence. Mozart understood what we so often miss in our busy days when he said, "The music is not in the notes, but in the Silence between." Without Silence, notes would just be a jumble of noise.

As in music, the power of a person's speech is felt in the quiet space between her words. It is Silence that encompasses the setting, the speaker's facial expressions and body language, and her history with the subject matter.

Silence is often synonymous with wisdom, perspective, and a desire to listen. This is why the silent person is so often well regarded. The Silence-wisdom relationship is shown in this comment on growing up by a Hawaiian woman, Haunaniokawekiu: "I had to . . . leave long silences for wisdom to grow."[1] Ohiyesa, a Santee Dakota from the 1800s, elaborates: "We believe profoundly in silence—the sign of a perfect equilibrium. Silence is the absolute poise or balance of body, mind, and spirit. Those who can preserve their selfhood ever calm and unshaken by the storms of existence . . . those, in the mind of the person of Nature, possess the ideal attitude and conduct of life."[2]

Our relationship with Silence affects not only our view of ourselves and our relationship with other people but also our connection with all of life. Silence is the gateway to the Natural Realm. If we do not nurture a relationship with it and are hesitant to slow down, Becoming Nature will remain to us a mystery.

 ## To Reenter the Silence

- **Be honest with** ourselves about how we fill our time.
- **Reintroduce** quiet space back into our lives.
- **Sit with the discomfort** brought by quiet until our hearing returns.

And we will effect these results:

- **Quality of life** will increase.
- **The state of dynamic Silence** will return.
- **More information** will fill us than any verbal language ever could.

Empowering Silence through Listening

"So now you want to know some things. Where do you start? That's a good question for you to answer. Maybe just listen. Listen to the drum. Listen to the air. Listen . . . to the earth breathing. Listen to the stars go across the sky."[3]

MASANEA, KICKAPOO,
NORTHERN MEXICO

LEARNING TO LISTEN

Everything in the natural world occurs for a reason, and the reason for quiet is to help us listen. Many people believe that a Bird sings to be heard. If this were true, he would stop singing if there was no one around to hear him. However, he sings to impassion the Silence, so that he might better listen. As covered in step 2, he learns the number of other males in the area, their locations, and the size and shape of their territories. He finds out if they are mated, how dominant they are, how secure they are in their territories, and how much of a threat they might be to his territory and mate. This information is vital to his well-being, his ability to provide for his mate and produce offspring, and perhaps to his very survival. He learns all of this from the Silence that follows his song.

Most animals are typically quiet, making noise only when it serves a purpose. An animal listens to find food and a mate, and to detect danger. The better an animal listens, the better—and longer—her life will be.

■ ■ ■

Although it is not always apparent, being quiet is our natural state of being; we are intrinsically listening creatures. Anthropologist Claire Farrer, who spent time with the Mescalero Apache, notes that their proper way of communicating is "giving a speaker sufficient time to think and reflect before rushing in to fill a silent space. Anglos are uncomfortable with spaces in conversations; Apaches cherish the quiet times as spaces for reflection and continued thought."[4]

An Elder's Lesson on Listening

I learned that lesson from a Blackfoot Elder back around 1980. I would seek out Elders and follow them around, peppering them with questions about the Old Ways. I would listen to their answers, but without really understanding them, as I interpreted them to fit what I thought they should mean.

Irritated by my endless string of questions while I tagged after him, he turned around and said, "Tamarack, when you talk, there's no room for listening. When you ask a question, you are not really questioning, because you think you know what you need to learn. If you'd let yourself listen, you'd get answers to the questions you don't know to ask. Only when we listen do we learn, and you've learned next to nothing all this time."

Shame seared through my defenses as I heard the truth of his words. Yet rather than discouraging me, it made me want to learn more about listening. If one Elder could teach me so much in just a few sentences, how much more was possible? The more I learned about how to listen effectively, the more my abilities to find and understand animals improved. I know the same can be true for you.

A good listener is every bit as present and engaged as the speaker. As a result, the speaker feels heard and valued.

When we listen well, we give three gifts.

- Silence
- Presence
- Active listening

To Be an Active Listener

- **Maintain contact** with the speaker
- **Show interest**
- **Encourage** the story

Show interest and encourage the story with
- **Body language**
- **Facial expressions**
- **Simple vocalizations** such as, "Wow!" "Really?" and "Hmmm."

Learning to listen well in our Human relationships helps us listen effectively in Nature and develops the skills we need to engage in Nature Speak. However, in Nature Speak, active listening is exhibited by active Silence. We remain quietly engaged in the present moment, open to all that is happening around us. When we enter Silence as active participants, we become true listeners.

LISTENING BEYOND WORDS

If we don't know Nature Speak, we probably never learned to truly listen. Vernon Harper, a Northern Cree from Canada, said, "In the Cree teachings, 'The Listening' means more than anything else to us. [We] learn how to listen to the environment, to the wind, to the rocks. We learn how to listen to everything."[5] Vernon's words might seem far-fetched, especially if we never thought the Wind could speak, for surely then we never would have heard her message.

True listening involves being able to hear both *symbolic* and *direct communication*. *Symbolic communication* is word and symbol based, while *direct communication* involves intuition, the senses, and other cues, such as facial expression, gesture, and body language.

We were taught that verbal language is the primary mode of communication, so we focus on words. However, Human communication is actually less than 10 percent verbal. We communicate the rest nonverbally. Native Americans, along with indigenous peoples around the world, learned to listen to their environment using their full range of capacities, whereas those of us from modern cultures relate to the world mainly through our minds. "It should be remembered that among Indians the whole body speaks,"[6] says Ohiyesa. "It is a fact that both voluntary and involuntary actions of the body tell truly the mind's purpose."[7] When we tune in to Nature without expectation and on its own terms, we can resensitize ourselves to the range of communication that occurs beyond the verbal.

Wolves' Wordless Language

I learned to connect with animals nonverbally when I went to live with Wolves. At first, I thought we spoke different languages, as I couldn't understand their words, and they were lost with mine. Initially I thought I could train them to recognize some of my words, as I did with my Dogs. However, the more I got to know the Wolves, the more I saw how complete they were already, and the more I felt like an outsider. Making them join my world by learning my language just didn't seem right—I realized that I would be demeaning them by implying that my language was superior to theirs. I humbled myself before them and began listening instead.

Although I learned many of their words by listening, I soon realized that I was still missing something. I began to notice that their communications went well beyond the few words they used. Ever so gradually, I grew more sensitive to the silent voice on which they often relied.

What a revelation it was to be immersed in a world of sharing that was not voice reliant but instead based on intuition. Had I insisted on word-based communication, I would have only stymied my reawakening. And I would likely have drawn the conclusion that Wolves were simple creatures, capable of only basic communication.

A few years ago I learned about a young woman who spent her early childhood locked away in a corner of her house. She had learned only the rudiments of spoken language, so when she was found and rescued, the social welfare team put great effort into getting her verbal skills up to speed.[8]

Because of their focus, it took them awhile to recognize that she could communicate very well without words. If only they could have listened at the onset.

To listen is to honor. Every human, animal, plant, and supposedly nonliving entity has something to teach us, and as soon as we recognize this we can start to truly listen. When we listen to Nature without a goal or objective, we learn amazing things and cultivate new relationships. Along with that, we gain new insights regarding our place in the Hoop of Life.

HONING OUR LISTENING SKILLS WITH SHADOWING

One of the most effective methods to improve listening is an exercise called Shadowing. It reawakens an innate skill that our Ancestors relied upon to move silently and inconspicuously while hunting or traversing dangerous territory. *To Shadow something is to leave our own identity, thoughts, and feelings behind and Become so at-one with another being that we move as he moves, think as he thinks, and feel as he feels.* In doing so we Become as present, inconspicuous, and unobtrusive as a shadow. It is then that we can best listen, as we are totally attuned.

I practice and teach three different types of Shadowing exercises: Shadow Walking, Shadow Talking, and Shadow Miming, which work together synergistically to improve listening skills.

Shadow Walking

Walk in someone's footsteps and move synchronously with him, as though we are his shadow, and we are Shadow Walking. Unlike a choreographed dance, where everyone is trained to move together, the Shadow Walker attunes herself to the person she is Shadowing by picking up subtle cues from both the person and the environment as to why, how, and where he is going to move.

Shadow Walking can be easily practiced anywhere, indoors or out.

To Practice Shadow Walking

1. **Randomly slip in** behind someone walking by.
2. **Stay one step behind** a person, walking slowly, increasing the distance based on how fast he is moving. This can also be practiced while running.
3. **Watch for cues** indicating his next move, such as where he is looking, how he shifts his weight, the length of his stride, how he places his steps, and any preoccupation in which he is involved.

Shadow Talking

Say what another person is speaking, as he is speaking it, and we have essentially become the speaker's parallel voice. This can be the most challenging of the three exercises, as it takes a high degree of presence and attunement to the one we Shadow.

Characteristics of Shadow Talking

- **The more we Shadow a particular individual, the easier it becomes,** as we all use repetitive phrasings and structures of speech.
- **The louder we Shadow Talk, the more difficult it becomes—** and the more irritating for the person being Shadowed.
- **The more quietly we Shadow Talk, the easier it is to keep attuned to the speaker,** as we have committed less vocal energy.
- **After we have become proficient, we can practice Shadow Talking inwardly,** any time. It keeps our skill honed, and it helps us give our undivided attention to the speaker. *Shadow Talking is best learned by engaging the voice, so practice it silently only after becoming proficient at doing it aloud.*

 ## To Practice Shadow Talking

1. **Get permission** from the person you will be Shadowing.
2. **Speak in sync,** rather than echoing the person.

3. **Watch for cues,** such as changes in facial expression, posture, and volume, to foretell what the speaker might say next.

Tip for Beginners

If you end up struggling when first attempting to Shadow Talk, try Shadow Singing. Choose someone singing a song you don't know, and join in with her. The melody, poetic structure, repeated lyrics, and the fact that most songs are slower than speech, make singing easier to Shadow than talking.

Shadow Miming

Mirroring another's fine-motor movements, Shadow Miming is similar to both Shadow Walking and Shadow Talking. We have the potential to practice whenever we are with other people. Meals are an ideal time.

 ## To Practice Shadow Miming

1. **Pick an appropriate meal and person,** and sit across from him.
2. **Imagine eating in front of a mirror** and observing your image.
3. **Arrange your table and plate just as his is arranged, adopt his posture, and mimic his every movement,** right down to chewing.

Warning: This exercise can hold high entertainment value for others, so be prepared for a few chuckles until they get used to what you're doing.

We are creatures of habit, so the more we practice these exercises, the more we get into the habit of being attuned to those around us. These Shadowing exercises are excellent habit breakers; at the same time, they help to establish the habit of attentiveness and the active listening skills that are the cornerstones of listening to animals.

Ask Permission

The Shadowing exercises can infringe upon others' personal space and cause irritation. Unless we are very discreet and proficient, it is best to practice these exercises on others only with their consent.

BIG EARS: A DEEP LISTENING EXAMPLE

The ability to hear beyond normal perception is called Deep Listening. After Shadowing hones our listening skills, we will have built the foundation for improving our Deep Listening ability.

Deep Listening Allows Us To

- **Listen not just to what we hear** but also to what lies outside and underneath that.
- **Trust in what we hear,** even though we can't understand it or see its source.
- **Hear the Silence** in which sounds occur.

It is essential to hear the Silence, as that is where we find the unexpected and unfamiliar voices that extend our sight beyond the reach of our vision. Listening is like enjoying a painting for what it is, whereas Deep Listening is like knowing the canvases beneath paintings and all the potential they hold for expression.

The following story, which is from Abel Bean, a fellow staff person at the Teaching Drum Outdoor School, shows the characteristics of Deep Listening and how they work.

Characteristics of Deep Listening

"I was out in this clearing gathering greens," he said, "when I looked up into the eyes of a Deer, about thirty paces away. She was out there doing the same thing as me: gathering greens. I didn't want to startle her, so right away I went back to picking. She flicked her tail, showing she was a little nervous, then she went back to browsing. Out of the corner of my eye,

I noticed that she'd look my way every once in a while, but I didn't pay her any mind, and we did well together."

I told Abel that he was like a Wolf minding his own business. "A pack," I continued, "can wander in among a herd of Caribou, and all will remain calm—as long as the Wolves are not hungry. The Caribou can tell the difference, and it's not in the Wolves' nature to deceive them. If the Wolves did, it would be to their detriment, as the Caribou would no longer let them anywhere near."

I went on to explain that when the Wolves do get hungry, they stealthily stalk up as close as they can, and then they break into a final rush. The Caribou are shocked and bolt away, with the old, sick, and lame standing out like sore thumbs. Usually the weakest one is chosen, and the pack brings him down. In this way, both Wolf and Caribou keep sharp and healthy. A trust develops between them: each knows what the other is up to and why.

Continuing his story, Abel said that after a while a family of three Gray Jays came into the clearing. One sailed by him, light as a feather, as is their flying style, and raised a ruckus. This is the role she performs in the Hoop of Life: acting as a sentry and sounding the alarm. The animals trust in her.

"The Deer's tail went up," Abel said. "She snorted, and she bolted away."

Did she have to? It may not seem so to us, as Abel was no threat. The Deer knew that. Yet the Jays were thinking beyond the Deer, and beyond themselves. The Deer had no idea who the Jays were notifying everybody about, yet she knew to trust in it. False alarm or not, she couldn't take the chance. She often never finds out why the alarm was raised, yet her trust in Jay, or Squirrel, or the Silence that precedes a predator's appearance, never wanes.

This is a survival trait that is imprinted in the Deer's genetic memory. Those who had doubted the call of sentinels were eliminated from the gene pool long ago.

Here is a potent example of how we are all connected and how we all listen to each other, whether consciously or not. Each animal is like the organ within an organism, performing a separate and valuable function.

We can do the same when rejoining Nature, by getting outside of ourselves and trusting other voices. The various animals are truly sisters and brothers: they care for and trust in each other. As discussed earlier in the book, if we were to stay in our heads and hang on to the "I-know-best" and "seeing-is-believing" way of life, we would sooner or later die. On the other hand, if we could get out of our heads, think less, and listen more, we would greatly increase our chances of surviving.

A Deep Listening Exercise

Whenever we are around someone who is not speaking, we have an opportunity to train our listening skills. We do it by listening with our other senses, which can tell us so much more than our hearing alone can. It is important to remember that people (and all animals) are always speaking, even when they are saying nothing. What people think, believe, and feel, along with what they expect and regret, or what they have and have not accomplished, can be more easily—and often more accurately—"heard" by attuning to their senses rather than listening to their words.

Nonverbal Cues to Watch For

- **Posture:** how the body is carried, leaning into or away from conversations, length of stride.
- **Physical condition:** body fat, muscle tone, degree of physical activity, injuries.
- **Facial expression:** tilt of head, character of eyes and lips, set of jaw, tightness of cheeks.
- **Skin tone:** tanned or not, type of makeup, skin health, signs of exposure or accidents.
- **Comfort level:** clenched or relaxed hands, fidgetiness, eye movements.
- **Dress:** degree of casualness, cleanliness, age, style, body coverage.

- **Handheld items:** purse, keys, book, type of snack food or drink, extra clothing.
- **Grooming:** hairstyle and condition, shaven or not, cleanliness, state of fingernails.
- **Daily schedule:** wake-up and bedtimes, leisure-time activities, degree of promptness.
- **Social patterns:** kinds of friends kept, level of gregariousness, family involvement.

These suggestions are only to get us started; we can add to the list as we practice.

The primary reason for this exercise is to improve our listening skills in the Natural Realm. As stated earlier, communication is less than 10 percent verbal, and that applies to virtually all animals as well as Humans. Fortunately for us, our sensory intelligence does not distinguish between Humans and other animals, so practicing Deep Listening with our friends and coworkers is going to help us with both our human and nonhuman relationships.

DEEP LISTENING AND TIME

Our ability to listen deeply is constrained by our concept of time. When we relegate the passage of time to a prescribed system, we will find it hard to be fully present and attuned to Nature's rhythms. Every animal and plant, every change of the weather and the season, has its own time sequence. As shown in step 4, we can sensitize to these sequences by spending time uninfluenced by our second-minute-hour based system.

Doing so is a big share of what makes immersion in the Natural Realm such a tantalizingly exciting experience. The immersion experience includes Deep Listening, which is how we hear Nature Speak.

To Deep Listen is to become invisible. It allows us to receive clear information, without the filters and distortions of our personal feelings and perceptions, which include our concept of time. The more transparent we become, the better we can Envision what Deep Listening brings us.

When Our Minds Won't Let Us Listen

We all have times when our mental chatter is just too distracting for us to be present and open to other voices. The next time you find yourself in such a predicament, ask yourself, "Where will the next voice come from?" The mere act of asking opens us up to other possibilities.

LOOKING VERSUS SEEING

Deep Listening is seeing. When we can hear what lies beyond hearing, we can Envision it as well, and Envisioning is seeing. Some of our goals in evolving our relationship with Nature are to be ever alert, perceptive, and spontaneous, which I call the "state of seeing."

Our perspective guides our focus. When we *look*, we narrow our field of perception, and we miss what falls outside of it. In the same way that I can think without thinking, I can see without looking. *Webster's Third New International Dictionary* defines *looking* as "to direct the eyes or one's attention."[9] *Seeing* is defined as "to perceive."[10] *Looking* could then be understood as seeking, as it is directed and intentional. Alternately, *seeing* can be understood as observing, as it is unguided and spontaneous. *Looking* is active, while *seeing* is passive.

To demonstrate the difference, let's say I have two red balls, three yellow balls, and one green ball, and I throw them down on the floor together. How many balls are there?

If your answer is "six," that is looking, as you are focusing on the number of balls I had and not seeing the possibility of other balls already being on the floor. If you answered something like, "as many balls as appear there to you," that is seeing.

If I told you to keep your eyes open, I would be encouraging you to look: to focus and watch out for something specific. On the other hand, if I encouraged you to be aware, that would have expanded your field of vision and perspective.

In Nature, seeing cannot occur with just our eyes, as it takes all of our senses to observe what is unfolding before us. When we are in our Animal Minds and seeing, we are only seeing. We're not worrying about the future or thinking about something back home. This leaves us fully available for seeing, so we can do it—and meet our present needs—with minimal effort.

Nature Provides When We Listen

I was paddling up a stream to explore a new section of wilderness. The sun was about to set and I knew I had a distance yet to paddle to reach my portage trail. Rounding the next bend I came upon a large Fir Tree that fell across the stream and blocked my way. Finding a tunnel through the branches, I looked up when I got through and was immediately flooded with golden light streaming through the low-hanging branches of a vast forest of ancient Tamarack Trees. They were all dead, having been flooded out by the backwaters of a Beaver pond the size of a small lake.

I pulled my canoe over the dam and paddled into the enchanted grove. Losing all sense of space and time, I drifted around between the trunks of the great Trees. Then I felt something. Or more accurately, it was the lack of feeling that got my attention. It was quiet—too quiet. Even though the place had a reverent, churchlike feel, I still felt the vacuum. Something was holding back, something very much alive and all around me.

All of a sudden I found myself in the middle of an explosion of frantically beating wings, as more than a hundred Ducks rose like helicopters straight through the canopy. They were bedded down in that quiet backwater for the night and were now likely headed to the stream's headwater spring ponds.

Catching my breath, I noticed a Duck lying in the water about a canoe length ahead of me. I picked her up and felt that she was still warm. Giving thanks not only for the Duck but also for the whole enchanted day, I paddled to shore, cleaned the Duck, and returned home for a thanksgiving feast with my family.

Even though it was thirty years ago, I clearly remember the vibrant flavor of that Duck's meat. Through her, the inaudible voices I heard that day became a part of my voice, and the gift that I received for listening has continued to inspire me.

A month or so later, I was exploring farther downstream and realized

I was hungry. I had not taken any provisions with me, which has long been my custom, as I trust I will be provided for.

Coming to a stretch of stream laced with the floating emerald-colored leaves of Eel Grass, I spotted a silver reflection off to the side. It was a large Brook Trout, bejeweled with bronze speckles, floating on her side. I made a fire on the open bank ahead and feasted my thanksgiving.

I was out paddling again a few weeks later, even farther downstream, and again I had packed no provisions. As dusk approached, I set up camp on a high bank overlooking the river valley. As I stood there immersed in the moment, I felt an urge to go down and slip my boat into the water. Paddling back in the direction from whence I came, I looked off to the side, and there lying in the shallow water between two hummocks lay a healthy-looking Muskrat that had just died.

Although these may sound like stories of how to get something with little or no effort, I actually put a tremendous amount of dedication and training into awakening my Animal Mind and hearing Nature Speak. Even though being able to recognize the abundance around me is such a gift, what I most appreciate is the sense of relationship I experience with the animals and plants. We speak to each other, and I feel at home with them, just as I do with my Human family.

The animals and I trust each other. It's not because we won't hurt each other, because sometimes we do. We trust each other to speak our intent and listen to what the other says. We trust each other to be true to our natures, to be fully present, and to take full responsibility for our actions. There is no remorse, no guilt, and no blame. There is just the eternal dance of life begetting life, begetting life.

A Listening-Is-Seeing Story

"I'm feeling a little peckish," says Trevor, who hired me to guide him on a wilderness trek. He starts to look around on the ground for something familiar to nibble on, as we haven't brought food with us.

"Good idea," I reply, as I look up into the Trees.

"What do you see?" asks Trevor.

"Nothing yet. I'm tracking my lunch."

"In the treetops? Can you find something edible up there?"

"In a roundabout way," I reply. "The Trees tell me what's growing beneath them much quicker and easier than I could find out on my own. Why run all over the woods if I can just see what's there at a glance?"

"Makes sense," says Trevor. "And then again, it doesn't."

"Here's an example of why Deep Listening is important. Without it our mind will reject possibilities that it can't make rational sense of. Remember, the rational is designed to give us answers, while the Animal Mind keeps us ever-questioning."

"Boy, ain't that the truth about the mind—mine, anyway. All right, you've got a captive audience. Show me how to accomplish something by doing the total opposite. That'll be a big help the next time I don't wanna go to work."

"Perhaps. But I don't want to be held responsible when your boss tells you you've lost your mind and you try to tell him you actually just found it." After a brief pause, I continue. "What I'm doing here might seem like some shamanic hocus-pocus, yet it's just Deep Listening. Remember those deep Moose footprints we saw earlier that were holding water? When we took a close look, we discovered that each one was a mini pond teeming with life. Trees leave footprints too, only much bigger, of course."

It's important to remember here that everything has a voice that can be heard, because everything is alive. If we can embrace and honor this, we'll step through a doorway to another reality. Some think this is just a quaint old Indian belief. Unfortunately, those people may never hear what the Indian hears. His ability is nothing mystical: he merely respects all life, so he can hear all life's voices. If you don't recognize or regard somebody, are you going to listen to what he has to say? Of course not, and that is why we're shut down to so much of what goes on around us.

Gissis Makwa, an Ojibwe Elder with whom I studied forty years ago, told me that if a philosophy doesn't grow Corn, he doesn't want to hear about it. The Native way is not a belief system; it is practical reality. All who live within the Natural Realm know this, because it's how they survive. We modern Humans, however, have forgotten it, which is why our survival prospects don't look very good. But our Animal Mind remembers; we just have to start listening to it again.

> *Trevor steps back a couple of paces and gazes up into the treetops.*
>
> *"If you think the Moose's track was big," I state, "a Tree's is as big around as the Tree herself. And just like the Moose's, a Tree's footprint creates a unique habitat that's suited for certain plants and animals. The Tree sings this information for all to hear. She wants to attract foragers to spread her seed, prune her undergrowth to make room for her offspring, and contribute nourishing scat and urine. If I see the Tree as my sister, my brother, we can talk to each other and help each other out. That's really all there is to it."*
>
> *"That's it, eh? Piece a'cake!"*
>
> *"It is, seriously. Just like listening to your living room or yard: you walk in and you've got the story, with no effort. What I do is find a high, open place and listen for the song that pleases me. I don't think, 'Oh, this Tree tells me she has such-and-such plants and animals hanging out under her, and that Tree says she has these others around her.' It's more like the sense you get the moment you step into your house. Just like you, I'm listening from deep within my Animal Mind and drawing upon ancient memories."*

I'll sometimes close my eyes and hear the unique voice of each Tree. Young Aspen flutters softly yet vociferously, while elder Aspen flutters harshly and quietly. Pine sings through her needles with a high, hissing sound, even in a gentle breeze, like she's breathing through clenched teeth. Red Pine's song has a little rattle, and White Pine's tone is tinged with the wispy sound of escaping steam. Oak's voice has a tinny clack, clack, clack, and Maple's sound is like tearing paper. And then there's the voice of Canoe Birch, which reminds me of fingernails scraping over a bed sheet. Grasses and bushes each have their own sounds as well, and they have another set of sounds when they are wet or icy.

Every single being sings in her own unique way about her age, size, health, and feelings, along with describing the family of plant and animal Relations who live within and around her. This song is heard often by the eye, which can hear as well as see.

I think we show our innate awareness of this when we say, "I see," and we actually mean, "I hear you." Sight is closely related to hearing, as both the optic nerve and acoustic nerve evolved from the same neural brain connection. Even though our rational brain has largely taken over sight, it's still connected with our deep ancestral brain. When we pick something up "at a glance," we're not referring only to sight, but to a deeper, fuller connection. Beethoven, who grew deaf around mid-career, was said to have heard with his eyes, which allowed him to continue composing without compromising the quality of his work.

"You're getting a peek at how effortless this can be," I tell Trevor. "At the same time, I see how overwhelming this is for you right now, and I just want to encourage you not to throw in the towel. I assure you that you were born and made to be a Deep Listener. Just remember that there's nothing to learn: you only need to peel off the layers of conditioning that keep the ability buried beneath your consciousness."

"Peeling off those layers . . . that's a tall order," says Trevor.

"Keep in mind that it took a long time to accumulate them, so we have to be realistic and accept that it may take awhile to become fully ourselves again. Hopefully what the animals and plants and I share with you will show that the seeing we are doing here is just the exercise of an innate ability. In the same way that a Wolf doesn't need lessons to follow a scent and a Falcon doesn't need lessons to chase down a Jay, neither do you or I need lessons. We're predators, just like them, and we've been at it for millions of years, just like them. Training and practice don't give us the skill; they only make us more effective."

"I know you're right," says Trevor. "I can feel it. But it's overwhelming. It's a lot at once."

"It is, yet it's a lot of the same thing. I can walk over mountains, through jungles, across deserts, and still it all boils down to walking. So don't be daunted. I can dance a few words around what we're doing, yet that doesn't mean I know any more than you." I pause for emphasis and then continue. "But hey, enough chitchat. You came for wilderness adventure, right? How about if we continue on and listen to each Tree's song and see who lives beneath her?"

"Sounds great," says Trevor, "but our talking is doing me good too. It's opening me up to this experience. Already I can tell I'm thinking less and listening more. It gives me a little shiver to imagine the possibilities."

We amble through groves of Maples where we feast on Leeks, Spring Beauties, and Violets. In an Aspen savanna we find some very satisfying Ant larvae, which we top off with a garnish of vinegary Sorrel from under the big Pines. Then it's back to the savanna for a dessert of late Raspberries and early Blackberries.

THE PROBLEM
WITH SEEING TOO MUCH

While hunting, a Serval (a midsized African Wildcat) may pause for up to fifteen minutes at a time, close her eyes, and listen for rodents. Blind people have a similar skill: many of them can hear solid objects in front of them. They are also able to develop an acute sense of touch, to the point where many of them can read with their fingers. We see the same trait in other animals who have a weak sense and another correspondingly stronger sense. Most Birds do not have a well-developed sense of smell, yet they can have acute hearing or eyesight.

I used this information to help someone new to Nature's ways. "I'm a highly visual person," he told me. "I'm constantly distracted—my eyes are darting all over the place. I can't seem to keep focused on the trail."

"Your affliction is your gift," I replied. "You've been given this great visual ability for a reason. Much sign is missed when people stay focused on the trail. Your only problem is that you happen to live in a visually oriented society. That only encourages you to be more vision dependent than you already are."

To help him engage and exercise his other senses, I suggested the following exercise.

 Spot Search Exercise

1. **Choose a piece of ground** about the diameter of your foot.
2. **Mark it off with sticks or pebbles.**

3. **Get down close to it and allow your senses to expand into it, noting every essence, movement, and particle.**

How many Ants can you find, and what are they up to? Notice how looking under the Grass is like peering into a forest. What do you smell and feel? What does it remind you of? Are there signs of death as well as life?

At first the exercise might seem restrictive. Yet if we practice it every day—a must in order to break our visual dependency—we'll find that it opens a window to a vast world within a world that we did not know existed.

A LESSON IN LISTENING

Scent Tracking

John, a visiting friend from out East, asked if I would demonstrate scent tracking, as he had never heard of Humans doing it. "You came to the right place," I replied. "Out here in the bush, we don't mind sniffing around like Dogs—we don't have much pride."

We had no trouble finding a scent, as the conditions were near ideal: a humid, midwinter afternoon with a faint, variable breeze and the temperature hovering around freezing. The vinegary-musky odor was strong, yet we couldn't go any more than twenty paces in any direction without losing it. We tried zigzagging, a technique I commonly use to get a bearing on the source of a scent, but it didn't help. The breeze was too weak to carry a strong enough scent trail to follow.

"Now what?" John asked.

"Well, I'm humbled," I replied, "and mystified. We could stand here frustrated for a few minutes, and then curse our luck and go home."

"I don't think so," said my stalwart friend. "That doesn't sound like you. Besides, that scent has to come from somewhere."

"You're right," I responded thoughtfully, "and it smells like opportunity. In fact, I'm getting psyched."

I realized that I had a chance to learn more about Deep Listening. It still never ceases to amaze me that the more I learn, the more I'm shown how little I know—or better yet, how much I can look forward to learning.

We decided to methodically radiate out in all directions to define the perimeter of the scent trail. However, all we came up with was an ill-defined, shifting oval.

While contemplating under a large Hemlock near the center of our oval, I felt a cool draft down the back of my neck. At that instant I experienced what a Chipmunk must feel when he becomes suddenly aware of the Hawk perched on the branch above him. There, looking down at us from a large limb about five body-lengths up was a medium-size Porcupine. I hope she got as good a laugh out of being "discovered" as we did.

How can we explain what happened? Let's not attribute it to lack of awareness, as it would be easier on my ego to turn to physics. The interior of the Hemlock funneled a downdraft of cool, shaded air to compensate for the warm air rising off her sun-drenched outer needles. The downdraft laced itself with the bark-eater's scent, then hit the snow and spread out like an inverted Mushroom.

The next time I'm with someone else and come across a mysterious scent, I'm just going to ignore it.

Animals can read each other's feelings quickly and precisely—they have to to survive. As we have learned, we possess the same intuitive ability, only we tend to get stuck on words and tangled up in theories. In the next step, we are going to awaken our animal senses so that we can again Become Nature.

STEP 7

Energize and Attune Your Senses

Imagine a telephone line that links only two phones. That is what ego-based communication, our modus operandi, is like. I am centered in my reality, you are centered in yours, and we connect. This gives us a narrow and often simplistic view of things.

Now imagine a vast web of lines interconnecting telephones over a great area. When we function from our Animal Minds, rather than from our egos, our voice reaches the entire Web, even though we may be speaking to only one person. Not only do we hear the voice of the one who is speaking to us but also the voices of those speaking through and around her.

Herein lies one secret as to how some people can perform seemingly miraculous feats of perception such as reading minds and seeing the unseen. Yet there is nothing special happening here, as these abilities are perfectly normal and achievable for all of us. The only reason we can't perform them is that we have become numbed by a lifetime of ego-based existence. Much of our mental capacity goes unrealized (see step 4), and our sensory, emotional, and intuitive powers have atrophied due to lack of use.

Jennine Elberth

The good news is that, like our muscular system, our other capacities and powers can be reawakened and strengthened through exercise. We will accomplish this in three parts: the first will give a sense of where we are going, the second will use stories to show the normal functioning we can expect, and the third will give us the tools to get there.

THE AWARENESS

Anesthesia Teaches Mindfulness

Recently I had an operation requiring spinal anesthesia. This meant that during the procedure I was in a coma from the waist down, while I was conscious and functional from the waist up. As my legs began to fall asleep, I felt my anklebones and buttocks in contact with the operating table, and I imagined feeling them in that position throughout the operation.

After the operation was completed and my wound was dressed, the nurse lifted my legs to see how they looked. I stared wide-eyed at what she was lifting, not believing they could be mine. They looked like my legs being lifted, yet I felt them still lying on the table. She moved my legs around, but it made no difference. My eyes tried to convince me that they were my legs; however, my conscious self recognized them as just two chunks of meat. She moved them around some more; it didn't help.

What was happening? I couldn't bridge the gap between what I was seeing and what I was feeling—I could not own those legs. The reason is that our senses do not give us direct input. When blind people first have their sight restored, they typically see nothing but electronic impulses or meaningless mélanges of colors and shapes. What we "see" are impulses translated into something meaningful by our emotional, intellectual, cultural, and habitual selves.

My experience with my legs impressed upon me the fact that I can't trust just one of my senses, nor can I rely merely on my intellect or my feelings. One-dimensional input will give me a one-dimensional answer.

To get around this pitfall we need to listen to all of our senses, along with our feelings, intellect, intuition, ancestral memories, and those other often undefinable voices. Our decisions then come from a place of wisdom and perspective—a place of balance—rather than from knee-jerk reactions that we often regret later. You may have heard this concept expressed as walk in balance, walk with heart, be mindful, *or* Oneness.

When a traditional tracker functions from this place of balanced perspective, he hears the song of the track. If he were to track an animal by listening to only one or two voices, he'd be slowed down and could end up going in the wrong direction or losing the track altogether. When he remains open to every voice in the song, including those that enter and leave the chorus, he changes perspective with the song's mood and melody. This process causes him to constantly refine and redirect his trailing. We function from this same type of awareness when we immerse ourselves in Nature rather than merely observing.

OVERCOMING THE BARRIERS

First: The Ego

As already mentioned, the ego can impede our progress toward Oneness with Nature. An understanding of the ego and how it functions can help us partner with it rather than seeing it as our nemesis. *The ego is the aspect of our psyche that distinguishes self from other.* When we encounter dangerous situations, the ego helps to keep us safe by engaging our fight-or-flight response.

However, when our fight-or-flight response is inappropriately triggered, our ego can isolate us from others by making us self-conscious and inwardly focused. *If when out in the Natural Realm we feel fearful of some animals for no solid reason, or we just feel like we don't belong, we are likely approaching Nature from our ego mind.*

To Become Nature, we want to remove the ego-created barriers that keep us separate from the animals. As covered in step 6, the Shadowing exercises can help us create relationship. Yet if we practice the exercises from ego consciousness, we will fail to connect with the true being we are Shadowing. We'll only know the image created by our ego.

When we approach the world from our ego mind, we see and interact with everyone as separate beings. *When we function from our*

Animal Mind, we become multidimensional beings not dependent upon *ego* for our sense of identity. If we can relate to an animal as a multi-dimensional being we will be able to see beyond his ego-self as well. We'll then recognize him for who he is, rather than for what his shadow projects. This is pure relationship, and the Coming to Oneness exercise on page 143 is designed to take us there.

Second: Limited Life Experience and Prejudice

These are notorious for creating additional barriers to awareness and attunement. They both play big roles in shaping how we view the world, often causing us to miss what could otherwise be seen. I remember when I was young and many coniferous Trees looked the same to me. Once I learned their distinguishing characteristics, they appeared as distinct from one another as Dogs are from Cats.

We often categorize for the sake of convenience. I might decide to ignore deciduous Trees for the moment so that I can focus on learning the coniferous Trees. Prejudice is something different: it is categorizing out of bias. I don't like Cats—they all look and act alike.

Whether it is lack of life experience or prejudice, it blinds us from seeing groups or individuals for who they actually are. It doesn't matter if it's Spiders, Butterflies, or Muslims; they become cloaked either in our ignorance or the erroneous opinions we hold.

Third: Having Answers

We can dissolve our prejudices and grow in life experience in two ways: *being in the now* and *being as a question*. Steps 1 through 4 have brought us into the now; being as a question means engaging life in a way that encourages an endless stream of inquiry and wonder.

Questioning keeps us engaged in the now, whereas answers cause us to move on and tune out any further information. While it may be uncomfortable to be as a question in a culture that heavily favors answers, it is usually those who embrace the questioning path who become our trailblazers. Albert Einstein, who is noted for his intellect, recognized the incredibly valuable role of questioning when he said, "I have no special talents. I am only passionately curious."[1]

Where an answer will feed us once, a question will teach us how to find food. An answer will show us a crystal, and a question will take us inside, where we will be drenched in kaleidoscopic splendor.

Now that we are mindful of these barriers, we can work on keeping them from interfering with our sensory attunement. The following stories will give real-life examples of how it can be done.

THE STORIES

Shoreline Tracking

An Eagle glided low over the beach that my students and I paddled toward. Pulling up on the sand, we noticed the tracks of a small animal trailing down the shoreline. As this was a Nature-awareness class, everyone was immediately down on their hands and knees, trying to figure out who went by.

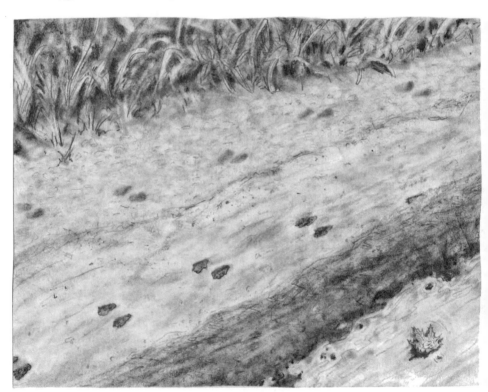

"Maybe it's a Squirrel," one of them offered.

"No," said another, "a Squirrel has only four front toes, and I see five."

"Look at the pads on this footprint . . . looks like a baby Raccoon."

"How about Muskrat?"

"Step back and take in the Web," I encouraged them.

They all got up and literally stepped back, yet they were obviously confused as to why.

"It is possible to know the animal, and in fact the whole story, at first glance," I told them. "Do we get to know a plant by studying just the blossom? Look down the beach and see how the animal zigzagged. As you know, Muskrats are drawn to vegetation, and there's hardly any here. You've seen Raccoons working the waterline for morsels, and even wading in for Crayfish."

"Raccoons and Muskrats would probably be walking instead of bounding down the beach like this guy," said one of the students. "I think Skunks mostly walk too."

"Let's use what's going on here as an example of what I call Web Consciousness. Imagine that the tracks are one strand of a Web, and when we focus on it, the rest of the Web goes out of focus. That's what we did here. Do you see the high-water line etched in the sand by the waves from last night's thunderstorm? Now take a look at the wave line closer to the water's edge."

"That must've been made by this morning's breeze," offered a student.

"Aha!" exclaimed another student. "The tracks are between the two lines, so they had to be made sometime last night after the storm and before the morning breeze."

"That rules out Squirrels; they're not active at night," commented someone else.

"As always, there's more to the Web," I said. "See those tracks up there?"

"Looks like they're from the same animal," stated a student, "only they're higher up on the beach, above the storm-wave line."

"How do they differ from the tracks between the two wave lines?" I asked.

"They're definitely older looking," offered a student. "They're pretty washed out, so they had to be made before or during the storm."

"What does that say?"

"That the beach could be part of the critter's regular rounds."

"Notice that both sets of tracks show the animal poking around in some of the same cubbies," I add.

"Wait, I've got an idea!" exclaimed one of the students. "Could this be a female Mink with cubs?"

"You got it," I said. "What did you put together?"

He replied that it was the size of the animal and the fact that she was bounding, along with her focusing on this particular section of shore.

We then sat down in the sand and talked about how the fascinating part of the story wasn't so much about identifying the animal, which we could have done right away by pulling out a tracking field guide. It was more about Becoming the Web: the interplay of the beach, the storm, the waves, and the animal. That's what gave us the *hows* and *whys*, and that's how we got a glimpse into the eyes and mind and heart of the animal.

Wolf Tag

Years ago in my youth I was privileged to live with a pack of semi-domesticated Wolves. Simbut, which means Silver Wolf in Mohican, was the alpha female. We met when she was eleven days old and her eyes hadn't yet opened. I was right there when they did, and we bonded instantly. We grew up as pack mates, which gave me an intimate view into the life of a being who dwelled in natural Oneness.

From time to time I'd notice Simbut going off by herself to find a quiet place, perhaps slightly elevated, with a good view of her surroundings. There she'd sit, sphinxlike, and in short order she'd look very relaxed. Her breathing slowed, her eyes were half closed, and she seemed oblivious to her surroundings, ready to drift off to sleep.

"What an opportunity!" I'd tell myself. Sneaking up behind her, I'd attempt to give her tail a tweak. It was the form of tag we played, with her nipping at my ankles to tag me.

However, it was hardly a fair game, as she nearly always bested me.

I hate to admit that, so I usually just say that she hated having her tail touched. And it's true: any time I got close, she'd tuck it between her legs and scoot her hindquarters away from me as fast as she could.

It seemed as though she was overreacting just to be comical. Whether or not she intended it, she looked so silly with her rear end practically rolled underneath her belly that I'd end up writhing on the ground in a fit of laughter.

Worse yet, she'd then exploit my vulnerability by rushing in to nip my ankles.

Yet her love of the game overruled how much she detested having her tail touched. She would flirt her derrière confidently before me, knowing the odds of me actually nabbing it were close to nil. So I didn't at all see that I was taking advantage of her when she was half asleep; I just figured the odds were closer to even.

I would take my time stalking, moving stealthily when the breeze rustled the branches, then freezing when the breeze stilled. Detecting no change in Simbut's demeanor, I'd grow hopeful that this would finally be the time I could best her.

The only movement I could detect from her would be an ear moving ever so slightly. Wolves, like many other animals, periodically turn their ears to catch sounds from various directions. Yet Simbut's ear movements were so casual and seemingly disconnected from her consciousness that I'd just pass it off as twitches.

When I got close enough, I'd extend my hand very carefully, inching closer and closer to that elusive tail. Just as I was about to wrap my fingers around it and surprise the heck out of her—finally giving me a point— she would bolt like lightning, with her tail between her legs and that silly scramble with her hindquarters tucked under her belly.

And would I jump! What a master of deception—she had to be watching me the whole time. I'd then be so pumped up with adrenaline that I'd scramble after her and make an even bigger fool of myself. She, of course, would let me get close enough that my fingertips just barely breezed over the tips of her fur, then she'd scoot off again.

Once she was a safe distance away, she'd stop and look over her shoulder at me, as though to say, "Is that the best you can do?"

At first I thought Simbut's super-awareness was something special, yet as I got to know the other Wolves in the pack, I came to realize that they all had the ability. So do domestic Cats. If you want to experience sensory attunement animal-style, your Cat might be glad to demonstrate it to you. When she is perched on a banister or on the back of the couch, seemingly oblivious to her surroundings, test her as I did Simbut.

I've observed this state of attunement in many animals, and also in Native people. As with animals, Natives use it to rest and conserve energy, while at the same time maintaining alertness. Hunters, both Human and animal, will use this state to help them remain invisible. They dwell on the Shadow side of things (see step 9), which lets them move within the greater movement and send out as little revealing energy as possible.

It takes firsthand experience to truly know the difference between ego consciousness and Animal Mind attunement. Words simply cannot capture the Animal Mind sense of being alerted to someone's presence by sensing him staring at you. Yet others' experiences can give a taste, so I will share three short stories, to help you recognize attunement when you achieve it.

Deer Crossing

While paddling a shallow river, my eye caught a break in the underwater vegetation. Being in my Animal Mind, I knew right away what caused it.

Glancing down, I switched to rational consciousness and quickly assessed the narrow, stripped-away swath that spanned the river from bank to bank. This Deer crossing, I thought would be a good place to Count Coup (see step 12) or set a snare. Being creatures of habit and pattern, just like us, Deer cross streams at the same time and place each day.

I learned that habit by observation, which made the Deer both familiar and vulnerable to me. Deer realize that they are vulnerable in the water, so they like to choose crossings with good visibility and solid footing. Using this immediate information, along with other strands from the surroundings, prior experience, and ancestral memories, I gained perspective on the Web and Envisioned how I would Count Coup.

Paddling on, I returned to my place in the Hoop—not as me, but as a Deer. I watched myself crossing the river several times up ahead. Most of the time when I reached the spots, I saw that they were actual Deer crossings.

Shrew Thinking

One autumn a Shrew moved into my upstairs bedroom. I had space to share, as she was tiny and didn't ask for much. However, she took to chewing up nearly anything that was once alive, including Turtle shells, Bird wings, rawhide containers, and anything tied with sinew.

Entering my Animal Mind, I became a strand in the Web and listened. As you now know, Animal Mind listening has little to do with picking up sound waves and more to do with sensing the rhythms of the animal and the interplay of related factors. Returning to my rational mind, I set a trap and went downstairs to hang out with a visiting friend.

To test myself, I told him that I had just set a trap upstairs for a Shrew and that she would be caught in ten minutes. He glanced at the clock on the wall, then we lost ourselves in discussion.

We heard a snap. My friend looked at the clock and gave me a disbelieving look. I went upstairs, brought down the Shrew to take outside, and we returned to our dialogue.

Invisible Meal

The day was warm and the grassy spot overlooking the pond in front of my house invited me over. I gladly obliged and relaxed into the languid mood of the afternoon. Nothing stood out, and I didn't notice any conspicuous signs of animal life.

Once settled in, I Became the touch of the sun and the smell of the water, and another dimension revealed itself to me. A flicker of light at the edge of the water became a Frog, a couple of Mosquitoes hovering a forearm's length from that Frog revealed another one, and then a third. An Ant taking a shortcut over my leg drew my attention to dozens of ants around me, busy scurrying between succulent Fiddleheads and tender Raspberry and Strawberry leaves. In the shallows at my feet were cattail roots and tender shoots, along with floating Duckweed.

Out of the corner of my eye I caught a wisp of orange flitting among the plants behind me. Turning around, I watched a Monarch Butterfly laying eggs one by one on Milkweed shoots that I hadn't seen when I sat down, even though I had looked for them.

Right there within reach was all the food I would need to sustain me for the day: protein, fat, carbohydrate, and greens. It didn't come to light because I was looking for it when I sat down to write. Rather, I had drifted into my Animal Mind, which put me in a state of attunement that held neither expectation nor attachment to outcome. I melded into the Hoop of Life and became no more intrusive than a shadow. What was initially invisible to me then emerged as though someone pressed a button, raising Frogs and Fiddleheads from discrete subsurface chambers.

THE EXERCISES

Start with Not Doing

When I'm asked what I did to reawaken my senses and broaden my awareness and attunement abilities, I reply that it is actually about what I did *not* do. As discussed in step 4, when we are constantly bombarded by sensory input we become overstimulated. Out of self-protection, our sensory receptors start to desensitize. If they kept functioning at normal capacity, we'd be overloaded with sensory input and in time probably go psychotic.

The upshot of overstimulation is that we become deadened to our surroundings and end up tuning out a good share of the natural world. This awareness, which we covered in step 4, is so important that it cannot be overemphasized.

I took one giant—and simple—step to bring back my sensory acuity, and that was to quit inundating it. I went for years without seeing a movie or playing recorded music, I lived without electricity, I drastically reduced my reading time, I got rid of my alarm clock and avoided routine jobs, and I distanced from friends whose lives rotated around these practices.

"So what was left of your life?" people ask. I reply that it was quite the reverse: life started flooding in. I had been living as a passive receptor, for the most part coasting along and merely existing. I was barely connected to the means and ends of my existence. Eliminating that deluge of canned sensory input bathed my senses in what they were designed to receive: natural light, Nature's music, and natural sights, along with friends of like awareness. The change in me was miraculous.

Everyone is different, so don't think you have to be as radical as I was to accomplish the same goals. The following exercises will give you the essence of what I have done, in ways that you can incorporate into your everyday life.

The Foundation Exercise

When we attempt to connect with Nature but are not in our Animal Mind, we typically either consider our effort a failure or it feels too much like work. Rather than settling for frustration and limited results, give the following exercise a try. I learned it from my Wolf friends, and I've watched a variety of animals do the exercise before going on the hunt. A Native Elder showed me the exercise as well, which she called "Coming to Oneness." It does wonders to dissipate the fog of civilization and bring us to Oneness/Animal Mind consciousness. Some people describe it as an active meditation.

Coming to Oneness Exercise

1. **Find a location, preferably outdoors,** that gives an overview of your surroundings and is relatively free of the noise and distractions of everyday life.
2. **Choose a comfortable place to sit.** Avoid discomforts such as extreme temperatures and wind exposure, especially when first practicing. Sit erect and cross-legged: a posture conducive to Oneness.
3. **Breathe deeply and slowly,** to relax into your posture. Give mental and emotional static neither attention nor inattention, as feeding static makes it grow and suppressing it only causes it to crop up again. Left alone, it will drift by like a cloud over the sky.
4. **Let your attention get caught up in something close by,** such as a pebble, an Insect at your feet, or a leaf that is turning golden. Allow

yourself to be absorbed by the item and taken into relationship with everything connected to it.

Let's say you chose a pebble. Notice that it is surrounded by other pebbles. From there, your attention is drawn to the stones of all sizes that cover the hillside before you. You realize that the next hill must be sprinkled with stones as well, along with the unseen hills beyond that one. Your consciousness is now comprised of all the pebbles and hills that roll before you and all that touches and is touched by them.

The Wolf pups would focus on a little something that caught their attention, such as a Butterfly, and let her movements take them from being caught up in themselves to flowing seamlessly beyond self. A serenity would then overtake them that unbounded them from their physical forms and emotional involvements. They commingled with their surroundings like a breeze flowing through the Trees.

When It Doesn't Work

When we get distracted or hung up on any step, we just start over. Because we are breaking an entrenched pattern, it may take a number of attempts to progress through the steps.

Another option is to let our distraction be our doorway. Whether it is rain, a noisy Bird, or a wild thought, it can draw us out of ourselves and into the world. Following is a story from the Zen tradition about how this can work.

There was once a Seeker and an Elder who were walking together down a country lane.

"Honored Elder," spoke the Seeker after a time of silence, "where can I find the doorway to awareness?"

"Do you hear that stream flowing over there?" asked the Elder. "Let that be your doorway."

"But I can't hear it," replied the frustrated youth after he strained to pick up the sound he expected to hear. "Those rickety old carts and noisy Oxen and Donkeys going up and down the road drown everything out."

"Then let that be your doorway," replied the Elder.

When we resist what is given to us, we often trigger an emotional response such as frustration or resentment. These act as barriers to openness and connection. On the other hand, when we let thoughts and feelings flow freely, regardless of whether we consider them positive or negative, we remain mentally and emotionally clear. As Jiddu Krishnamurti says, "The ability to observe without evaluating is the highest form of intelligence."[2] Without judgment or frustration as barriers, we're able to look at something as an opportunity rather than an obstacle.

The beautiful part of Coming to Oneness is that there is nothing to learn. All we are doing is sidestepping the clutter that keeps us from relationship. As Oneness is intrinsic to our being, we are merely returning to our normal state, with no further effort needed.

Yet most of us will need to repeat the exercise regularly until we break the habit of relying upon our controlling ego. In time we will be able to switch to Animal Mind consciousness without the exercise. In fact, it will often occur spontaneously.

Many of us will find the exercise easy, as we are essentially distracting ourselves from the rational mind-set, which we are already adept at doing. Only here we can view distraction as something positive. We could view distractions more affirmatively anyway, as they are typically the mind's attempts to return to its natural state.

Once we have returned to Oneness, we are in the most conducive state to reawakening our senses.

Four Sensory-Attunement Exercises

1. Everyday Practices

Most of these take little or no extra time and will fit right in to our regular routines.

- Wear soft, thin footwear and clothing.
- Identify the sources of sounds.
- Notice what people are wearing. Choose jewelry one day, shoes the next, and so on.

- Eat outside.
- Find a pattern in the carpet, tile, or sidewalk, and follow it.
- Take stairways rather than elevators/escalators.
- Spend time with a child under six years of age for four consecutive hours every week.

2. Aerobic Exercise

Physical attunement is a cornerstone to sensory attunement. It can be done nearly anywhere with little or no expense.

- Choose any activity that engages the major muscle groups, such as swimming, jogging, tennis, or fast dancing.
- Start slowly, working up to a 30-minute activity period.
- Perform at 60 percent of your peak heart rate.
- Mix up your routine to avoid repetitive motion injuries.
- Exercise every other day for maximum benefit.

Start Smart

If you are overweight, have a chronic health problem, smoke, drink, lead a sedentary lifestyle, or are over forty years of age, consult with a health care practitioner before beginning.

Benefits of Aerobic Exercise

- Weight loss
- Increased stamina
- Lower heart rate and blood pressure
- Improved cholesterol profile
- Greater sensory awareness
- Stronger immune system
- Less sickness
- Reduced fatigue
- Increased muscle strength
- Improved mental health
- Increased life span

All of these benefits will help us be more present, aware, and functional in the Natural Realm, along with increasing our quality of life in general.

✿ 3. Urban Attunement Training

Here are some basic ideas to get you started.

- **Take a tour of one city by following the map of another city.** The inherent contradictions activate our senses and force us to attune to our surroundings.
- **Follow a random algorithm,** such as *go north for two blocks, then east for one, and south for three, and then repeat.* Use the cardinal directions rather than *right* and *left*. (See "Getting into Animal Mind-Set" on p. 67).
- **Hang paper and pencils in public places** for people to answer questions such as, "When was the last time you cried?" And "What smell comes immediately to mind?"
- **Put something out of place,** such as a nearby trash-can lid on a park bench, and watch people's reactions.
- **Use your imagination** to come up with other ways for pulling yourself and others out of normal, disconnected routines.

In the city we usually proceed from point A to point B and miss nearly everything in between. We ignore smells and sounds and the memories attached to them. We pass by curiosities and miss what they might bring us. We note the weather only if it poses some inconvenience. Yet it doesn't have to be that way: we don't have to wait until we can get out in the woods to work on awakening our senses and attuning to natural rhythms. We can do it anywhere in the city, even on the job or when we are out for the evening.

Guiding Points for Urban Awakening

- **Have an abstract structure** so that you will be neither goal oriented nor aimlessly wandering.
- **Notice the patterns**—or lack thereof—in people, buildings, and landscape.

- **Keep attuned** to weather, location, and direction of travel.
- **Immerse yourself** in whatever feelings, memories, and sensations that arise.
- **And above all, have fun!**

4. Wind Direction Exercise

Here is a quick are-you-paying-attention check-in that can be done any-where and anytime outdoors. With students, and even with friends, I'll spring the exercise at random times. Here's how it typically goes, step-by-step.

> **First:** "Everybody close your eyes, and keep them closed."
> **Second:** "Now *quickly* point in the direction the wind is coming from."
> **Third:** "Now open your eyes and see how close you got."

Those new to the exercise often get a chuckle out of how far off most of them are, and those accustomed to the exercise swear by it, as they've seen how much it has improved their awareness in general.

Four Passion-Awareness Balancing Exercises

Too much passion suppresses awareness, and not enough passion leaves us in sit-and-watch-the-show mode. When passion and awareness are in balance, they feed each other and keep each operating at maximum efficiency. The following everyday exercises help maintain the balance.

1. Mental Pattern Breaking

- **Use your opposite hand** when eating, brushing your hair, and writing.
- **Step first with your opposite foot.** If you typically start walking with your right foot, switch to your left.
- **Look for other opportunities** to do things differently from what you are accustomed to.

This simple exercise has the power to rewire our brains so that we will rely less on knee-jerk reactions and foregone conclusions and instead be more open to listening and attuning to the Hoop of Life.

🏵 2. Balancing Practice

- **Stand on one leg** whenever standing in one spot. Switch legs periodically.
- **Tuck unused foot behind opposite knee** to increase the exercise's effectiveness.
- **Do it blindfolded** when you need a greater challenge.

This exercise builds leg strength and balance, which will increase our mobility and gracefulness. In addition, improved physical balance promotes mental and emotional balance.

🏵 3. Blindfold Walk

- **Choose a familiar trail section** that you can safely walk blindfolded. A narrow trail works best.
- **Blindfold yourself.**
- **Take small steps,** proceeding slowly and deliberately. Come down on the balls of your feet. Let your feet and your memory become your eyes.
- **Freeze, then backtrack,** as soon as you realize you are off the trail.
- **Stop when you are mentally or emotionally fatigued.** Fifteen minutes to a half hour is a reasonable amount of time to begin with.

Along with helping to enliven our sense of sight (by not taking it for granted), we will invigorate our senses of hearing, touch, and taste. Over time we should notice our feet becoming sensitized to the point that we start seeing with them. With even more experience, we'll begin to see images of the trail ahead.

A variation of this exercise is to walk at night without a flashlight (which also helps cure fear of the dark).

✿ 4. Becoming Invisible

- **Choose something to Shadow** whose movement you can easily mimic, such as a person, a pet, or a plant blowing in the wind (see p. 115).
- **Make sure you have left your ego mind,** so as not to send out "look at me" energy.
- **Take each step with the intent of leaving no trace** of your movements.
- **Make no extra effort to become invisible.**

Shadows are paid little or no attention, so we (as with other animals) can be in full sight yet not be seen. A stalking predator becomes a shadow and adopts Shadow Consciousness in order to move within the shadows—a shadow within a shadow. I have a theory that we Humans, having evolved as predators and evaders, are genetically programmed to be shadow movers. All we need to do is dust off that innate ability and give it a tune-up.

We can be identified by what we leave behind—unless we are shadow, which leaves no trail. Following is Shadow Consciousness as expressed two centuries ago by an unknown Zen monk.

> *The shadows of Bamboo leaves move not an inch*
> *although they sweep the ground*
> *The reflection of the moon leaves no scars on the water*
> *although it drills to the bottom.*

As we discussed in step 6, to Shadow something or someone is to leave our own identity behind and become so absorbed and at-one with another being that we move as he moves and think as he thinks. We are no longer limited to ourselves, nor are we attached to what we Shadow. Our Animal Mind Becomes the mind of all. We see, hear, feel, and sense all that is going on around us as well as within us. Ego-based feelings of fear, separation, and mistrust disappear. Vast, seldom used portions of our brain now connect with so much of life, in many ways that were previously unavailable to us.

In time, Shadowing can again become second nature to us: we will drift across the landscape like an unidentifiable wisp, and everything will be as it was before we arrived.

If you have trouble with any of the above exercises, try the Coming to Oneness exercise (p. 143) as a warm-up. I encourage students in my courses to practice Coming to Oneness any time they feel out of sync. For more related exercises, see part 4 of my book *Journey to the Ancestral Self.*

Six Sensory-Awareness Games

These traditional games are sensory and intuitively based, which makes them difficult to describe in words. Games 1 through 5 have accompanying videos of the games being played, which will help tremendously in understanding them. You'll find the videos on the Teaching Drum Outdoor School's website at **http://teachingdrum.org/ becoming-nature**.

The games do not need to be played in any particular sequence, as each will meet you where you're at. Expect to be tremendously challenged, as I chose each one to both stretch cognitive skills and encourage Animal Mind consciousness.

The Rules for All of the Games

- **Nothing matters**
- **Don't think**
- **Don't compete**

Analyzing only gets in the way and causes frustration. The key is to remain aware and observe with all senses. A competitive spirit switches us to ego consciousness, which shatters the Nature Speak Web that connects the players with each other and with the playing pieces.

---

1. Secret Stone Game

Number of players: 2 or more
Materials: 11 varied stones

a. **Arrange the stones in a circle,** with the players sitting in a circle around the stones.

b. **One player starts the game by choosing a stone,** without verbally divulging his selection. Yet in Nature Speak he lets his selection be known and points the other players to it.

c. **The starting player removes a stone** from the circle other than the one she chose.

d. **The next player going sunwise (clockwise) removes a stone,** striving not to take the unidentified stone chosen by the first player.

e. **The game continues in this fashion** until either a player removes the chosen stone or the chosen stone is the only one left.

f. **The next player sitting sunwise chooses a stone,** and the game continues.

When you become proficient—but not before—make up your own variations.

2. Stone Tracking Game

The purpose of this game is to use our intuitive ability to follow a stone that is being covertly passed between the other players.

Number of players: 3 to 5
Materials: 1 flat stone small enough to fit comfortably in the palm of everyone's hand, 1 lightweight stick, as long as you can spread your arms, from fingertips to fingertips

a. **The tracker sits facing the other players,** who are sitting close to each other in a line about 7 or 8 feet from him.

b. **One player shows the tracker the stone,** which is passed to another player, with hands always in full sight of the tracker but not exposing the stone.

c. **The players continue passing the stone** to each other—or making faux passes—in no particular order, in an effort to rattle the tracker's ability to keep track of the stone.

d. **The tracker attempts to continually follow the stone** by pointing the stick at the hand she thinks holds the stone.

e. **When the time is up, the stone is revealed;** 3 to 5 minutes works well.

f. **Each player takes four consecutive turns** at tracking.

3. Stick Game

Before playing, have only one player go to page 157 to find out the secret of how the game works, which is then kept from the other players.

Number of players: 2 or more
Materials: 9 hand-length or slightly longer sticks

a. **All players sit in a circle,** facing each other.

b. **The informed player arranges some or all of the sticks** before him in a random pattern.

c. **That player asks, "How many sticks are there?"**

d. **All players venture their answers.**

e. **When someone answers correctly twice in a row, that person takes a turn** at laying down the sticks, and so on, until everyone either gets the game or starts tearing their hair out.

4. Spiderweb Game

Start with having only one player turn to page 158 to get the secret of how the game is played. Keep it from the other players.

Number of players: 3 or more
Materials: Pointing stick (optional)

a. **All players sit in a circle,** facing each other in silence.

b. **The informed player spins an imaginary web** between several nearby objects, pointing with stick or finger as she says something like, "I'm spinning a web from this stone, to the end of that log, to Susan's left elbow."

c. **The spinner asks, "Whose web is it?"**

d. **Players offer their answers,** until someone correctly identifies the player possessing the web.

e. **The first person to answer correctly twice in a row is the next spinner,** and so on.

❁ 5. Drum Stalk

Number of players: 2 or more
Materials: Blindfolds and a drum or other noisemaker

a. **All players but the drummer disperse** throughout a wooded area, blindfold themselves, and spin around several times to disorient themselves.

b. **The drummer positions herself** as equidistant as possible from all players, in a spot challenging enough to meet the players' skill level.

c. **The drummer plays a few beats.**

d. **The players make their way toward the drum,** the goal being to stay on course and progress as quietly as possible. When players are no longer clear on their bearings, they freeze and wait for the drum to sound again.

e. **When all players have frozen, the drummer sounds.**

f. **The drummer silently signals players** who reach her to remove their blindfolds and clear the way for others coming in.

❁ 6. Cat-or-Dog Game

I can get obsessed with details. If you and I were out together and came across a feather, such as the Hairy Woodpecker wing feather I found yesterday, you might as well find a comfortable place to sit, because I'm going to stop and read its story. I'll look for compression marks along its quill to determine whether it was molted or torn out, and if it was torn out, who did it. I'll read the stress marks on the barbs, which give the history of the Bird's feeding pattern and physical condition. I'll then check for sheen, coloration, and wear to discover the Bird's age, activity level, and place of origin.

I often do the same with a track: How many lobes are on the leading and trailing edges of the palm pad? Are the toe pads teardrop shaped, oval, or elongated? Does the toenail imprint show acceleration, deceleration, or side motion?

However, I don't ask these questions when tracking an animal. Tracking evolved not as an analytical exercise but to bring home the meat. My goal—and the goal of every animal who hunts by tracking—is to read sign at a glance in order to keep moving and find the animal as quickly as possible. For me, this is the ultimate test in tracking. And the ultimate thrill: my senses are keened, adrenaline is pumping, and I'm high on the exhilaration of the chase. I was obviously born to track.

Yet when I come across a fuzzy track that could be either canine or feline, I'm still tempted to stop and ID it, then read it like I do a feather. The rational mind is a powerful tool that likes to be used. Instead, I've learned to pick up clues at a glance, which can be as definitive as a detailed analysis.

Please remember to view the videos for the games at **http://teachingdrum.org/becoming-nature**.

Easy-to-Read Clues to Distinguish between Canine and Feline Tracks

- Canine tracks tend to be longer than they are wide, while feline tracks are usually the reverse (see illustration below).
- Canines walk more up on their toes than felines, who put more weight on their palm pads.
- Canines have small palm pads and large toes, and felines have the reverse.
- Canine's toes, particularly Wolf and Coyote, are typically bunched together, with the short outer toes tucked partially behind the dominant middle ones. Feline's toes are spread out in a semicircle that wraps about 40 percent of the way around the palm pad.
- Canine's two center toes are the same length, while feline's inner center toe projects forward.

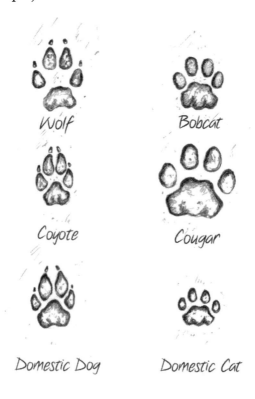

Typical canine and feline tracks

Read the front paw print rather than the rear. In both families the front paws are larger, more articulate, and show more personality than the rears. When we are in our Animal Minds, it is possible to feel the difference in the energy that canine and feline tracks project.

And Now for a Quiz

Why do felines have palm pad–dominant paws and canines have toe-dominant paws? You'll find the answer on page 158.

After you have familiarized yourself with the games, you may notice that they draw upon all of what we have thus far learned and reawakened. The pace is quickening; from here on we should be able to see and feel rapid progress as we strive to compensate for our upbringing in a Nature-deficient society.

The last two games, Drum Stalk and Cat-or-Dog, are both movement oriented. They were placed last in preparation for the next step, where we will learn how to move with the grace of Wolf and the stealth of Cougar.

THE ANSWERS FOR STEP 7

The Secret to Playing the Stick Game (page 153)

As the informed player, you are the first to lay out the sticks. Arrange them any way you like: complex or simple, touching or not. When you're done, rest your hands nonchalantly in your lap or in front of you, as long as all players can easily see them.

The answer to "How many sticks are there?" has nothing to do with how the sticks are arranged but instead with how many fingers you have extended. If you have one extended, the answer is "one." If you have seven fingers extended, the answer is "seven." Be sure to have your fingers naturally exposed, so that your hands do not draw undue attention.

The intention is not to mislead the players but to let them find their way through the preconceptions and focused attention that keep them from seeing with perspective.

When no one answers correctly, give the right answer and throw the sticks again.

If someone answers correctly twice in a row, yet after taking a turn at throwing the sticks it becomes obvious that she hasn't actually discovered the secret, the previous thrower resumes throwing.

The Secret to Playing
the Spiderweb Game (page 153)

As the informed player, you spin the first web. You won't know the answer to "Whose web is it?" until you ask the question, as the web belongs to the first person who speaks.

When a player misidentifies the owner of the web, simply answer "no" and repeat the question. Let the players keep guessing until they choose the right person. Continue playing until everyone solves the game.

If someone answers correctly twice in a row, yet after taking a turn at spinning the web it becomes obvious that he hasn't actually discovered the secret, the previous spinner resumes spinning.

Answer to Quiz (page 157)

Question: Why do felines have palm pad–dominant paws and canines have toe-dominant paws?

Answer: It has to do with movement patterns and hunting strategies. Watch a house Cat pad gracefully and quietly across a room, then compare that with a Dog's more forceful, direct steps. Where felines' padded paws are designed for walking (which they much prefer to running), canines' strong toes are made for speed and traction, and they think nothing of breaking into a run. Although both animals stalk, felines are typically much better at it, and canines generally excel at the chase.

STEP 8

Walk and Paddle Quiet as a Shadow

People who are at-one with Nature are fully immersed in each step they take. Walking is a meditation that brings them into their bodies and the now, which makes walking an awareness raiser and a vehicle for growth.

We who were raised in contemporary cultures tend to view the destination as more important than the journey. We make our choices based on how quickly and conveniently we can reach our destination, and we typically regard the time it takes to get there as an inconvenience. However, in Nature the journey is the destination: where we are going is seldom as important as how we get there.

To truly know animals, we need to walk and run quietly and efficiently through the woods and meadows, as they do. We must allow ourselves to venture forth without our ego shields and hear without words. We need to Become Nature, where the woods will be our classroom and the animals will be our teachers.

Here we will reacquaint ourselves with the way our Native Ancestors moved, which is the way we naturally move when we are fully present and engaged. We'll continue the work we began in steps 3 and 7 on

learning how to transition from being destination oriented to being present in each step of the journey. The exercises are designed to help us break through the shell of self-consciousness and reconnect with the innocent inquisitiveness of childhood.

At the same time, we'll learn how to incorporate the knowing perspective of our life experience into our movements. One of those experiences is Becoming the animal, an innate survival skill we will learn how to practice in step 11. When we Become an animal, we start walking like him: so purposeful that it appears purposeless. In the Natural Realm there is no other way to move. Every step takes an animal either closer to or further from death, so every step must be both solid and adaptable to instant change.

NATURAL WALKING

As we learn to allow the terrain to dictate each step, our feet glide with the grace of a ballerina and the flow of a t'ai chi master. Our choppy movements turn to liquid, and we find our way as smoothly as water winding through the rocks in a riffle. In essence, we merge with all other movements: we Become Nature.

This may sound poetic, yet it addresses a purely mechanical process. Every action has its equal and opposite reaction. For this reason we want to be as present as possible when we move, so that we can be as present as possible with whatever our movement triggers. With walking, this means having a visceral connection with every step.

Footwear
Think of walking as a form of touch. When we have sensory connection with every step it will likely be a conscious step. While I recommend walking barefoot as often as possible, we do sometimes need foot protection. Every time our feet (or hands) are excessively chilled or overheated, they lose a degree of sensitivity. Every cut creates scar tissue, which decreases sensitivity. At the same time, we want to maintain our tactile connection by having as little as possible between our feet and what they touch.

Heavy footwear is noisy and increases the chance of tripping. The best footwear follows the contour of the foot and is light and flexible to allow for complete and unencumbered movement. The closer footwear feels like wearing no footwear, the better it is. In essence, it should function as a second skin.

I know of only one type of footwear that meets all of these criteria: the moccasin (see illustration below). It was the footwear of our Ancestors, and it is still worn in various forms by Native people all around our Mother Planet.

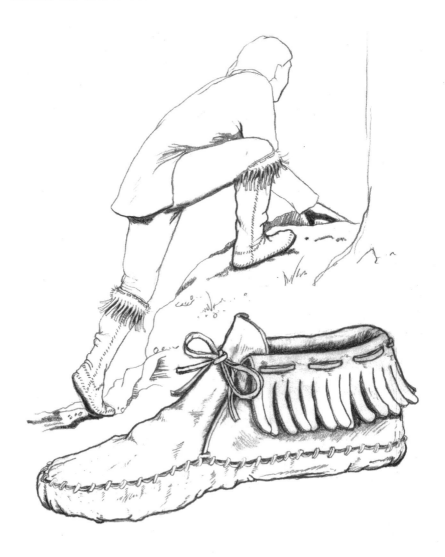

A Moccasin's Benefits

- **Thin:** Which allows the foot to see.
- **Quiet:** Flexibility and lack of sharp edges reduces snapping and crunching.
- **Breathable:** Which helps keep the feet dry and promotes foot health.
- **Strengthening:** Suppleness allows for all foot muscles and joints to aid walking, where most shoes force a few major muscles and the ankle joint to do most of the work.
- **Comfortable:** They are form fitting and adjust to the individual foot.

Moccasins custom-made for your feet are the best choice. Next best are commercial moccasins or moccasin-style shoes.

Commercial Footwear Criteria

- **Avoid heels of any sort:** They alter gait, reduce sensitivity, and increase the chance of ankle injury.
- **Avoid protruding soles:** Which catch on things and encourage flat-footed walking.
- **Choose flexible soles:** Which are thin, soft, and an integral part of the shoe.
- **Allow room for unencumbered toe movement.**
- **Size exactly to the length of your foot:** As overlong shoes cause tripping.
- **Choose below-ankle uppers:** So as to not inhibit ankle movement.

Relearning to Walk

Our Ancestors and those who grew up in hunter-gatherer communities were taught to move like the animals they hunted. They let the landscape and the moment dictate their movements. To someone who has no experience with natural walking, it can look like a chaotic mix of slow and fast dance styles injected with a good dose of free-form rock 'n' roll. Someone might take several flat-footed steps to get maximum traction on slick rock, followed by digging in the sides of his feet on a section of loose gravel. He might then be up on the balls of his feet to step over a couple of rocks, then on his heels to flow gracefully over a small rise. The next step could only be a touch-down on the tips of toes to slip between two close roots.

When I was a child, my friends and I called it Indian walking. I've heard it referred to as woods, Fox, Wolf, Native, and natural walking. I now call it Deerstepping or Bearwalking in honor of these two siblings who have shown me the intricacies of their unique ways of walking. Deer is usually up on her toes, and Bear is typically flat-footed. Both are able to adjust their steps in infinite ways to meet the situation.

A Thousand Ways to Walk

A visitor to my camp once commented that he learned six different kinds of walking at an outdoor-skills school he attended, then he asked how many walking styles I knew.

After a moment of feigned reflection, I responded, "I guess I don't know any." A couple of seconds later I added, "Then again, you could say I know thousands."

He was silent.

In a more serious tone, I said, "There can be as many walking styles as a person wants to invent. A chef's school could teach several different styles of cutting vegetables. Yet when we're actually doing it, don't we constantly adjust our cutting to the vegetable, based on its size, texture, firmness, and quantity?"

"I guess that's true," he replied. "So how would you teach that?"

"No need," I responded. "We already know it—it's our natural way of walking."

"Then why don't I naturally do it?"

"Because you were unnaturally raised. A Wolf brought up like a house Dog would be just as bumbling as any city person if she were taken out in the wilds."

We can easily restore our atrophied ability, I explained to him, by skipping the rational book or class approaches and asking Nature to be our teacher. We'll then quickly learn to adapt our step spontaneously to the continually changing situation. All we need to do is allow ourselves the freedom to do it.

Let the Animals Be Our Guides

Deer taught me the fine points of jumping and sidestepping while keeping my head directed and steady; Wolf showed me how to walk efficiently with a group through snow and dense vegetation; Cat gave me variations on how to counterbalance my leg swing with my body rather than with my arms. Rather than watching, I learned through feeling, by Becoming these animals (see step 11). I am enchanted by every animal's waltz and every Tree's sashay, and I shirk no opportunity to Become them and have them continue to teach me.

Have you noticed that the most fleet and agile of animals walk on the balls of their feet, or even on their toes? It's true for the fleetest of Humans as well, from basketball players to ballet dancers. Most predators who give chase are Deersteppers. They have elongated hind feet and high ankles that function as additional leg joints, which give them additional leverage and speed. Along with the Deer family, canines are a good example.

Bearwalkers, who are down on the flats of their large feet, are not known for their speed. Instead, they are either large (like Bear), have other defenses (like Porcupine), or escape by other methods, such as climbing (Raccoon) or swimming (Beaver).

We are unique among the animals, as we can Bearwalk, Deerstep, and everything in between. That makes it possible for us to learn something from practically any animal. The following exercises will help prepare us for that, as well as for how to become invisible in the wild (see step 9).

Toning Up

Our goals here are twofold: develop the musculature involved in walking and restore connective tissue flexibility. Our flat-surface walking style has caused our foot, leg, hip, thigh, and lower back muscles to develop in ways that are not conducive to Deerstepping. On top of that, a lifetime of chair sitting has shrunk our tendons and stiffened our joints.

The following exercises can restore all of our walking-related capacities. The major drawback of exercise routines is that most people abandon them. Not so with this one, says my students, as there is no special equipment needed. The exercises can be done practically anywhere and anytime, in conjunction with normal routines.

Toning Exercises

1. **Sit cross-legged:** Which will eliminate the majority of your chair use. The many benefits include strengthening and lengthening foot and leg muscles and connective tissue, correcting the common tendency toward duck-footedness, and improving hip-joint rotation.

2. **Sit and rise without the help of hands:** This multiplies the benefits of sitting cross-legged, along with strengthening the lower back.

3. **Sleep cross-footed:** With legs outstretched and heels next to each other, overlap your toes. This practice is especially effective in correcting duck-footedness, as the body regenerates during sleep.

4. **Squat:** It improves balance, promotes knee-joint mobility, and strengthens and stretches the Achilles' tendon and calf muscle, which Deerstepping constricts. Work to keep your heel on the ground. Natives typically squat to rest, relieve themselves, and keep from sitting on cold or damp ground.

5. **One-foot balance:** Whenever standing, raise one foot and slightly bend the other knee. To increase effectiveness:
   • **Tuck raised foot behind opposite knee**
   • **Raise and lower yourself**
   • **Blindfold yourself** (merely closing eyes is not as effective, as you know you can open them at any time)
   • **Dress and undress** (including shoes and socks) in this position

6. **Toe stand:** Rise up on your toes just enough so that your heels clear the ground. Progress in this order:
   a. **Flex one calf for two seconds,** relax it, and flex the other. This stimulates a slow walk or stalk.
   b. **Keep the relaxed leg in a state of dynamic tension,** which simulates instant readiness (rescue and military organizations call this "stand-by alert").

   c. **Rise up a little farther with each flex,** so that after a dozen or so flexes your heel is raised to its maximum.

   d. **Reverse the process,** returning to the point where your heel almost touches.

7. **Ankle stretch:** Start by standing on one foot, and then:

   a. Stretch out the other leg and point toes downward and inward, with toes just off the ground (see illustration below).

   b. Hold that position until you feel a good buildup of tension from the ligaments and muscles on the outside of your foot and ankle stretching.

   c. When releasing tension leaves your foot feeling somewhat numbed, as though you've been sitting on it for a while, switch to the other foot.

   d. Repeat the exercise until your feet feel fatigued.

Ankle stretch

8. **Skipping:** There is no simpler way to strengthen calves and thighs, or to get in the habit of moving on the balls of your feet.

How to Deerstep

When I give my knees a slight bend and step lightly, I enter a moving meditation in which I Become my animal self. I am a silent stalker, walking in the shadow of the Deer before me. His faint essence tickles my nose as it hangs in the damp air. In that moment I am his blood brother, possessed by the spirit of his kind as I move with the light touch of my hooves on the trail. I turn my ears this way and that to catch a rip in the familiar patchwork of sounds that clothe the forest.

The instructions below will allow us to slip in to the shadow of the Deer. They'll be especially helpful for those who have no experience or who have trouble getting started. Once we have these basics down, we'll be able to quite easily pick up the finer points of Deerstepping on our own.

Getting Started: Body Posture

Watch the instructional video called *Native Walking* at **http://teaching drum.org/becoming-nature**.

1. **Center yourself in your belly:** It is our gravitational center. Let the body rotate around it rather than the head. Relax, loosen your arms, and release control of your senses.
2. **Keep knees bent:** They act as shock absorbers, along with helping

to maintain steady and smooth movement. The rougher or more unfamiliar the territory, the more we should keep knees bent to avoid the shock injuries caused by knees fully extended.

3. **Transfer weight to one foot:** Otherwise we will wobble with our first steps as we narrow our straddle (the width between our feet) to get our feet directly under our center.

4. **Maintain a stationary upper torso:** When one leg goes forward so does the opposite hip, instead of using the opposite arm to counter balance. The shoulders and arms can then remain stationary, which reduces choppy movement (see illustration below) and enables one to carry items or use the arms and hands for tasks other than having to swing them back and forth for balance.

✦ Movement Guidelines

1. **Push off and step down on the full forefoot rather than just the outer edge:** We'll then be able to feel instantly what's underfoot so that we know whether we have sound footing or should not commit to the step (see illustration below). On uneven terrain, the forefoot gives a broader, more flexible, and better gripping surface than the heel. Forefoot walking creates considerably less ground vibration than heel walking.

Forefoot walking

2. **Use your ankles:** When we walk on the balls of our feet, our ankles act as another set of cushioning joints to augment the knees, as with Dogs, Horses, and many other animals. This helps to protect both our knees and ankles (the easiest-to-damage joints) from injury.

3. **Choose every step:** It takes only one false step to twist an ankle or disturb a Hornet's nest. When we are not attuned to every step, we miss much more than just where we plant our feet.

4. **Shorten stride:** Short steps are solid steps; they reduce the chance of injury and allow us to react quickly.

5. **Reduce straddle:** The wider our straddle, the more we sway from side to side and advertise our intrusion. When we walk without straddle, our weight is centered over our feet, and we maintain solid control of our movements (see illustration below).

6. **Break up methodical walking patterns:** Stopping to listen and slowing down in rough terrain is typical animal behavior and helps us enter the Silence.

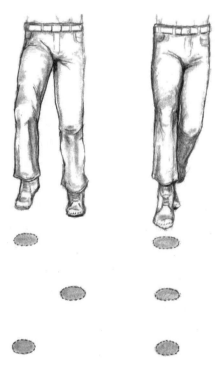

Wide straddle versus no straddle

To Avoid Injury

Be very well practiced at Deerstepping before trekking unfamiliar types of terrain, and especially before running.

Trail Protocols

- **Keep two or three paces behind** the next person, so we can see where to place our next step and not be concerned about abrupt stops or branches snapping back.
- **Maintain balance and a narrow profile** by carrying heavy loads on front or back rather than at our side.
- **Step over obstacles** rather than on them and over depressions rather than into them to keep a low profile and reduce the chance of injury from slipping.
- **Bend down** when approaching dense brush, as it is often open close to the ground, where branches have died off.
- **Go around or duck under branches** rather than pushing them away, to create less disturbance.

Practice Suggestions

Our sense of belonging and our ability to flow with Nature have more to do with the way we walk than with any other awareness or attunement technique we have covered so far. In Nature our feet rather than our hands are our primary touch organs. Whether or not we can see or hear, we *must* feel with our feet.

What is most important here is not that we feel, but *how* we feel. One beauty of practicing Deerstepping is that it can be done virtually anywhere, anytime we are on our feet. Whenever we are on our feet, we are feeling.

Vary the practicing terrain and circumstances as much as possible: crouch, carry things, go up and down hills, through thick Grass, over gravel, or whatever else is around. The more variation, the more flexible, adaptive, and aware we become.

Practice Exercises

1. **Keep the sun at your back** or walk into your shadow on a wall to assess progress at eliminating waddling.

2. **Have someone command you to stop at random times.** The more belly-centered we are, the better we'll be able to freeze midstep.

3. **Practice at night or blindfolded.** Like the Drum Stalk exercise in step 7, this enlivens our foot-touch sensitivity and the Animal Mind in general, which is where our natural walking ability is centered.

4. **Wear a pendulous, weighted necklace.** The less it swings, the less choppy our steps.

5. **Carry an arm-length stick** in each hand, pointing in the direction of travel. Have someone observe while we walk by to see how smoothly the sticks are traveling. To help the observer, tie brightly colored flags to the sticks. At night, attach a flashlight or candle lantern (see illustration below).

6. **Practice on loose soil** so that we can assess our tracks.
   - **If the heel is indented,** we're heel walking rather than forefoot walking.
   - **If there is a push-up behind the forefoot indentation,** we're pushing off before our weight is centered over our other foot.
   - **If there is a side push-up pattern,** we are twisting our foot in a way that could be harmful.
7. **Wear slick-soled footwear.** It challenges us to walk with finesse and leaves little tolerance for mistakes.

Wolfwalking

If you've ever walked any distance through deep snow or heavy undergrowth, you know how energy sapping it can be. Now imagine that you're with others and everyone in the group is struggling similarly. Wolves and many other large animals have found a way to greatly reduce that difficulty: travel single file, with the leader breaking trail and the others stepping in her footprints (see illustration below). I learned the technique from my Wolf pack; so in honor of them, I call it Wolfwalking.

The Benefits of Wolfwalking

- **The pack expends considerably less energy** as a whole, which enables it to travel faster and farther than if not Wolfwalking.
- **The leader chooses the trail** and acts as primary scout, which allows the rest of the pack to relax.
- **Everyone takes a turn leading,** which gives everyone leadership training.
- **It masks the size of the pack,** as only one set of footprints shows.

My students and I practice Wolfwalking for the above reasons, whether or not there is snow or dense vegetation. Wolfwalking is a powerful Shadowing exercise (see step 6), as well as a way to greatly reduce the trampling of vegetation and small animals that typically occurs when a group moves through an area. Whenever you are out with one or more persons, I encourage you to take advantage of Wolfwalking.

Woods Nearsightedness

One habit that negates much of what natural walking has to offer is keeping our eyes glued to the ground. Yet it's understandable that we would want to watch where we're going, as there are sticks, stones, roots, and who knows what else waiting just about everywhere to trip us.

The upshot is that when we focus our attention on where we're walking, we're not giving much attention to what we are walking through. I call it "woods nearsightedness," and it comes from unfamiliarity with natural landscapes. For many of us it's a crutch we've learned to rely upon so heavily that we forget we did just fine without it when we were kids.

Fortunately, it's like most other habits and can be kicked.

Five Steps to Curing Woods Nearsightedness

1. **Slow down:** Reduce expectations as to how far and fast you're going to travel.
2. **Stay centered in your belly:** Remember to see with your feet.
3. **Glance down only every few steps,** more or less often depending on terrain, and hold a mental image of what is coming up ahead.

4. **Deliberately listen, smell, and touch** what is around you, to encourage engagement with the surroundings.

5. **Practice consistently,** as any reversion to the old pattern only reinforces it.

Remember that the exercises in this section are needed only until our natural walking rhythm returns. How long that will take is directly related to how often we practice. Fortunately, these exercises generally bring quick results, so we'll have strong positive reinforcement to follow through.

SHADOW CANOEING

Canoeing Eye-to-Eye

In the headwaters wetlands of Wisconsin's wild Eagle River, Wolves and Bears scout the shorelines; Beaver, Muskrat, and Otter ply the waters; and a host of Birds grace the scene with song and color. Expanses of Marsh Grass, Wild Rice, and Cattails blanket the shallows, while golden Water Lilies dapple the surface of the deeper waters.

This morning I take my time stalking the river's backwaters by canoe, with no intent other than to be at-one with my favorite habitat. Just before a bend, I come across a nose and a pair of eyes skimming the surface of the water, with several sedge leaves in tow. The assemblage passes about two canoe lengths ahead of me, leaving in its wake a perfect V to spread across the mirror-smooth water.

Back and forth, back and forth, go the nose and eyes, packing leaves into the den under the roots of a shoreline Birch Tree that had fallen into the water.

My first urge is to paddle-stalk up to the Tree trunk, perch above the den entrance, and Become a part of the Tree to surreptitiously watch the Muskrat's comings and goings. Perhaps I'd dangle my hand over her, so that one finger, like a bent-over branch, would skim the fur on her back as she swam by.

This time I want something more intimate. Drifting silently up to the den entrance, I position my craft so that when she comes out she'll be swimming right beside me.

My timing is perfect: just as I get in place and lean over the side of the boat to get down to her level, she emerges and swims toward me. Right at the point where I could have shot my hand out and touched her, she glances up. Our eyes meet, and she dives faster than I could ever imagine moving.

Leaving Muskrat to her labors, I round the next bend and slowly approach a head mounted atop a long, arching neck. I'd make more of a disturbance diverting my course, so I just allow myself to drift toward him.

With three canoe lengths yet between us, he gets jittery and slips silently under the surface. Half a minute later he reappears seven or eight canoe lengths downstream. Seeing that I'm still there, he dives again, arching his back sinuously out of the water like a breaching Whale.

Knowing Otters as I do, I figure his curiosity won't allow him to go far. Becoming him, I see a large form drifting slowly downriver toward me. Though it feels intimidating, it's not threatening, as it isn't employing any diversionary or stalking tactics. Yet I need to be cautious, as that thing is big!

At the same time, I'm curious. Hugging the shoreline, I swim underwater around the bend, come up for air, and wait a bit to see what's going to happen. If I don't pick up any warning signs, I'll swim back upstream and take another look.

Returning to myself in the canoe, I stick my hand down into the tannin-stained water and see that it quickly disappears from sight. I don't have to worry about casting an alarming underwater shadow. I paddle discreetly, without breaking the water's surface, creating ripples, or knocking the side of the boat. Slowly I drift to where I imagine he's going to surface for a breath and orient himself before rounding the bend.

I lean over the side of the boat, he surfaces, and we look into each other's eyes. Startling each other, we both jerk back. He executes his classic arched-back dive, only this time in fast motion, and my boat sends shock waves across the water.

As with Muskrat, I could have attempted to Count Coup (see step 12) when Otter surfaced, only I didn't have it in me to cause such fright just to prove I could do something. Neither was it the best setup, as I would have had to be not just in the general area of his emergence, but spot-on, to touch him in the brief instant that his head would be above water.

Furthermore, I realized that being face-to-face with him and looking into his eyes would be more fulfilling than besting him. Ultimately, it's all about relationship: embracing an animal's soul while he embraces mine. We each wanted to know what the other thought and felt, and in that instant of eye contact, we achieved it.

From there I paddle a mile up a clearwater side stream and let myself drift into a small, shallow bay. So that I don't have to break the surface to maneuver, I keep my paddle in the water. Aquatic animals are very sensitive to underwater vibration, which can be caused by even the smallest movement. Yet I've found that I can get away with quite a lot of disturbance, as long as it fits within the animals' realm of experience, such as when I make my movements sound like a splashing Swan or wading Deer.

On the far side of the bay, perhaps three canoe lengths away, floats a young adult Beaver. The uprooted plants floating on the surface tell me that she's feasting on roots and tubers. I drift to within a canoe length of her, she notices me, and with a furious slap of her tail, she is gone.

Becoming her, I realize right away how much I enjoy munching the succulent new growth. I'm not ready to leave, so I duck into the nearby Cattails and wait until the intruder leaves.

Returning to myself, I realize that I can stay right where I am and she'll probably come back. If she detects no further disturbance—which she would feel rather than see—she's likely to reappear pretty quickly.

I get distracted watching a pair of Great Blue Herons, followed by a pair of American Bitterns, landing in the marsh across the stream, to the serenading ker-cheeee of Red-winged Blackbirds. I grew up with their call, and every time I hear it I'm taken back to the wetlands and hayfields of my youth. Once again I'm catching Butterflies and figuring out how to protect Blackbird nests from the farmer's haymower.

American Bitterns have long been favorites of mine because of the male's call, which is not remotely similar to that of any other Bird. My neighbor Ken calls Bitterns plunja Birds, because of their ker-plunk sounding call. Imagine a deep, resonant gulp, amplified loud enough to reverberate over a 200-acre marsh, and you have the call of a plunja Bird.

Ker-splash! *I jerk back and spin around quick enough to see Beaver's back rolling under the surface. As with Otter, I may have been able to Count Coup on her had I been present and seen her coming, as she had swum up right beside me. Yet my hunch is that I would have again chosen not to do so. This time, even without interacting, my yearning for knowing the same curiosity and hunger is fulfilled. The sense of kinship comes from having the same clarity and confidence to make decisions and act spontaneously upon them, along with learning from experience.*

Paddling on, I sense something more to my sharing with Muskrat, Otter, and Beaver than the feelings of elation and fulfillment on which I ride. Clearly, any day that I get to experience what it's like to be another animal is a day to cherish. But why? Maybe it's because we modern Humans look at ourselves as some kind of oddity—we just do not fit with Nature. Or is it the empathy I gain with a wildling that takes me another step closer to dissolving that boundary? Then there's the invaluable knowledge and skill honing. All I can say with clarity is that it's a good day to be alive.

The Magic of Canoeing

We live in a water world. In order to truly know the land and her creatures, we need to know the streams, lakes, and marshes and the creatures who dwell there. We terrestrials came from the water, and you and I can return there to discover roots that lie shrouded in the mists of distant time.

The aquatic realm is a magical place that functions on its own set of rules. Yet like night and day, land and water are not only complementary but also vital for each other's existence. To glide on the water and Become a creature of the water is to gain an intrinsic understanding of the most vital domain in the Hoop of Life.

In the story above, I enact the aquatic parallel to natural walking, with my canoe as my skin and my paddle as my feet. I can move as a shadow on the water, just as I can on land, only much easier. I heartily encourage you to allow the silent paddle and nimble canoe to Become you, as it could do wonders for you on your journey to Becoming Nature.

Oneness with a canoe is Oneness with all that she touches and experiences, all her journeys and discoveries. It is Oneness with all who have touched paddle to water ever since the first Human ventured forth in the first dugout. All the guidance we need awaits us in the water, all of the strokes are in the paddle, and the canoe already knows how to move. All we need to do is sense what wants to happen and dance it into being.

Choosing a Canoe

With clothing, shelter, tools, and most other outdoor-related things, I like to get by with as little as possible. This allows me to become as intimately involved with Nature as I can. I apply the same approach to my canoe, which to me is clothing, shelter, and tool.

On long trips I sometimes use a tandem canoe because of the capacity and efficiency she affords me. Yet her bulk and size severely limit the exploring I like to do. I prefer a canoe that is short for precise maneuvering and light for easy portaging over rough terrain. At about one-third the weight of a typical tandem canoe, a solo canoe gives access to typically inaccessible waters. I especially enjoy small streams not generally considered canoeable, because they are the majority of streams, I have them all to myself, and they bring me up close to animals.

Most Natives would consider the 15- to 17-foot tandem canoes that we typically use recreationally to be freight canoes. Such boats are high-sided and heavy, with up to half a ton of carrying capacity. I know a local Native family of four who, along with their Dog and gear, traveled to summer camp in a craft of such size. For two people with little or no gear, using such a boat is overkill. With compromised maneuverability and the hassle of lugging her around (which cuts in to time on the water), people are sometimes discouraged from going out at all—especially alone.

My fiberglass canoe is ten and a half feet long and weighs eighteen pounds. She is patterned after a cedar strip boat known as the Wee Lassie, which was made in the late 1800s by J. H. Rushton. On a whim, I can hoist her to my shoulder with one hand and take her down to the pond behind my house, or I can quickly slide her into the van and take off. When two of us go out we still generally prefer two solos to a tandem, for the personal freedom and feeling of intimacy with the water world that the small boats provide.

In its agility and responsiveness, a solo canoe is much like a kayak. One sits on the floor, which creates a low center of gravity and makes the boat quite stable (see illustrations on page 185). The boat is maneuvered with body movements as well as the paddle. Sitting low enough to easily see into the water and touch it gives a feel of intimacy. Whether observing, harvesting, or setting nets and traps, it goes better at water level than on a high seat.

On inland waters a solo canoe has advantages over a kayak in that it is shorter, tracks better, and is open, which makes it more suitable for transporting goods, foraging, and hunting. The Algonquin Natives of my area used solo canoes for both travel and hunting, and they quickly became popular with explorers and recreationists. However, they fell out of favor in the early 1900s, and there are now only a few manufacturers. To find one, check with your local canoe shop or search online.

Choosing a Paddle

A solo boat's light weight and easy maneuverability allow for low-effort paddling and the use of a short, light paddle.

What to Look for in a Paddle

- **Wood:** It's warm to the touch, repairable on the canoe trail, biodegradable, and nonreflective. Choose a paddle with straight and clear grain.
- **One piece:** Has length-of-grain strength. Avoid laminates, which are prone to cracking.
- **Flexible:** Cuts down on fatigue, as it absorbs some of the shock that would otherwise be transferred to arms and shoulders.
- **Unfinished:** A rough surface cuts down on the slippage that causes blisters.
- **Thin blade edge:** Slices quietly and efficiently through the water.
- **No rib:** A ribbed blade (see illustration on page 182) creates noisy eddies when the blade slices through the water.

paddle with ribbed blade

Paddle Length

The general rule is to choose a paddle with a neck the same length as our arm. Measure arm length from shoulder joint to the middle of palm, and measure paddle length from the top of the upper handhold to the middle of the lower hand grip (which should be just above the blade). When holding the paddle in paddling position, our two arms and the paddle should create an equilateral triangle (see illustration below), which creates an efficient transfer of energy.

We need a longer-than-recommended paddle if we cannot bury the blade in the water without having to bending over.

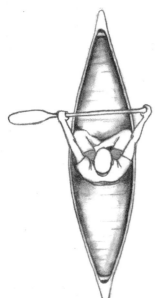

The equilateral paddling triangle

Blade Style

There are three basic styles, each of which is designed for a specific type of paddling (see illustration below).

1. **Ottertail:** Best for deep water. Its narrow width allows for paddling close to the side of the craft, where energy transfer is most efficient, and its long blade provides maximum thrust.
2. **Beavertail:** For shallow water. Its short and wide profile grabs the water for easy maneuvering around obstacles common to creeks, shallow rivers, and wetlands.
3. **Point:** For rapids and rocky shallows. This versatile combination provides for poling and pushing off from rocks and other objects, while still retaining the benefits of a paddle.

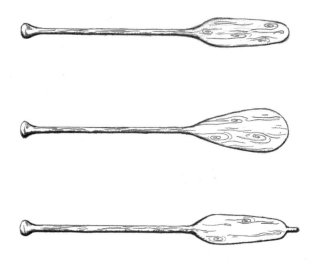

Ottertail (top), beavertail (center), and point (bottom) paddles

The Best Wood

I prefer a paddle made from Pine or Spruce, which is usually light, flexible, and fairly rot resistant. These softwoods make for easy repair and modification (I like to carve the blades down to a thin edge). Yet Ash and other resilient hardwoods make good paddles as well.

Paddle Care

- **Prevention is everything.** Store paddles off the ground (they are favorite Porcupine chews), and don't use them for anything but paddling.
- **Keep out of the sun,** especially when wet, to prevent warping and cracking.
- **Oil periodically** to preserve and waterproof. Any light oil will work. Add about 10 percent turpentine (preserves and aids penetration) and apply warm to a warm paddle.

Boarding and Exiting a Solo Canoe

If you want a lesson in humility, try to board a solo canoe without guidance. If you are already humble, read on.

A Safe and Easy Boarding Technique

Start by positioning the canoe parallel to the shoreline and a few inches out, with the paddle resting on the boat. Follow the illustrations on page 185, and view the video called *Solo Canoe Workshop* at **http://teachingdrum.org/becoming-nature**.

1. **Stand on shore next to the center of the canoe,** facing the bow.
2. **Step into the center of the boat** with your offshore foot. Keep knees slightly bent. If your foot is off center, the boat could tip.
3. **Lean over boat, grabbing both gunnels.** For more stability, place your shore-side hand on the ground next to your shore-side foot; or grab something nearby, as in the bottom illustration on page 185.
4. **Lift your shoreside foot into the boat and slowly sit down.**
5. **Sit either cross-legged or with legs outstretched.** Keep your knees in contact with the sides of the boat, to aid maneuverability.

To exit, execute steps 1 through 4 in reverse.

1

2

3

4

Boarding a solo canoe

A stable way to board and exit

For the Sake of the Canoe

Rather than running the bow up on shore to exit, pull up broadside, which is quiet and prevents damaging the hull.

Paddling

Think of yourself in the middle of the canoe as the craft's pivot point (see illustration below). As much as possible, execute paddle strokes right next to the boat, for the sake of efficiency and to maintain a streamlined profile. Although right-handed people paddle best on their left sides, and vice versa, learn to paddle equally well on both sides to reduce fatigue and give yourself the most maneuvering options.

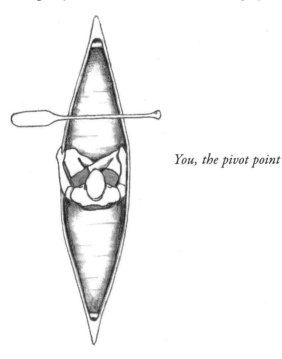

You, the pivot point

Use Your Body

Beginners tend to paddle with arms bent, which requires a tight grip and stresses the biceps, forearms, and wrists. Instead, keep your arms straight and power your stroke with your torso and shoulders, as shown in the video and in the illustration on page 187. This allows

Paddling with torso and shoulders

for a relaxed grip and more efficient paddling with less fatigue and a more enjoyable time.

Thumbs Off

When we've progressed to the point at which canoeing becomes a dance on the water, we'll naturally start letting the paddle find its own momentum. We'll guide it less with force and more with finesse.

The biggest inhibitor to this transition is the lower thumb. We tend to lock it around the paddle neck, which interferes with the sensitive communication between paddler and water. Keeping the thumb on the same side of the neck as the fingers (as shown in the video and the illustration under "Paddle Length," p. 182) frees the paddle to respond quickly to both paddler and water.

At first, we are likely to think that we are gaining sensitivity at the expense of control. However, when the marriage of craft and self is complete, we will discover that the command our grip gave was merely a substitute for the flow that was yet beyond our reach.

Another important benefit of the no-thumbs grip is protection of our all-important thumb from injury. Paddling can easily bruise the joint at the base of the thumb, along with the adjacent connective tissue. In addition, a wrapped-around thumb is prone to being sprained from a jolt to the paddle.

Be Prepared

Carry an extra paddle, and tie it to your boat. The first time you lose your paddle on a portage or watch it go floating downstream, you'll understand why. Include a roll of duct tape for canoe repairs and some cordage for lashing broken paddles (see illustration below).

On-the-spot cracked blade and broken neck repair

Basic Strokes

A good share of my paddling consists of combinations of strokes along with moves that defy categorization. Yet it's good to begin by learning the basic strokes in order to have a foundation from which to draw.

🌸 Rudder Stroke

This basic rudder stroke provides both thrust and steering. A variation of the traditional J stroke, it is used at all times other than when a special maneuvering stroke is required.

1. **Reach forward right alongside the boat** with arms fully extended and paddle held vertically (see illustration series below).
2. **Lower the paddle** until blade is fully submerged.
3. **Draw the paddle straight back,** alongside the boat, as far as you can reach.
4. **Roll your lower hand out,** rotating the paddle 90°, so that the blade sits vertically in the water.
5. **To turn left** when paddling on the left side (as in the illustration below), rotate the upper edge of the blade outward about 45°.
6. **To turn right, do the reverse.**

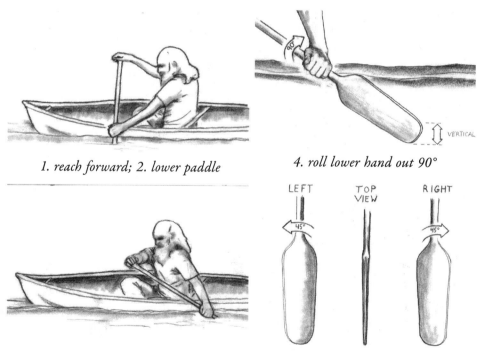

1. reach forward; 2. lower paddle

4. roll lower hand out 90°

3. draw paddle straight back

5. turn by rotating paddle 45° right or left

Rudder stroke steps

When paddling slowly, we only need to give the paddle a slight turn with each stroke to keep on course. When going fast, especially with a canoe that tracks well, we'll only have to rudder with every third or fourth stroke.

🌸 Bow Turn

With the bow turn stroke we make little noise while smoothly turning and maintaining velocity. The following steps are for turning right when paddling on the right side.

1. **Lean forward as far as you can and grab the right-hand gunnel** with your extended right hand (see illustration below).
2. **Clasp the paddle shaft tightly to the gunnel** to help maintain stability and control.
3. **Point the paddle about 30 degrees to the right** of the direction of travel while holding the blade vertically above the water.
4. **Lower the paddle into the water** by raising the grip end.

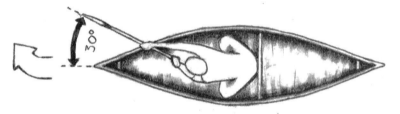

Bow turn

🌸 Cross-Bow Turn

To turn in the opposite direction:
1. **Clasp the left gunnel with your right hand,** as in step 1 above (see illustration below).
2. **Follow steps 2 through 4 above,** adapting them to the left side.

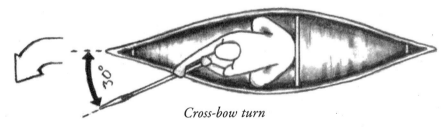

Cross-bow turn

❀ Sweep Stroke

To pivot when not moving, the sweep stroke can be executed on either side of the boat.

1. **Extend the paddle forward,** just as with the bow turn, only do not grab the gunnel (see illustration below).
2. **Slice the paddle into the water.**
3. **Sweep the paddle in a wide arc** all the way around to the stern of the boat. The farther out we reach, the more effective the stroke.

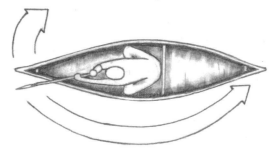

Sweep stroke

❀ Draw Stroke

The draw stroke moves the canoe to the right or left while maintaining the same direction of travel. It is especially useful for sidestepping obstacles in fast water and to pull up broadside to something when not moving forward.

1. **Slip the paddle vertically into the water** at arm's length from the side of the boat and perpendicular to it, holding the face of the blade parallel to the side of the boat (see illustration below).
2. **Pull the paddle directly toward the boat,** which will pull the canoe toward the paddle.

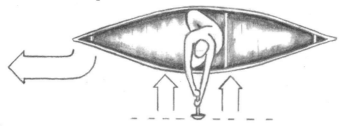

Draw stroke

To Move Backward

All of the strokes can be done in reverse, with opposite effect. They will take additional practice and caution, as they can be destabilizing.

Stopping

Here is the most effective method for stopping.

1. **Slice the paddle into the water** at your side and pull toward the boat (see illustration below).
2. **Undercut the boat as much as possible** to keep the boat from turning while stopping.
3. **Push lower hand forward.**

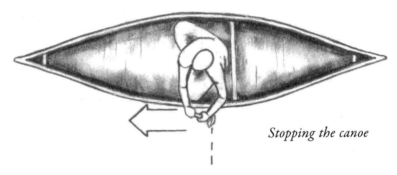

Stopping the canoe

Portaging

Long Distance

1. **Lay two paddles on canoe** (see illustration series on p. 193).
2. **Grab the paddle necks and gunnels together.**
3. **Flip the boat upside down over your head.**
4. **Lower the boat, with paddle blades resting on your shoulders** and the crotch of the V formed by the paddles coming down around your neck.

Short Distance

Merely hoist the canoe to your shoulder, as in part d of the illustration on p. 193, and stabilize by holding on to the gunnel while walking. To cushion your shoulder, use either your life preserver or a piece of folded clothing.

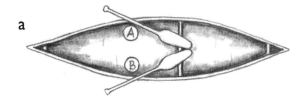

a

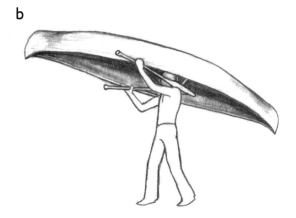

b

Long-distance portaging:
(a) Lay paddles on canoe
(b) Grab gunnels and
paddles together and flip
boat over your head
(c) Lower paddle blades
onto shoulders

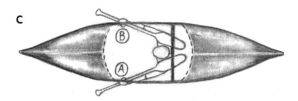

c

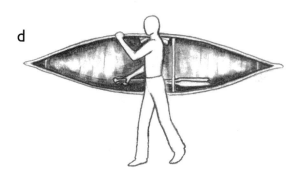

d

Short-distance portaging:
(d) Hoist onto shoulder
and grip gunnels

This makes for a comfortable portage, as the blades disperse weight evenly across the shoulders. Padding increases comfort level. Where some people like to tie the paddles to the thwart, I leave them loose so that I can adjust them without having to stop and lower the boat.

Being a Shadow on Water

We are now going to learn how to move even more silently. Making noise wastes energy, and as we know from step 6, Silence is essential to Becoming Nature.

Tips for Silent Paddling

- **Move the paddle at your speed of travel when you cut it into or lift it out of the water** so that the paddle is stationary in the water. This greatly reduces splashing and noise.
- **Don't hit the boat with the paddle,** as it sends a shock wave through the water. Too many times I have ruined a silent stalk by banging the boat. Now when I brace against the gunnel for a stroke, or to just lay the paddle down for a rest, I use my hand or leg as a cushion.
- **Keep the paddle blade in the water** as much is possible. Any time we break the surface we risk alerting keen ears.

Silent Strokes

The ultimate goal in Shadow Canoeing is to paddle as though we are merely gliding through the water. With the following strokes, which are variations of the rudder stroke, the paddle is not lifted out of the water, so there is no noise either from dripping water or breaking the surface. These strokes are best suited for slow travel.

Slice Stroke

The slice stroke is a simple stroke that offers precise control by giving maneuvering potential at both the beginning and end, as well as in the recovery.

1. **Begin as with the rudder stroke** but a short distance out from the boat (see illustration on p. 195).
2. **Pull the paddle in toward you,** which turns the boat slightly toward the side on which you are paddling. It compensates for the remainder of the stroke, which turns the boat in the opposite direction.
3. **Continue by following steps 3 to 5 under "Rudder Stroke"** (p. 189).

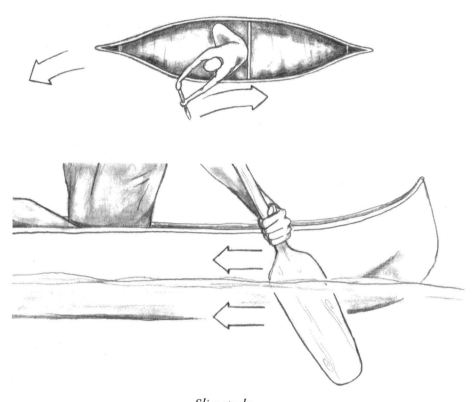

Slice stroke
(upper) 1. Submerge blade away from boat. 2. Pull toward you.
3. Follow through.
(lower) 4. Slice forward, keeping nearly all of the blade submerged.

4. **Recover by keeping the blade submerged and slicing forward**
   to begin the next stroke. To prevent the neck from cutting noisily
   through the water, keep the very top of the blade above water.

❀ Sculling Stroke

When even arm movement is too much, use the sculling stroke, which
is the most discreet one I know.

1. **Position the paddle alongside the boat with the blade in the**
   water and vertical, as in the rudder stroke step 4 position (see illustration on p. 196).

2. **Twist the paddle neck to rotate the top of the blade 45° toward you and push outward with your rear arm** about a foot, holding your front arm in position.

3. **Reverse the motion** by rotating the top of the blade 45° away from you and pulling the blade inward.

4. **Repeat steps 2 and 3 to keep the back-and-forth motion going,** which in effect keeps water flowing over the top of the blade.

5. **To turn, stall the paddle at either end of the stroke,** which replicates step 5 of the rudder stroke.

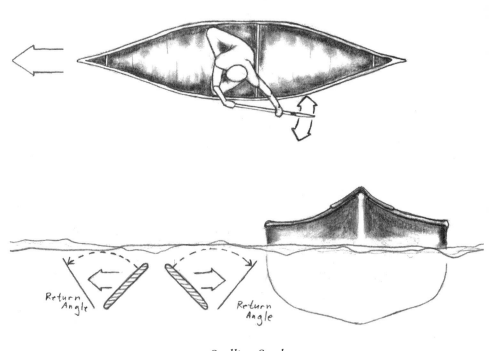

Sculling Stroke
(upper) Use a back-and-forth motion and blade just below the surface.
(lower) Alternate blade rotation as illustrated.

Clearing Overhead Obstacles

If we lean forward rather than back to duck under a fallen Tree, bridge, or other obstacle, we better maintain our Silence and center of gravity, as well as being in paddling position as soon as we clear the obstacle.

After a certain period of practice with a new skill we usually reach a threshold where reflexes become automatic and the skill becomes us. However, there is a veil over the threshold: we cannot see it, nor do we know when we are going to reach it, until it happens.

With canoeing, we've arrived at the threshold when a paddle of the right weight, balance, and flex is the only one that will do. Familiarity between paddler and craft has grown to mutual trust in each other's abilities. We can now direct our energy elsewhere than to the basic skills, such as learning to move as a shadow over the water.

While practicing the skills in this step, we will do well to remember that we evolved to Shadow: the skill set is imprinted in our DNA. For millions of years our Ancestors flowed as shadows while foraging and traveling. Wolfwalking like a Deer or seeing through the eyes of an Otter while gliding seamlessly on the water has more to do with unlearning than with applying new skills. Let us trust in Nature's children to help us recall what our Animal Mind already knows—what has been buried beneath years of cultural norms and modern convenience.

One of those norms is the belief that wild animals naturally fear us. What they actually fear is the cultural mask that we wear. In the next step we'll learn how to slip out from behind that mask. With the animals no longer fleeing in fright, it will seem as though we have disappeared; yet the only thing that has actually gone is how we typically identify ourselves.

Jennine Elberth

STEP 9

Turn Invisible
and Instill No Fear

A Blue Jay's Sweet Song

One afternoon I went alone to my old wilderness camp, which was nestled beneath an immense Aspen perched atop a rock bluff overlooking a lake. Getting there took a long hike and a paddle across the lake—a journey I cherished. It gave me the chance to leave myself behind and Become the Deer trail, the dappled sunshine on my shoulders, and the earthy smell of the great, crumbling Tree trunks over which I stepped.

On this particular day, I arrived at camp with neither a project in mind nor an inclination to go out scouting. I was content with being merely an ethereal presence, without form or direction. I did carry out one task though: I decided which Tree to sit under. Within minutes I heard something above me so pleasant and whisper-soft that at first I didn't care from whom or where it came. But that didn't last long; it was too otherworldly for my curiosity not to get the best of me. The song lacked the intensity of a Warbler, and it didn't have the flute-like resonance of a Thrush. It simply defied categorization.

After a brief silence, the song started again. I glanced upward and saw a Blue Jay. "Nah, it couldn't be," I thought. She then partially spread her tail and wings, the way a Red-winged Blackbird does when singing, and again she performed that heavenly pastel melody. It was the most gentle and sweet birdsong I had ever heard.

Seeing is believing, yet my rational mind kept arguing: It makes no sense that the singer is a raucous Jay. Besides, I didn't think I had turned invisible, so why would a Jay let me witness such a soft part of her life?

Even with that rationalizing, I could have died right there, and I'd have considered my life complete. The upwelling of emotion made me feel as though I could float away. I wanted to share the experience with everybody I knew and cared about, but who would believe me?

I see now that it was actually me who couldn't believe—I didn't trust that other people could turn invisible.

Since that day I've come to realize that Blue Jays are raucous when I'm raucous: when I create a disturbance, they pick up on it and mirror it back to me. On the other hand, when I lose myself and Become the forest, I become privy to their complex personalities and the range of emotions they can express.

As we've already seen in previous steps, everything is connected. Our relationship with self, as well as with the outer world, is tantamount to our relationship with Nature. If we approach the Natural Realm as passive observers we will remain only observers. However, if we approach Nature as we would any highly sought-after relationship, humbling ourselves in the knowledge that we are just one part of the whole, we will be accepted by the wildlings as one of them, and their home will be ours as well.

The Four Advantages of Invisibility

- **We no longer disturb the animals,** as we do not create disturbance.
- **Animals stop "hiding" from us,** as we realize that their disappearing was no more than our blindness.
- **We become privy to Nature's secrets,** as invisibility improves hearing.
- **We understand and accept what Animals tell us,** as invisibility enlivens our Animal Mind.

Now we can take what we've gained in the first eight steps and apply it so that we can experience the four advantages of losing the self to Nature.

SEEING THROUGH OUR BIGGEST BLINDERS: PREJUDICE AND FEAR

We have already discussed prejudice and fear as they relate to previous steps. Here we take a look at how they make us conspicuous and what we can do to change that.

When we Become Nature we are at-one with our surroundings. We move among the animals and plants as if the forest were our home. Our sense of awareness comes from knowing ourselves as one part of an already existing whole. There is no need for reaction or fear, as we are immersed in the flow of the life around us—we are in relationship rather than in tourist mode.

Yet if I were to walk down an unfamiliar city street at night, I'd be on alert. Everything would be unfamiliar, and I wouldn't have a relationship with those who live there. All I'd know about this city would be from the news reports of its decay and crime rate—secondhand knowledge that would have instilled fear in me. I'd peer into the shadows and tense up with every noise I heard.

Someone who had grown up in this neighborhood would likely be more at ease than me. She'd have relationships with those who lived here, and she'd be familiar with its sights and sounds. She'd know what constitutes a real threat, as opposed to my imagined ones based on my fear of the unknown.

Whether or not we grew up in the city or in the wilds, it would be natural for us to base our perception of reality on our experiences and on the beliefs we were taught. Beliefs can lead to prejudice and fear, which keep us in ego-rational-mind consciousness. Although the ego mind can serve us well by keeping us safe, our ability to Become Nature is hindered when we are kept separate from our surroundings.

To understand how the ego mind fuels beliefs and undercuts our connection to Nature, let's take a look at the factors that help create our reality.

Our perception of reality is based on:

1. **What we are *able* to see, hear, and smell.** Limitations include sight and hearing disabilities, along with environmental factors.
2. **What we *think* we see, hear, and smell.** If we mistake a floating log for an Alligator, it *is* an Alligator, and we pattern our actions accordingly.
3. **What we *allow* ourselves to see, hear, and smell.** We are subjective creatures. Trauma and stress cause us to shut down some of our perceptive abilities to guard against sensory overload. Beliefs contribute to the shutdown. If I were raised to think that nakedness was evil, I'd avert my eyes at the merest hint of a naked person. Out of fear, I could deny the experience or even erase it from my memory.

If you and I shared the same belief, we wouldn't recognize it as a prejudice, as it would be our shared reality. It's only when we have *different* beliefs that they then stand out from one another. The same is true when we enter Nature with a belief system.

As we discovered in step 7, when we are in our ego minds we reinforce our perception that we are separate from all others in Nature. We then think we need to camouflage ourselves in order to blend in with them.

Though we may see camouflage as a way of blending, it is actually a way of hiding. Many of us hunters use camouflage to gain advantage over our prey. We do it because we believe we are separate and different from our prey. This belief limits our perception and, even more importantly, our knowledge of who we are and of what we are capable.

Without knowing that there is another way to be, what we were taught becomes anchored in our consciousness and forms our perception of reality. Simply knowing this can help us relax around our beliefs and conditioning, which we must do to learn how to become invisible. Otherwise we are just masking our presence by resorting to some form of camouflage.

The Best Defense

Several years ago I was talking with Robert Wolff, the author of *Original Wisdom,* about how a Native strives to be invisible by moving as a shadow rather than as a shadow maker. Using an example from the Malaysian Senoi aborigines with whom he lived, he said "If they didn't want a confrontation, they became invisible—exactly as many animals can seemingly 'disappear.'"[1]

HOW TO BECOME INVISIBLE

In an absolute sense, *invisible* means *unseeable.* However, we use the term here in a relative sense, which means that someone can be seeable yet not actually seen.

Two Ways the Seeable Goes Unseen

- **Stepping in to physical blind spots.** All animals, including us, have variable fields of vision, which create blind spots. Mine is a vertical strip in the center of my field of vision. When we learn other creatures' blind spots, we can step in to them and in effect disappear.
- **Creating emotional and psychological blind spots.** Our brains fabricate what we think we see, based on operating systems programmed by prior experiences and beliefs. An Owl could glide by in front of me, yet I might not see her but instead think she is a ghost.

Utilizing these awarenesses, we can become invisible without the aid of camouflage, often while remaining in full view. When we lack awareness, we resort to methods such as camouflage and stealth.

Disadvantages of Camouflage and Stealth

- **They require additional energy,** whereas invisibility is part and parcel of Becoming.
- **They call for constant vigilance,** as the least unconscious movement could expose a person.

- **They are reliable for the short-term only.** The longer the duration, the more chance there is of discovery.

If I want to sit down in the woods and remain unseen, I could camouflage myself so that I am literally invisible, or I could Become a Tree stump. Camouflaging myself would take work, and it could compromise my ability to see and hear, whereas Becoming a Tree stump could be as easy as sitting down or lifting an arm over my head, as in the illustration below. I can stay out in plain sight and someone could look directly at me, seeing only a stump.

Becoming a Tree stump

Who is to say that I'm not really a Tree trunk? When we have Become something else (see step 11) we are no longer ourselves, so we have nothing to hide and therefore no reason to hide. More than a way to turn invisible, Becoming is a way to turn in to Nature. We join in rather than disguising from; we revel in our sameness rather than reinforcing our differences.

Become a Moving Tree Trunk

To keep out of sight when someone walks by the Tree we're hiding behind, we can plant our feet and rotate our upper body around the trunk, to keep on the side of the Tree opposite the passerby (see illustration below). When we don't move our feet, we don't create noise. If a foot does become exposed, it will likely be taken for a flared trunk or exposed root.

Invisibility in Visibility

If a person dressed as a clown were standing in line to purchase tickets for a concert, he would stand out. His ego chose to wear a clown suit, as one of the ego's jobs is to increase visibility by creating distinction and separation. No matter what his reason for standing in line, he will be noted for his singular appearance.

Contrast this with someone who has Become her surroundings. She is neither trying to stand out nor hide. Not coming from her ego mind, she is able to Become the sidewalk, the buildings, the sky above, and the ticket line itself. Even if our gaze were to pass over her, we would probably not be able to recall her presence. She has become transparent.

When we are transparent in the Natural Realm we don't need to camouflage ourselves to be invisible any more than the woman standing in line. Why become invisible to the wind and the Trees if we *are* the wind and the Trees?

To Become Invisible at Night

Flashlight and headlamp beams put us in the center of attention by pointing directly at us, along with blinding us to everything that falls outside the beam. When we turn off the light, we disappear into the dark. Our eyes adjust to night vision and our senses come alive, allowing us to see, hear, smell, and feel much more than when the light beam defined the night world.

Invisibility Is Movement

In addition to leaving our ego minds behind, invisibility requires that we know how to move within Nature. As we covered in the previous step, how we move will determine how well we blend in and are accepted by the Natural Realm. If we walk through the woods as we walk down a city sidewalk, we'll stick out like cowboys at a Star Trek convention. On the other hand, if we want to be present and move invisibly, we need to think and act like a shadow, making no wave and leaving no trace of having been there.

Invisibility is not stillness. As T. S. Eliot said, "We must be still and still moving."[2] It bears repeating that if we don't move in rhythm with the greater movement, we stand out.

On Disappearing in Front of Snapping Turtle

I remember standing at the upper end of a shallow pool on a tiny stream early one morning and watching a large Snapping Turtle slide into the pool at the lower end. Realizing that I was right on her trail, I forgot about her and went back to listening. When a gust of wind tugged at the nearby bushes, I bent as well.

Catching her in my peripheral vision every now and then—which was easy with the water being so shallow that it didn't cover her shell—I kept track of her progress. My gaze drifted here and there, to whatever attracted it. When she reached my end of the pool, she passed by me without a flinch, even though I was standing in full sunlight and was so close that I could have bent over to pick her up.

The Criteria for Becoming Invisible

- **Flow *within* the flow,** rather than just *with* it. This does not mean merely Shadowing movement, but rather moving within the movement's shadow.
- **Be in Animal Mind consciousness.**
- **Function as a vital organ in a dynamic organism.**
- **Let our feelings both touch and reflect the greater feeling** in which we are immersed.

Consciousness Is Everything

Several years ago we had a midwinter thaw that melted all the snow and left everything brown—except the all-white Snowshoe Hares. I remember one who continually sat tight when I walked by, even though I passed only a few steps from her. She stuck out like a sore thumb, yet she assumed she was invisible. For her, invisibility was instinctual, where for us it has a conscious component.

Ditch the Camouflage Gear

Here's a story to give life to the discussion already started on camo clothing and gear. An understanding of this topic is not enough—it has to resound in our Animal Mind if we are going to live and breathe it.

When Whip-poor-wills Turn to Stone

I used to live in an area of granite outcrops, where Blueberries grew bountifully. I happen to be fond of Blueberries, so I spent some time on the outcrops during the berry season.

On one of my berryings, I cut across a bald knob in the hope of bluer pastures on the far side. I got about a third of the way over when a Whip-poor-will fluttered down a couple of paces to my side, looking like she had a broken wing and crying out as though she was in horrendous pain. I knew the play and froze in my tracks, with my left foot suspended in midair.

At the same time, I noticed the two fist-size granite stones I was just about to step on. They were too symmetrical, too identical to be random stones that just happened to roll next to each other. I knew what they were, yet my rational mind couldn't accept it—they did not look or act like Birds. They were granite on granite: the sparkle of their eyes was mica chips; the speckles of their plumage and their scattered droppings were bits of milky quartz embedded in the rock. They had no smell, and they had no nest. When they moved, I wasn't sure they did, as they immediately became the rock again as soon as they sat still.

They were "nested" in such a conspicuous place that it would never have occurred to me to look for them there. If the odd vagabond (such as me) crossed that knob, mother would divert their attention, if not their path.

Until Whip-poor-will highlighted my ignorance about camouflage, I thought it was mostly about not being seen. Besides the breath-catching moment I reexperience every time the story comes to mind, I have been enriched by several insights on invisibility.

Tips for Invisibility

- **Everything takes the imprint of its surroundings,** but only to the degree that it is a part of those surroundings. Becoming invisible is not as much about disguising as it is about Becoming.
- **Odor and movement are as important as visibility.** When we eat foods native to the area, our body odors cause little alarm. Stimulating foods throw our rhythm out of sync with Nature's rhythm (See "To Make It Easier" in step 4).
- **Use animal calls for sound invisibility.** I can say *stop, come, look up, look down, east, south, north, west,* and more with a set of birdcalls.
- **Earth-tone clothing is all that's needed.** Checkered or plaid patterns are better than stripes.

Because of our visual orientation, we tend to place a lot of emphasis on disguising our visible presence. In actuality, animals are usually aware of our presence long before they see us, from the audio and olfactory signals we send out.

Using camouflage paraphernalia to give us a sense of belonging is akin to getting our car painted and expecting it to be a different vehicle. When we camouflage ourselves, we are attempting to hide. We're saying, "I'm not good enough to be seen, I'm not connected enough to be accepted, and I'm not attuned enough to be myself." We set ourselves up to observe wild animals in much the same way as animals in a zoo. We create the illusion of being with wildlife without learning *how* to be with them.

Anything that disguises us is the antithesis of Becoming. If we are not there to touch, taste, and feel what the animal does, we're getting close to Nature only as observers. Can we smell the animal and hear him breathe? Are we getting to know him through feeling his energy and eye-to-eye contact? Relationship requires communication. As with all relationships, the closer we get and the fewer boundaries between us, the easier it is to communicate.

The Magnifying Effect

Camouflage gear artificially magnifies our personal ability. A good example is camo-pattern clothing, as it helps us blend in when we aren't actually capable of doing so. The ads promise instant attunement, yet we are only masquerading. Like any costume, camo is a guise that allows us to imagine we are something that we are not. The upshot is that our short-term gain backfires and becomes our long-term loss: we tend to grow complacent and do not learn the skills of invisibility and Becoming.

TO STAND OUT IS
TO BLEND IN

When we learn the ways of invisibility, not only can we become invisible, but we can also see others who were formerly invisible to us. There are two seemingly diametrically opposed approaches to invisibility, which Eagle and Owl will illustrate for us.

Owl's and Eagle's Disappearing Acts

Eagle is a child of the day, whereas Owl's realm is the night. Sight is Eagle's sharpness, and Owl is keen of hearing. Eagle is upfront and visible, while Owl lurks in the shadows. Eagle soars high and sees with perspective, and Owl roosts low, focusing on detail.

With Bald Eagle's bold color pattern and yen for perching in conspicuous places, he seems a poor example of invisibility. Yet two days ago, when I was paddling toward a root snag in the middle of a lake, I got to within three canoe lengths before a large, mature female Eagle whom I hadn't seen took off in front of me. She skimmed the water's surface, gained altitude, and landed on a high snag overlooking the shore.

It happened again yesterday when I was paddling along the shoreline. I saw an Eagle up ahead, perched on a gnarly piece of driftwood. As usual, I just kept to my business, not giving her any attention, other than occasionally catching her in my peripheral vision, so that I wouldn't alarm her. I passed her by, and she didn't take off, which wasn't so surprising. What did trouble me was that she seemed so stoic, almost as though she were a lifeless decoy.

Unfortunately, I couldn't even find comfort in the fact that I was duped by a plastic look-alike—it was just a twisted branch.

The contrast of the Eagle's white head and tail and dark body breaks up her outline, especially against a light background. An Eagle can be perfectly visible, yet our mind can't piece together its body outline. The mind then either registers nothing or makes something else of it. Either way, the Eagle in plain sight is as good as invisible.

The same is true for Owls. I hate to admit how many times I've stared at an Owl— sometimes at very close range—and all I saw was Tree bark. Feather coloration, patterns, and texture that simulate bark are crucial contributing factors. In addition, an Owl can sit still and be taken for a broken-off Tree branch, which his body shape often resembles.

BE THE LANDSCAPE

Just like animals in the wild, *we can sometimes best become invisible by being blatantly visible. The easiest way is by allowing animals to become accustomed to our presence.* I have an affinity for Beaver dams, and I sometimes hang around one enough that the Beaver colony gets so used to me that they carry on with their affairs as though I belong, right there with the Ducks and Water Lilies. I've done the same with Deer, Squirrels, Grouse, and other animals, who in time allow me to be fully present with them.

 ## To Familiarize Animals with Our Presence

1. **Move gracefully,** in rhythm with the surroundings.
2. **Go about our business,** oblivious to the animals.
3. **Move closer gradually, with no pattern to our progress.**

Even though we make ourselves blatantly visible, we must still Become the shadow of our surroundings. We can do so by gathering berries, canoeing, setting up camp, or any other activity that shows we are engaged in our lives just like every other animal. When we act as though we are in a zoo by passively observing and analyzing wildlife, we stick out like a steel fence post in a sea of waving Grasses. When we let the wind move us with the Grasses, we become invisible simultaneously with being visible. Another layer of life, previously unseen, then appears before us.

Animals who sing together in a chorus of indistinguishable voices, such as many Frogs and Insects, are a dramatic illustration of how overwhelming visibility can create invisibility. In the midst of a sea of potential prey, predators struggle to key in on an individual songster.

VISIBILITY: A SURVIVAL STRATEGY

Animals can protect themselves through speed, size, concealment, numbers, deterrents (such as spines and poisonous skin glands), and high visibility. The latter is used by male Birds to draw attention from their mates at nest. Some Insects and amphibians with poisonous properties, and who also live out in the open, have bright coloration and bold patterns so that their predators can easily identify them and leave them alone. Individuals sacrifice themselves for the survival of the species, as a Bird has to eat an attractively colored but acrid-tasting Butterfly in order to learn to avoid the species.

Discovering that, I began to wonder why other animals have not evolved escape strategies or defenses and why their predators haven't become more efficient at preying upon them.

Imperfectly Invisible Clams

One bright afternoon while gathering Clams on a quiet river, the Clams enlightened me. They were nicely camouflaged: the same color and texture as the silt in which they were partially buried, except for their projecting white feeding tubes. When they detected a disturbance, they would withdraw their tubes, close their shells, and disappear from sight. To find them, I had to stalk in close enough to see their feeding tubes before they clammed up.

Why weren't their feeding tubes pigmented the same as their shells? That would make them less detectable and give them a higher survival rate. Yet there was already a sizable Clam population, as I had just gathered what had to be close to a hundred in less than an hour. The piles of shells at feeding stations along the shoreline told me that a number of Raccoons and Otters also had no trouble gathering their fill.

If Clams were harder to find, I reasoned, it would mean less food for predators, hence fewer predators. A higher-than-normal Clam population could lead to crowding, disease, and starvation. Perhaps in certain contexts there is a real benefit in not being as invisible or efficient as possible. Does that mean I would also benefit from not being perfectly invisible?

The Benefits of Imperfect Invisibility

- **Helps predators keep the population lean,** sharp, and clean by gleaning the slow, weak, and old.
- **Feeds predators to keep them healthy and bountiful** so they can perform their service.

- **Insures that predators do not become overefficient,** lest they grow lazy, overpopulate, and starve from exterminating their prey.
- **Keeps prey sharp and active** by challenging and exercising them.
- **Gives us an additional training challenge.**

In step 6 we entered the Silence where animals dwell; in step 7 we learned how to hear and see animals; in step 8 we learned how to move silently so that we wouldn't scare animals; and in this step we learned how not to be seen by them. Now we're ready to find animals and get up close to them, and the next step will show us just how to do it. Following are the two core principles from the previous steps that we want to take with us.

To Become Invisible and See the Invisible

1. **We must become invisible to ourselves.** That means forgetting about who we are and from where we came. Our mother is now the Earth, and our siblings are now the plants and animals around us. We let the sun in our eyes and the leaves brushing our face help erase our past and connect us with the now. When all becomes quiet, we become self-conscious and reluctant to move, lest we disturb the peace.
2. **We need active engagement.** Sitting and watching only reinforces our separation from Nature. A Buffalo moving with the herd goes unnoticed; however, if she were to sit on the hillside and watch the herd go by, she would become the most conspicuous Buffalo of all. When we join the herd we feel as though we belong, and the animals accept us as one of them.

The Best Tricks for Seeing Animals

Our exploration of Silence in step 6 comes back into play here, as many of us have grown accustomed to Silence when we move through a natural environment. We could end up mistakenly thinking this quiet is typical of Nature. What we don't know is that just prior to our arrival the area was probably rich with various sounds and activities.

As we discussed earlier in the book, the animals lay low because we send out a wave of disturbance, which is caused by our fractured relationship with Nature. If we were to Become an ignored shadow and stay in the area long enough, the animals would begin to stir and the chorus would resume. The reason for their disappearance is not *that* we move into the area, but *how* we move in (see step 8 for details).

Following are some additional tips selected specifically to help us move in a way that we can get up-close and see animals. These pointers will be especially helpful for those new to Nature's ways.

 ## To Get Close to Animals

- **Wear quiet.** Leave noisy packs and canteens behind, and wear clothing that is quiet when you move.

Jennine Elberth

- **Approach scentless.** When we walk into the wind, our scent will not announce our presence. Avoid wearing perfume or scented personal care products.
- **Keep to the shadows** so that you do not cast a shadow, which is like having an extra body to conceal.
- **Keep out of sight** by taking advantage of hills, ridges, and gullies.
- **Approach by stalking.** It puts our senses on alert.
- **Consciously smell and listen** for anything that stands out from the background odors and sounds.
- **Look a distance ahead.** When nearby animals disappear, those at a distance may not yet be alarmed.
- **Look both upstream and down.** Animals will swim with and against the current, and shoreline hunters and foragers can come from either direction.
- **Take advantage of noise.** Use rustling leaves or rushing water to disguise the noise you make when moving.
- **Blend in when stopping.** Lay low in open areas, sit down in a thicket, or stand next to a Tree.

Following are the tricks I use for seeing animals. I chose them to give options for a wide variety of circumstances so that there would nearly always be at least one to utilize.

Ten Tricks for Seeing Animals

Trick 1: Move to Find Motion

Here we enter another level of motion awareness as we introduce new ways that our movements affect our ability to see animals. Let's start by taking a lesson from an animal common to all of us: the house Cat. Watch her as she stalks very stealthily through a flowerbed by moving between and within the movements immediately around her. In this way her movements complement the activity that is already occurring rather than disturbing it.

What she has effected is of primary interest to us, as it is the one trick for seeing animals that allows all the other tricks to work.

How the Cat Sees Animals

1. **She recognizes their dance**—awareness.
2. **She joins their dance**—movement.
3. **She Becomes their dance**—Becoming.

What a Cat does to see animals is just what we will be doing. We have already gained tremendously in terms of awareness, so let's go back to Cat and learn more about movement.

If Cat were to sit still instead of moving, her perception of life around her would be hit and miss. That's because stillness creates a two-dimensional field of vision. Though we can see what stands out, we have trouble distinguishing what merges with the background.

When we move, objects—especially stationary objects—appear to move in relation to their background, which gives us the three-dimensional perspective needed to see those objects. With each footstep we expand our ability to see, as we move into new flow patterns and territories. It is akin to playing a game rather than sitting and watching. Who best knows the game: the observer or the participant?

✿ Trick 2: Watch for Wallflowers

In step 9, I introduced the awareness that if everything is in motion the one who sits still stands out (the exception being those who use stillness as a melding or hunting strategy). All members of the Natural Realm are in a dance of relationship with one another, through which they are continually moving: faster, slower, changing partners, choreographing new moves. At all times they are actively engaged in the means and ends of their existences. There are no wallflowers—nobody stands aside and watches.

At least not for long. Anyone who falls out of rhythm does not find food, shelter, or a mate. What she does find—and usually sooner rather than later—is a place in somebody else's meal.

Wallflowers are typically easy to spot. At the same time, it is important for us to know that many out-of-sync animals are not slackers. They could be sick, injured, feeling threatened, or with slow-moving young. Whatever the case, we should exercise caution and keep our distance. A female could abandon her young if we approach too close, and wounded or diseased animals are often unpredictable and could prove dangerous.

Yet I don't want to discourage anyone from observing these animals. They are a part of the natural order, and much can be learned from them.

Safe Ways to Observe Potentially Threatening Animals

- **From a different habitat,** such as from water when the animal is on land.
- **From a different elevation,** such as high on a ridge.
- **From behind a barrier,** such as a dense stand of saplings.
- **From a Tree stand,** for nonclimbing animals only.

✿ Trick 3: Go Back to the Future

The path into the future is directed by the path we walked in the past. To know where we are going, we need to know where we have been.

That will tell us what brought us to this point in time: our needs and pleasures, what distracts and draws us, and the ways in which we travel. With that knowledge, we know in which direction to proceed and how to best do it. The process merges past, present, and future into the continuum—the flow of our lives.

Every movement leaves its track, and every track leads to the source—and cause—of the movement. The track is the continuum that can either lead us forward or take us back. By backtracking we get to know the animal and learn what brought her to this place where our trails have crossed. At the same time we find out where she's going and how she's going to get there.

The more we backtrack an animal the more we learn about her and Become her. We get to know her desires, delights, and disagreements. Let's say we backtrack an animal and find out that she has a den with pups. Other sign that we came across on her trail now falls into place, and we realize that she is out hunting to feed her pups.

Foretracking may not have given us this complete a picture of her life. As well, if our goal was to see her, we could be heading farther away from her if she were on her way back to the den with a fresh kill. By backtracking we found out where she is going to be in the shortest possible time; so to see her, all we need to do is wait.

🌸 Trick 4: Tap In to Clan Knowledge

The life skills that social animals pass down from generation to generation are known as *clan knowledge*. When someone discovers a new waterhole or trail that proves reliable, it becomes part of the group's clan knowledge. We can learn a group's clan knowledge through observation and participation, which is the same way young animals pick it up from their Elders. The more we increase our clan knowledge of a flock or herd, the more predictable its actions become and the easier it is for us to find and see.

For years I've watched flocks of wild Doves to learn where they nest and roost and where they go to feed and drink. Once I learned a flock's patterns, I could revisit them four or five years later, and even though all the Birds were replaced, I still knew their movements.

Unless there is some significant environmental change, the cycle of their lives and the pattern of their movements remains essentially the same over time.

With as much as we can gain by learning clan knowledge through observation, it's still best for our awakening as Nature's children to keep direct experience as our primary teacher.

✿ Trick 5: Leave Expectations Behind

The Scruffier the Forest, the Better

Not long ago someone I know stopped by and said he had just cut through a patch of woods so thick that he had trouble getting through it. "It was choked with scrawny saplings," he scowled, "and there was a tangle of dead wood lying around. And then a lot of the Trees were crippled and diseased."

"Sounds like a rich and beautiful forest grove you came across!" I replied.

"Huh?" was all he could say. "All I saw was waste," he added a moment or two later, "stunted little Trees that aren't going to amount to anything. Half of the big ones looked like they had one foot in the grave."

"What makes a forest?" I asked.

"Trees."

"And what should a forest look like?"

"Well, there should be healthy Trees with space underneath them so you can walk."

"More like a park?"

"Well, yeah."

"Why?"

"The Trees are more useful then. I took this class at an outdoor-skills school where they said we should adopt a gardener's approach and prune and thin things, so that what's left can grow stronger and straighter."

"Why would the forest be better off that way?"

"The Trees would be more useful, and it would look better."

"From whose perspective?"

"Ah . . . from mine, from Human perspective, I guess."

"Was there anything else living in that scruffy forest?"

"Well, sure. I saw Squirrels and Birds, some Insects, Mushrooms, a Salamander, Wildflowers, I saw some Bear scat . . . all kinds of life, I guess."

"Were they all part of the forest?"

"Now I see what you're getting at. I guess they are. But I always saw a forest as Trees and figured that any animals there just kinda hung out."

"Bear with me a bit yet. Where in the forest do those animals and plants that you just listed live?"

"Let's see . . . Squirrels live in hollow Trees, and some Birds do too. Bears could den under the upturned roots of windfalls. I found the Salamander under the loose bark of one of the rotting Trees. And come to think of it, I usually see Rabbits and Grouse in brush. Birds too. They nest all over the place: in brush piles, in the berry bushes and Wildflowers. The Flowers attract Butterflies, and Insects can be found just about anywhere. The same with Mosses, Ferns, and Mushrooms—anywhere it's damp."

"It sounds like the Trees are getting outnumbered."

"How about that. The woods can sure look different from the inside out."

How Expectations Keep Us from Seeing

- **They deaden our senses:** When we anticipate something, we devote only as much attention as is needed to meet the anticipation. If we are listening for the grunt of a bull Moose, we might miss the whiny call of the cow Moose, or the Goshawk flying overhead.

- **They limit our sight to what fits the expectation:** What falls outside of that oftentimes won't register, even if we do see it. As hard as it is to let go of how we think things ought to be, it is necessary to do so in order to see things as they are.

- **Many animals dwell where we don't think to look:** Because thinking can't take us there, someone could point to where an animal lurks, and still we might not see him. Prior knowledge of where to find animals helps, as long as we realize that there is so much more that we do not know.

🌼 Trick 6: Walk the Edge

The transition zone where two habitats meet, such as forest-grassland or river-bank, is called an *ecotone,* or simply, *edge.* Many of us avoid edges, as they're often brushy and hinder visibility. In doing so we avoid seeing most animals as well.

How Edge Helps Us See Animals

- **Visibility:** We can see out from just inside the treeline better than looking into the Trees. At the same time, we remain invisible.
- **Species diversity:** Edge holds a high number and variety of plant and animal species due to the overlapping habitats and the shelter afforded.
- **Animal trails:** On their way from feeding or hunting in one habitat to denning or loafing in another, animals typically cut across edge. Traveling animals often run their trails parallel to edge.
- **Predators:** Wolves and Cougars, along with a host of smaller predators such as Bobcats, Coyotes, Foxes, and Badgers, work the edge because of the concentration of prey species.

It is wise to hug the edge while paddling as well. The majority of aquatic life is found in the shallows along the shoreline, which is called the *littoral zone.* A fringe benefit when there are offshore winds is that paddling is easiest close to shore, where there are less wind and waves than farther out. And we are less conspicuous to anyone around or on the lake, including wildlife, than when we are farther out.

🌼 Trick 7: Leave the Dog at Home

As fun as it can be to wander the wilder places with your pet—especially when she enjoys it so much and is a great motivator to get out—she *is* a predator. No matter how harmless she might be, and even if you keep her leashed, most animals react to the presence of a predator. If they don't outright run and hide, they'll switch to alert mode, which means you will not be able to observe them carrying out their daily activities.

Even fellow predators will react, as they are prey as well, and predators compete among themselves.

Perhaps the most obtrusive aspect of Dogs' behavior is their demeanor. Being much more high energy than their wild counterparts, they create a wide arc of disturbance. They need to sniff and see up-close what Foxes, Coyotes, and Bobcats will usually pick up from a distance. Added to that, most Dogs have little concern for moving as a shadow. Altogether, their environmental impact goes far beyond that of a wild predator, which can significantly reduce the quality of our animal-seeing experience.

Shadow Peeing

Many animals use urine scent to communicate and mark boundaries. When they smell our urine along a trail, they may read it as a threat or competition for territory and therefore avoid the area. If it's an area that we or other Humans frequent regularly, it's best if we relieve ourselves some distance from the trail.

Trick 8: Know Where to Look

In order to see an animal it helps to know where and when he will most likely be found. All animals have preferred habitats and niches within those habitats, along with regular and predictable movement patterns. Learning what they are is one of the most helpful and time-saving things we can do to see animals.

The Questions to Ask

- Are the animals migrating, breeding, nesting, or hibernating?
- What is their preferred habitat in this season?
- Are they loners or social animals?
- Do they form pair bonds?
- Are they found with other species, and do they mingle?
- Are they prey or predator, scavenger or hunter, herbivore or omnivore, and how do each of these affect where and when they are found?

Where to Find Answers

1. **Direct observation:** Jump-start by accompanying a knowledgeable and experienced person on his outdoor excursions.
2. **Stories:** Invite an experienced outdoors person to talk with you and your friends or family about her adventures and discoveries.
3. **Nature centers, parks, and preserves:** They often have wildlife exhibits and offer naturalist-guided programs.
4. **Media resources:** Books, videos, and online resources can provide a wealth of information. Be careful about overusing them, as they can easily become inadequate substitutes for direct experience.

How many times have you kicked yourself for not seeing that animal right in front of you before she spooked? The question and answer sections above have gotten us to the right place at the right time, and now we could use some tips on what to look out for.

Spotting Clues

- **Sign:** Gnawed bones, piles of feathers, patches of fur, chewed vegetation, nests, dens, rubs, lays, dust beds, claw marks on Trees and ground, and tracks indicate animal presence.
- **Color and pattern contrasts:** Brightly colored Birds, Red Foxes, and chestnut-colored Deer against a green background; Coyotes and other animals with unpatterned coats against a busy background of branches or rocks.
- **Shapes and lines that don't fit:** A horizontal line in a grove of saplings could be a Deer's back (see left-hand illustration on p. 224); a nondescript patch on a pebbled streambed might be a resting Fish (see right-hand illustration on p. 224).
- **Appendages:** Legs, muzzles, ears, or tails can stand out even though the rest of the body is camouflaged.
- **Movement:** Twitching ears and tails can be conspicuous when animals are standing still. Watch for contrary movements, such as an object going diagonally to a stream flow or a Heron standing still in waving sedges.

What Animals Watch For

The spotting clues listed above are the same ones that give us away to animals. In addition, they are particularly keen on out-of-place forms. A common one is a slouched sitting Human (see illustration on p. 204). When sitting erect, we can pass for a Tree stump.

🌸 Trick 9: Use Trapping and Hunting Know-How

How Trappers and Hunters Find Animals

I remember one day about thirty-five years ago when I was out scouting a trapline with my friend Bob. We skirted an open field, followed the edge of a Pine plantation, and wrapped around a granite outcrop before crossing a small stream and dipping in to a Cedar bog.

"We're crossing quite a few runs," I commented. "Don't we want to pick up on one of them and trail the animal?"

"I'd starve if I did that," Bob replied. "Finding where a Raccoon is denned up for the day isn't going to give me the pelts I need to pay the bills."

I understood—he wanted a trapline that intersected as many trails as possible in the least amount of time so that he could efficiently prepare and check a number of sets. And intersect trails we did: a Deer trail leading into the field, the remains of a Fox-killed Grouse by the plantation, a Coyote scat-scent marking area on the outcrop, and Mink tracks along the stream.

However, if we were hunting we'd have done the opposite and taken the Deer run to find an advantageous spot to either set a snare or sit and wait.

The hunter wants to follow one trail to the source, while the trapper wants to find as many trails as possible. A hunter will generally cut across a stream valley while following a trail, whereas a trapper will walk up the valley to intersect trails. On a beach a hunter might pick up a trail and follow it inland, and a trapper will more likely stick to the beach to cross as many trails coming down to the water as possible.

We can take advantage of these two approaches to find the runs that will help us see animals. The best conservation wardens use this knowledge to apprehend poachers. I knew someone who took advantage of the knowledge to raid traplines. The awareness has helped me with search and rescues and to avoid hunters and trappers. Yet I most often use it for the main reason I'm sharing it with you—to immerse myself in the world that calls to my heart.

🌸 Trick 10: Follow Their Hunger

Although this has already been mentioned, it deserves special attention, as it is one of the most successful ways to see animals. In order to eat, nearly all animals need to move, and this is when they are the most visible. When we know an animal's feeding patterns we can often see her quite easily as she moves to and from her feeding area. Whether herbivore or carnivore, she typically sits tight when not eating, which makes her hard to spot.

Animals are most vulnerable to predation when they are eating. When they can, predators will usually take their kills to a safer place than the kill site itself for consumption. Herbivores are particularly vulnerable when eating, as they must often come out in the open to graze. In addition, they spend a good share of time grazing, as it takes large quantities of plant matter to sustain them.

The Ultimate Trick

"You must have real love and sympathy for [animals] and be consistent and straightforward in your dealings in order to gain their friendship."[1]

OHIYESA

WHAT TO DO WHEN WE SEE AN ANIMAL

Now that we know how to find and see animals, what can we do so that we don't spook them? *Above all, we want to stay in the deepest available shadow.* It's hard to peer into darkness and easy to see into light. Following are some more pointers.

If We Are Moving

- **Keep moving:** Any change in speed or direction could alert the animal to the fact that you've noticed him.
- **Avert our eyes:** Have you ever felt someone staring at you from behind? Animals have a highly developed intuitive sense—it's how they survive. We can focus on something else, or we can keep focused on what we were doing, in either case watching the animal out of the corner of our eye.
- **Approach diagonally:** To get closer, we can approach the animal

indirectly, all the time looking preoccupied. If he gets nervous, we angle away from him.

- **Retreat:** If he gets nervous he'll often relax if he thinks we're leaving. We can then approach from another quadrant, as he'll be keeping an eye on where we disappeared.

If We Are Still

- **Freeze:** If he hasn't seen us yet, keeping still could be our best chance of remaining invisible. We can move closer only when the animal has seen us and remains relaxed, is looking in another direction, or is preoccupied with something.
- **Lay low:** A rule of thumb is that the higher we are, the more visible we are.
- **Find cover:** Peering through thick vegetation or around the base of a boulder or Tree trunk is very effective.

As French author Marcel Proust wrote, "The real voyage of discovery consists not in seeking new landscapes, but in having new eyes." When we leave our expectations behind and come ready to explore with a heart aching for discovery, we open a great doorway to the Natural Realm.

For those of us who have not yet Become or touched an animal, it is important to remember that what we currently see is limited by what we currently know. To grow beyond this, we must first acknowledge where we are and have a yearning to expand our awareness. This change does not happen all at once, but bit by bit as we learn to see anew.

In the next step we will learn how to Become an animal through Envisioning. It adjusts our lens of perception to blur what we typically see, which brings into focus what lies beyond. With Envisioning, we can circumvent the limitations of time and distance, which allows us to learn things without having to directly study or experience them.

Jennine Elberth

STEP 11

Become the Animal

This is the place where everything we learned thus far comes together. In the first ten steps toward Becoming Nature we became reacquainted with our Animal Mind and Nature Speak, learned how to enter the consciousness of the wilds, and honed our immersion skills and awareness. Now we are going to put it all to practice by Becoming a wild animal. In doing so we will awaken our ability to experience the inner lives of many animals.

Before we get into this magical experience, it would be good to revisit anything covered earlier in the book that was not fully understood. We'll be grateful for doing it when we see how much it benefits us in this step.

IMAGINE

You wrap yourself in the skin of an animal and move within her movements. You see through the bright of her eyes and feel through the pads of her feet. You know how she perceives her world, her mate, and her enemies. Her hunger and her pain are yours; her lust and her courage are yours. Hear the crying of her young, feel the strain of her fears, know the how and why of all that she does.

229

To experience this we need to *be* the animal. The Kung San of the African Kalahari know what it feels like to be a Lion or an Elephant. "When I tracked with [them]," South African conservation officer Alan Howell told me, "they literally *became* what they were tracking."[1]

"Becoming one with the animal you seek," says my friend and special investigations tracker Tony Kemnitz, "is the spirituality of tracking."[2] Becoming their quarry was essential for our hunter-gatherer Ancestors, as it is for hunter-gatherers today. And it is equally important for us if we want to reclaim our place in Nature.

When we first Become an animal the experience is bound to turn our view of natural processes upside down. If we were to look at fishing or hunting from the perspective of the animal, we would see that we do not catch the Fish, but rather the Fish chooses the Worm and catches himself. Instead of us trapping an animal, she decides to walk in to the trap.

Becoming the animal has deep roots in Native traditions around the world. Through fasting, dreams, and rituals, often accompanied by trance-inducing drumming and dancing, people enter the bodies of animals to gain their skills or seek personal guidance. They sometimes journey to the homes of particular animals. Others will go and live for a time with animals, as I did with Wolves. These people are not outside observers—they learn and speak the language of the animals, and they join in their daily activities. In essence, they Become the animals.

Animal Guides

In the Upper Great Lakes region where I live, the indigenous Ojibwe belong to animal clans such as Bear, Marten, Sturgeon, Eagle, and Crane, with clan members exhibiting the qualities of their clan animals. Ojibwe people might also have individual animal guides with whom they share their essential being.

We all have the intrinsic ability to Become animals, which will help us find them, learn their language (see steps 1 and 2), and even touch them if we so choose (see step 12). Some of us simply want to get to know animals on their own terms, rather than from our usual detached perspective. We might want to become better naturalists or more effective trackers. Perhaps we have deeply personal reasons for growing in relationship with our nonhuman kin. Whatever the reason, the Becoming process will take us in to the heart of an animal's existence.

Following are the stages to Becoming an animal, which I learned from Native people and from the wild animals with whom I shared a home.

Nine Stages to Becoming an Animal

First: Change the Way We Learn

We have a tendency to interpret and analyze what we see, rather than simply taking it for what it is. In addition, our preconceived notions create blind spots (as discussed in step 10), which limit our ability to know animals for who they are and enter into relationship with them.

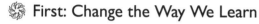

When We Become the Animal

- **We transcend our limitations.** The paw print or birdsong on which we once focused fades in importance next to the flood of information that becomes available to us.
- **We see something for what it really is.** It's as though what initially caught our attention has its mask ripped off. Think of it as X-ray vision: we can penetrate the image and grasp the reason and feeling behind it.
- **We know the cause-and-effect relationship that creates an event.** Therefore we can relive the event rather than just reading it.

It's easy for me to understand Birds, because I grew up with them and lived with them for decades. The same is true with Wolves. Yet what I have gained goes beyond Birds and Wolves. I don't have to take another lifetime to learn the ways of animals with whom I am not familiar, as I can apply my knowledge directly to other animals.

A Native connects with the song (or essence) of an animal because he knows that she is not just what he hears and sees of her. She is a ripple in the wind and the color in a blade of Grass. She is last summer's drought, autumn's bountiful acorn crop, and the way the hills roll in to the bogs. She is tomorrow's pups and yesterday's carcass. She is the fiber of her nest and the spirit of the animals she hunts. She is the reflection in our eye; she is the shadow we cast.

Whether she hears it or not, her heart jumps to the stone we accidentally kick, and her mind catches the thoughts we think. In communing with this song of the animal we can know her unseen, ethereal self and gain a feel for her moods and temperaments, thus allowing us to Become her more effectively.

If we search for a wild animal as one would look for a commodity on a store shelf, we will miss her song—and our doorway to Becoming. There is no relationship in the searching-for-a-commodity approach. In order to know a life, we must *be* that life.

The means of learning is most important, because it becomes the means of relationship. Learning to Become cannot be captured by study, because studying reinforces the idea that we are separate from Nature. Fact gathering certainly plays a role in gaining understanding, yet it is not nearly as important as directly Becoming Nature. The ability to Become cannot be studied, as it already lies within. Just as a mother experiences her child in order to know her, so must we experience Nature. Relationship is empathy, which is created not by study but by the experience of the heart.

We require the clear vision that comes from direct contact with life, so we must learn by the most direct and experiential means possible. Practice and the use of our entire being as an instrument brings us the clear realization of the animal as she actually exists. This unfolds through meditative focus, Envisioning, and intuition, rather than by study.

Second: Envision Being the Animal

The greatest aid I've found to Becoming an animal is to Envision the animal moving through her environment. I'm not talking about tracking, which can keep us focused on details that prevent us from getting a feel for the bigger picture of the animal's world. What I am referring to can best be conveyed by story, one of the greatest teachers. In this story, I take a student named Greg out in the wilderness for awareness training.

Envisioning Pine Marten

The sun has begun to slide into the afternoon sky as we make our way uphill through a grove of tall Red Pine. From the crest we survey the valley below and spot a little pothole bog ringed with Red Maple and Cedar. The bog shines like a green jewel in the dark shadows of the Trees.

A point jutting into the bog draws our attention. It's covered by a grove of close-growing Cedars and carpeted with soft Moss—a perfect place to sit and take a rest.

"How does one go about tracking a Squirrel?" asks Greg as we get up from our nap and shake off our drowsiness. The question is sparked by the local Red Squirrel's midden pile right beside us, which is made up of shredded pinecones that have accumulated under his favorite dining perch.

"It's funny you should ask," I reply, "because I was thinking about the same thing. More accurately, I was Envisioning a Pine Marten tracking a Squirrel." (Martens are members of the Weasel family, midway in size between a Mink and a Fisher.)

"Oh yeah?"

"Yeah. I started by seeing the valley as its own entity, independent of my perspective. In my mind's eye, I then saw a Marten working her way back and forth down the hill toward the bog. See that large White Pine at the base of the point? There in one of the lower branches sat a Squirrel, who was getting nervous. He took a break from adding to his midden pile and chattered."

"Hmm, I wonder why . . ."

"You got it—the tension was building. Marten rushed Squirrel, and sure enough, he fell for the trap and fled out onto the point. In hot pursuit, Marten drove Squirrel out to the very tip, where he had no choice but to take a flying leap out onto the bog. Marten was on top of him before he could reach the Trees on the other side."

"How did you do that without reading track or sign? Was it just a daydream?"

"In a way," I reply. "There was a timeless quality to the scene, like a dream. I saw it being played over and over through countless generations, first by parent, then child, then grandchild. It was a never-ending story: Squirrel was all Squirrels who have leaped out onto the bog, and Marten was all Martens who have launched out after the Squirrels."

"There should be Squirrel tracks all over here, then," says Greg.

"Perhaps. Can you find some?"

After a very brief effort, Greg concedes. The ground is mossy—one of the hardest mediums for a novice to track small animals over. Then there are the Trees; what does a track on a Tree look like?

"What about Marten tracks?" he asks.

"Where would you expect to see them?"

"All over the place. Probably up and down the Trees, but I don't think they'd show up very well either."

"Which Tree?" I ask. It's a vitally important question when one is surrounded by thousands of them.

In my visualization, Marten showed me which Tree would show her tracks. Are they actually there? I'm not sure—I'm never sure—so I'm exploring right along with Greg. He steps back a dozen or so paces to gain perspective and Envision Marten chasing Squirrel. "I can see it," he says. "I can see what you described."

It's time for Greg to confirm what he's already seen. I'm also thinking that it will help if he can see the power of impassioned claws and feel the drama of the chase.

"In your visualization, was there a particular Tree you saw the two run up?"

He walks over to a Cedar near the tip of the point and notices some shredded bark but no clear sign of a track.

"Do you know the size of a Pine Marten?" I ask.

He gives a hint of a smile, and in short order he's picking out patterns of pin-point stabs in the bark. "This is getting fun!" he exclaims as a self-satisfied grin spreads over his face. "It's awesome!"

With that experience, Greg made a great stride toward merging visualization and reality. When he is able to do so completely, he'll have transcended the species and time barriers, granting him the ability to Become the animal.

❀ Third: Start Where We're At

What if we don't have someone like me to guide us? That could be a blessing at times, as I can get in the way more than I help. Here is an old Zen story that shows how to reawaken our Envisioning ability with what we are doing right here and now, in the absence of a guide.

Being the Animal and the Knife

A customer came in to a butcher shop and found the butcher at work slicing up an animal. "How splendid!" said the customer. "Your skill level is unbelievable—you move as gracefully as though you were dancing."

"When I was learning the trade," replied the butcher, "my focus was entirely on the animal and how I was using my knife. In time I forgot about both, because I Envisioned being the animal and the knife. After that, it was as though the knife knew where to go on its own, slipping between bones and around tendons with no effort.

"Early in my apprenticeship," he continued, "I hacked more than cut and needed a new knife every month. When I got good at the craft, a knife would last me a year. This here knife and I have been one for going on twenty years, and we have long ago lost count of the number of animals we have prepared together. When a blade has no thickness, there is plenty of room between the bones. Meeting no resistance, this knife has stayed as fine as when it was first shaped on the grindstone."

❀ Fourth: Take Animal Perspective

Many times I've come across people who stop to rescue Turtles from the middle of the road. More often than not the rescuers will carry Turtles back from where they came. When I ask why, the common reply is that they assumed the Turtles inadvertently wandered out on the road and should go back to where they were safe.

Such reasoning implies that Turtles don't know what they're doing and that we Humans have some superior intelligence and know what's best for them.

Becoming the Turtles and Envisioning their journeys would create a bridge between our understanding and theirs, which would clarify their true intent. A Turtle's life is relevant unto itself, and we can see this more clearly when we don't try to view the Turtle's needs and desires from our own mind-set.

Just as we would have a reason to cross the road, so does a Turtle. She already made it partway across unscathed, but because a Human who thought he knew better came along and put her back, she now has to retrace her steps, increasing the odds that she is going to be flattened.

When we Become the Turtle we gain automatic empathy and the potential for understanding her intention. We might then be able to truly help her, by carrying her the rest of the way across the road.

Whenever I consider doing something for others, whether they are Human or nonhuman, I first want to gain empathy. I do so by Becoming. In other words, when I want to understand someone, I step in to his shoes.

What We'll See through Animal Eyes

When we start Becoming animals we'll discover things that we can now hardly imagine. As Hawk, with the sharpest vision of all the world's animals, we'll be able to see the nervous twitch on a Rabbit's face from a quarter-mile away. We could pick up the chest-breathing movements of a motionless Rabbit from up to a mile away. So much more awaits . . .

❀ Fifth: Prepare to Become the Animal

Becoming an animal is really a story of relationship: the interplay of wind, moisture, scent, desire, and so much more. An animal acts and reacts to the forces in her life like a pinball does to the flippers, bumpers, targets, and ramps of its world. Sometimes the animal scores points, and sometimes she gets nothing. If her relationship skills are not sharp enough, it is down the hole and her game is over. When we Become her, we have the opportunity to play her game of life.

The Four Preparatory Steps

1. **Be hungry.** An animal moves around and interacts with other animals primarily in quest of food. To feel her motivating hunger, it helps for us to be hungry as well. Where a full belly numbs the senses, hunger makes animals supersensitive: they can feel, see, and hear things they would otherwise miss. We are designed the same way: we move to eat, and we move best in the skin of another animal when we are hungry.

2. **Step out of the picture** and into the shadow of our surroundings. All shadows move, and not by their own will. When we become willful and make a decision independent of our surroundings, we stick out like a utility pole in a grove of waving trees. On the other hand, when we allow ourselves to move in rhythm with the wind, we disappear and another layer of life appears before us.

3. **Don't focus on the animal.** We are striving to refind ourselves in another animal. To do this successfully, we need to let go of the belief that we are all separate beings. This can be achieved by spending time on what is offered in steps 2, 3, and 4.

4. **Let go of expectations.** As irrational and counterproductive as it might sound, letting go of our goal actually increases the odds of achieving it. When we can fully Become the animal, our perspective and that of the animal merge. Time ceases to exist, and the drive to see the animal diminishes as the experience of being her takes over. The hunter and hunted have Become one.

Sixth: Attune to the Animal's Song

Here we will gain a solid feel for Becoming. The imprint an animal leaves on her environment through their interactive relationship is called her *song*. Attuning to the song is attuning to the animal, as her identity is formed by her relationships.

To be *in* relationship with another, we need to know the full breadth of that relationship, which in this case includes the animal and her environment. We have worked a lot on both up to this point, and now we are going to refocus on the animal. For this exercise, we'll need a wild animal we can hold in our hands. She can be either dead or alive. A roadkill kept in the freezer and thawed will work, as will a tamed wild animal. (My intent here is not to encourage taming wild animals

A roadkill kept in the freezer will work.

but rather to suggest that we take advantage of an already tamed animal or volunteer at a wild animal rehab facility.)

She needs to be wild, because her unique song is connected with her body structure and form, the color and texture of her coat, the way her eyes are placed, the length of her whiskers, the fullness of her tail, the condition of her claws, and so much more. Domestic animals differ from their wild counterparts in musculature, skeletal structure, and coloration, as well as their perceptive abilities and emotional responses.

The song of a wild animal is a resonant voice in Earth's chorus, while the song of a domestic animal is discordant. It tends to pull other songs out of harmony. Yet once we become accustomed to the songs of native animals, we will be able to quickly attune to the songs of domestic animals, as they are relatively easy to hear.

✳ A Song-Attuning Exercise

1. Hold the animal in your lap.
2. Run your fingers through the animal's fur, feel his whiskers, scratch his claws over your skin, close his jaw over your fingers.
3. Envision yourself lying in your lap.
4. Envision your surroundings: the Grass brushing against your fur, the low branch that your ears barely clear as you duck under it, the soggy ground under your paws.
5. Ask yourself (now the animal) the following questions.

Physique

What are my physiological adaptations to my lifestyle?
What is unique about the bone and ligament structure of my feet?
How do my feet grip surfaces?
How do I smell to others, and from where do these odors emanate?
What is the function of my odors?
What senses do I rely on most, and why?

Seeing

What does the world look like through my eyes?
What is my range of vision?

Do I see in color?

Can I detect motion easier than shape?

Are close or distant objects easier for me to see? Why?

Is my vision focused or panoramic?

Hearing

What am I cued to listen for?

Which sounds would raise my curiosity?

What sounds would trigger my fight-or-flight response?

Which sounds would I ignore?

Habitat

How do my surroundings look at the level I travel?

Do I use regular trails, and if so, what kind of terrain do they traverse?

How and where do I procure food and water?

Where do I sleep?

Where is my lookout location?

Where do I go to find warmth or keep cool?

How and where do I find refuge when I'm frightened? In severe weather?

How do I deal with biting Insects?

Lifestyle

Am I nocturnal or diurnal?

How does it feel to touch my feet to rock, sand, mud, or water?

How do I react to threats?

How do I clean myself?

Am I a stationary or pursuit hunter? What tactics do I use?

Do I have a special way or place for relieving myself? If so, why?

Am I solitary or gregarious? How and when do I socialize?

How, when, and why do I communicate with my own kind? With other species?

When and how do I seek a mate?

When are my young born? How do I raise them?

Relationship with Civilization

How do Human land-use patterns affect me?

Am I preyed upon or persecuted by Humans?

Do I benefit in any way from Humans?

Do domestic animals factor into my life?

Now we are fully in our new form, moving, feeling, sensing, and communing with our inner being and our Hoop of Life.

Let's Walk in Our New Skin

- Feel how our fur (or feathers) varies across our body, from head to toe, from front to back.
- Stretch. Jump. Hop. Run. Curl up in a ball. Climb.
- Imagine all the possible ways to compose our song.
- Watch how our passing presence imprints on a spiderweb, on dust-covered Grass, in floodwater silt.
- Feel our ears, eyes, whiskers, footpads, and nerve endings detecting vibrations, temperature changes, and any manner of other things going on around us.

When we repeat this exercise periodically, especially after some time has elapsed, we'll find our Becoming skill growing solidly over time. Let's give these questions our deepest attention, as they are our stepping-stones to transforming an animal from something that merely leaves a trail to a sentient being, even a family member.

Use What We Have

Once we've become fairly adept at Becoming, it is no longer necessary to practice with just wild animals. Our Dog or Cat will work fine, as will a friend or child. As I did with what I gained from Birds and Wolves, you'll be able to apply what you learn to other animals.

🌸 Seventh: Become the Predator

This exercise is optional, yet I strongly encourage you to do it if you can, as it could greatly accelerate your awakening.

To get close enough to an animal to Become him, we have to know him like our lover. That means being privy to the intimate details of his life: what he likes to eat, what he does for fun, his sex life, his friends, his bathroom habits, everything. We will accomplish this with what is essentially a two-day predator tracking experience. We'll be doing it without an instructor or guide so that we can immerse ourselves completely in the experience on our own terms.

It's okay to have one partner, as long as he or she maintains the atmosphere of silence and listening as presented in steps 2 and 3. Any more than one other person tends to become distracting.

We'll need a full weekend for this exercise, from Saturday dawn until Sunday dusk, along with snow-covered or sandy ground for easy tracking. Equip with seasonally appropriate gear, as we'll be out for the entire day and might be sleeping on the trail. To keep track of observations, bring a notebook or voice recorder, along with a topographic map.

✳ *The Coming-to-Know-You Exercise*

1. **Locate land,** such as a public forest or tract of private land that you have permission to trek.
2. **Start at dawn.** Early Saturday morning, locate the fresh track of a medium-to-large predator, such as a Fox, Coyote, Bobcat, or Fisher. If you live near Wolf or Cougar habitat and you're in good physical shape (they range widely), do consider them, as their trails are easy to follow and their sign is conspicuous. (Before tracking a Cougar, read "Safety Tips in Cougar Country" on p. 275 of *Entering the Mind the Tracker.*)
3. **Record your observations.** Note every action, whether it is a change of pace, urination, nap site, or dig. Describe chases, kill sites, feeding, joining/departing from other pack members, scat contents, and anything else. Number each entry and record the number at the appropriate place on your topo map.

4. **Recap and Review.** After you have returned home and rested up, go over your map and notes point by point as you Envision being back on the trail. However, this time you are the track maker rather than the tracker. Envision every movement and every action. Allow yourself to feel what the animal would have felt: the inquisitiveness of an exploration, the exhilaration of the chase, the contentedness of a full stomach after a feast of fresh meat, the fear and curiosity of coming upon a larger predator's sign.

5. **Tell your story as the animal.** Find an audience: a friend, family members, other interested people, or just your recorder. The composition of your audience doesn't much matter, as long as you have one, as storytelling comes alive only with an audience. This final step will bring the experience to life. Tell the story in first person—"I, the Bobcat" or "I, the Coyote"—and give it convincing feeling and continuity. What you're after is the same as becoming so engrossed in a book or movie that you lose yourself to the experience and Become the character.

Becoming Brings Safety

Learn to avoid confrontation with potentially dangerous animals by Becoming them. Our first reaction to a threatening animal is usually to distance from her, yet one of the best ways to keep safe is to know her intimately. When we can think and feel like her, we will know what to do to peacefully coexist. At the same time, realize that knowing is no excuse for taking risks.

Eighth: Cultivate Healthy Human Relationships

Our patterns of behavior typically manifest in similar fashion across different areas of our lives. Whether we get involved in codependent relationships or tend toward control or victimization, we approach our relationships with animals in the same way. Our interactive patterns are often intensified with animals, because they come to us as they are, without pretense. The upshot is that we struggle to be in genuine relationship with animals, because they are their genuine selves while we are trying to conform to how others want us to be.

Our dysfunctional relationship patterns are usually learned during childhood. As we grow older, they become habitual, to the point where we project them onto others without even realizing it. How we learn to be in relationship becomes our modus operandi: we can't help but treat all relationships the same, whether they are Human or animal. An honest, straightforward relationship with an animal becomes virtually impossible.

The good news is that the more we heal our dysfunctional relationship patterns by establishing healthy ones, the better we become at relating to animals. From personal experience I came to realize that the better I developed my Human relationship skills, the more successful I was at entering into relationship with Nature. Over the years I've noticed consistently that when I made a human relationship breakthrough, it showed right away in my sense of presence and engagement with Nature.

Even if our human relationships are problematic at present, we can still enter into healthy relationship with Nature. The good news is that healing works both ways: being in Nature is healing, and what we gain there carries over to our Human relationships. Let us come to Nature as we are. We know that our relationship patterns may interfere, yet we can be encouraged by the fact that the more we heal, the deeper and richer our Becoming will grow.

❋ Ninth: Revel in the Relationship

Every relationship needs its reward, or it soon grows stale. My reward comes when the animal trail I follow mirrors mine, and I feel the direct relationship. It sends a chill up my spine—a feeling that I am being Shadowed by the maker of the track I am following. It's as though I am the Deer following the trail I've just left behind.

When you experience this feeling for the first time, you'll know right away that it's what I am describing. The disparate voices will all come together and you will hear the chorus, and it will be sweeter than you can possibly imagine.

Becoming Deer

I was once out with someone who suggested that we trail the Deer up in front of us who we had just spooked. "Why waste the time?" I replied. "I feel inside where she's headed; we can just go directly there."

The Deer was heading east, down a narrow valley, and we forked off to the south, climbing the adjacent hill.

"Are you sure you know what you're doing?" my comrade asked.

"Not really. I just listen."

We reached the crest of the hill and kept our eyes on the lowland just to the south. It took several minutes for the Deer to round the eastern point of the hill, double back on the south side, and pass below us, as he had probably five times more distance to cover than we did.

Like the mother who knows the whereabouts of her children even though she may not see them, so does the Native frequently know the location and activity of his animal kin. Even though the animal has long passed by, the Native can still often hear her song.

Native people have long been admired for their ability to move invisibly and track and hunt flawlessly. They tell me it's no big deal to walk inside the animal who laid the track. Many of us take such a statement as a sign of humility, yet it is meant as plain fact. The only thing a Native will take credit for is listening, as it is the keen eyes of Raven, the telling voices of Squirrel and Jay, and the emotional temper of Deer that do the work.

When Natives refer to the Four-leggeds, Wingeds, and Finned as "all my relations," they mean it. This is not a religion or a philosophy; it is their truth, their consciousness. When we are once more able to Become our relations, we will again be Natives.

Just as with all the other skills taught in this book, we will discover that the benefits of Becoming extend in to our everyday life. We will begin to see subtle shades of colors and pick up aromas that previously went unnoticed. The once commonplace—the nibbled plant, the scat, the coming rain—will thunder into our consciousness as we Become them without even realizing it. Yet even more important, we are now able to Become the animal within, which is the most vital part of this journey home.

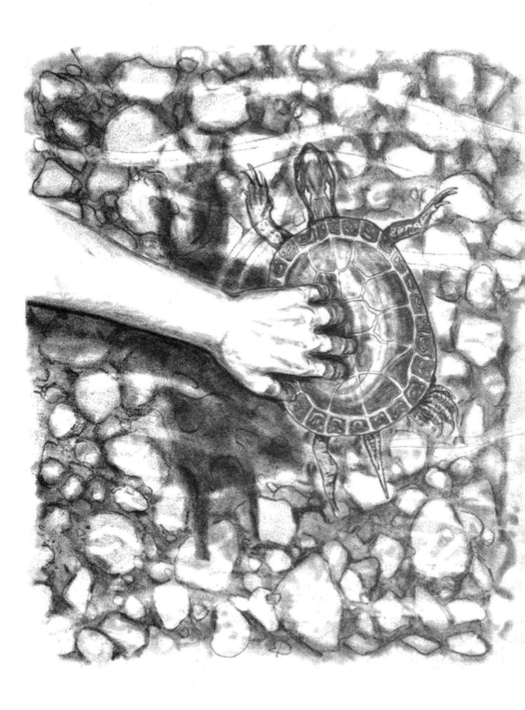

To Touch an Animal

Inattention to Attunement

The song of water riffling over the rocks of a woodland brook entices me down the hillside to take a closer look. Moving as quiet as an Owl, I keep attuned to my surroundings as I edge toward the water. Every step and every glance matters. I feel at home in the woods when I'm able to move discretely, as no more than a shadow among shadows.

Only on a sidewalk in the city could I afford to walk along with little concern for what lies before me. Here, I could trip or twist an ankle before I realized what happened. Even worse, I could miss the newborn fawn lying right beside me in the Ferns, or the Pine Marten peering warily from her den up in the old Sugar Maple I just passed.

As I step up beside a Fir Tree on the bank of the brook, my peripheral vision catches movement in the pool at the base of a downstream riffle. Going against the current, it has to be something alive. As it is lying low in the water, I take it to be either something small or the head of something large.

Whatever it might be is of no matter to me. It has to be that way, for if I show interest, I'll risk alerting the animal. I have no reason to be particularly excited anyway, as I regularly see animals in passing. When I get close to animals they usually feel comfortable with me being in their space, as the intensity of my presence is no more or less than what they would experience from their other forest kin. That's why a Coyote can saunter by a Rabbit, who will pay the Coyote no more heed than any other member of the meadow community—as long as he shows no more interest in the Rabbit than he does the Wildflowers underfoot.

Without looking, I'm fairly certain that the animal is still making her way upstream toward me. Note that I say "toward me" only to indicate her direction of travel. If I had really thought of her as coming toward me, I'd have placed myself in the center of an unfolding drama, which she would have picked up on and probably decide to no longer participate in. Instead, I stay relaxed into the bank, as though I am the trunk of an old Fir Tree rotting slowly into the needle-carpeted duff.

Why should I, or better yet, how can I, pay attention to whoever might be swimming by momentarily when so much else has my attention? Just across the stream a Pileated Woodpecker alights on the trunk of a half-dead White Pine, listening intently for the telltale gnawing of a juicy Wood Grub she might be able to chisel out. A little beyond her, in the pond hidden by the esker the Pine is growing atop, I hear the muffled nasal conversation of a pair of Canada Geese, interspersed with splashing. I can only imagine what kind of fun they're having.

Just upstream begins an Alder thicket, which is alive with the songs of Warblers newly returned from their winter retreat in the tropics. The thicket surrounds a small pond, the remnant of the lake that formed behind the esker when the glacier retreated ten thousand years ago. I imagine what the lake might have looked like before it broke through the esker and the Alders colonized its spongy bed.

The earthy smells tossed up by the frost leaving the ground underfoot draw my attention to the ruffled places where long-beaked Woodcocks probed the night before for arthropod morsels and where Star-Nosed Moles in search of the same pushed dirt up from their tunnels.

I mentioned that I was pretty sure the animal I caught in my peripheral vision had continued upstream, because if she were going to be spooked by me it would have more likely been by my approach than my presence. I worked my way down to the bank slowly and lightly, in sync with the wind-swayed Trees and their slow-dancing shadows. Not a sound or sight disrupted my flow.

If things did catch my attention, you'd never know it from watching me. A Tree answers to the breeze no matter what's happening around her, and I was no different. If I had allowed attention to lead to distraction, I'd have switched from participant to observer—a costly mistake for anyone who wants or needs to get close to animals. No longer in sync, I would have moved disjointedly and risked alerting the animals to an alien in their world.

In the Natural Realm, inattention is attention, and vice versa. If I decide that one thing is more worthy of my attention than another, I will need to divert my attention. What have I gained? The more relevant question is What have I lost? I'm happy when I can be as unobtrusive as a Tree nestled in a forest. It is not because I feel some sense of accomplishment—that would be self-defeating, as it would make me the main character of the story. Again, that would put me at risk of altering the outcome.

I'm in my bliss here on the bank of the brook, because it's my nature to be an intrinsic part of the Hoop of Life: to neither dominate nor deny myself, but rather to be a movement within the greater movement, to be a brother among siblings, to observe and be observed, to touch and be touched. I wear soft-soled moccasins and step gingerly so that I don't snap sticks or create ground vibrations. I observe with panoramic vision rather than staring. When I'm with someone else, we communicate silently, as do Wolves.

The Muskrat swims by in front of me, with her tail just breaking the water, as though it were a Snake swimming along behind her. The animal's identity comes as a side note, which is as it should be, lest I alert her with my attention. She looks this way and that, and if I didn't know better, I'd swear she's looking right up at me. I like to think that she figures she's looking at an old snag instead of me, but the truth is that she's nearsighted enough that she'd have to detect an out-of-the-ordinary sound, movement, or vibration in order to make me out as a potential threat.

She comes to within an arm's length of me. I consider Counting Coup, which in the glory days of the Plains Indians entailed touching an enemy and escaping without inflicting or incurring injury. Yet a touch would surely spook her, as I'd have to bend over to do it. It's not that there'd be anything wrong with spooking her—it could be a good awareness lesson. Still, just knowing that I could Count Coup is good enough for me. The only Contact Coup I go for anymore is when I can pull it off unawares.

A body length upstream is a hummock rising barely above water level. The Muskrat heads for it, nuzzles through the Sedge stubble, and finds a tidbit that she rolls around in her paws while nibbling at it. If I had my hunting club along and needed the food, this would be my opportunity. Again, knowing that I could do it is satisfaction enough. I have no reason to kill just to prove I can do it. Even though by Envisioning a strike I'm not actually striking, I'm still practicing the skills of the hunt that I could rely upon when I had to feed and clothe my family.

Snack finished, she slides quietly into the water and continues upstream through the breach in the esker. At this point I leave her story, along with those of the Pileated Woodpecker and the Geese, and I continue downstream for more storytellings.

COUNTING COUP: THE CONCEPT

I think there is something in Counting Coup that is intrinsic to the Human psyche. We've been hunter-gatherers for most of our existence as a species, and we have undoubtedly needed to derive emotional satisfaction from the hunt in order to continue with it. Imprinted in our DNA, the exhilaration of the stalk and outsmarting our quarry (which is essentially Counting Coup) now manifests in everything from a good mystery to a practical joke. When I pull a prank, a surprise party, or some other shenanigan, I feel the same sort of pleasure as when Counting Coup.

The Five Levels of Counting Coup

1. **Conscious Coup:** The animal knows she is being approached and touched.
2. **Scare Coup:** Approach the animal without her knowing, yet touching spooks her.
3. **Coup, then Scare:** The same as level 2, except our exit spooks her.
4. **Stealth Coup:** Touch (or nearly touch) the animal, then back-stalk (see p. 256) undetected.
5. **Mental Coup:** Envision touching the animal and exiting undetected.

The skills and awarenesses needed for Counting Coup are cumulative, so it is important to progress through the first four levels in sequence. Level 5 can be legitimately practiced only after level 4 has been executed flawlessly numerous times. Attempts at Mental Coup without progressing through the first four levels are merely fantasy. Even after reaching level 5, we need to perform Stealth Coups periodically to maintain our skill level.

For the sheer joy of it, I seldom pass up Stealth Coup or Mental Coup opportunities, whether it is on domestic animals, wild animals, or Humans. While successful hunting requires a certain level of expertise, Counting Coup calls for even more. A person who can hunt may not have the ability to Count Coup; however, someone who can Count Coup is bound to be a good hunter.

The Native Americans, prior to their subjugation, commonly practiced Counting Coup. The hunter-gatherer bands lived in a state of relative peace and stability, with minimal tension between them. Still, each band's Guardians would train to be ready for conflict, as well as for the personal fulfillment gained from perfecting and executing skills. They initiated missions to test their training, with the ultimate mission often being to descend into the bowels of danger and come back both unscathed and undetected—the ultimate Stealth Coup.

One training strategy was to brazenly confiscate an item from the lodge of a renowned Guardian from another tribe. Coup could also be counted during face-to-face conflict (a Conscious Coup) by plucking a feather worn by a Guardian or cutting off his scalp lock (a tuft of long hair tied atop the head in a conspicuous and taunting way; see illustration on p. 252) and escaping with it untouched—and still in possession of one's own scalp lock. Counting Coup was the dream of every young Guardian in training.

Standing Bear, an Oglala Lakota (Sioux) from the 1800s, left us this description of what his people called "touching the enemy":

A young warrior on meeting an armed member of the enemy tribe would throw his own weapons away, keeping for his protection only his shield. In his hand he would carry a long staff decorated with

Scalplock and Coup Feather

eagle feathers, which was a sort of flag or banner for the Sioux. With only the shield over his breast and the [staff] in his hand, he would ride close [and] . . . lightly strike the enemy's* body with the tip . . . then ride back out of danger as fast as possible.[1]

LEARNING TO COUNT COUP

Here is a skill to pull together everything that we have learned about Becoming Nature, as to be successful at Counting Coup, we need to use our attunement and awareness skills to the best of our ability.

 Tips for Counting Coup

- **Keep movements steady.** Animals key in to motion, especially when it is sudden and jerky.

---

*In the Lakota language, the term *thóka* means "alien" or "member of a tribe other than the Lakota" as well as "enemy." See Jan F. Ullrich, *New Lakota Dictionary* (Bloomington, Ind.: Lakota Language Consortium, 2011), 574.

- **Walk consciously, maintain balance, and move with Nature.** Review the natural walking section in step 8.
- **Direction matters.** Stalk into the wind, to hide our scent and disguise the noise we make.
- **Be dispassionate.** Getting pumped up on adrenaline makes us edgy and uncentered. To maintain perspective, cultivate a sense of gratitude for whatever happens by remembering that when training (which is always), failure is more valuable than success.
- **Have no expectations.** Many of my stories, including the one on page 219, illustrate this point.
- **Be prepared for any outcome.** Animals are complex beings, and Nature is filled with mystery, creating endless possibilities.

Safety First

Think twice before sneaking up on any animal and tapping him on the back. Even the smallest creature can react violently when startled, and medium- to large-size animals could inflict serious damage with slashing hooves, antlers, claws, or teeth. Be especially wary of sick or wounded animals and those breeding or with young. As with Humans, there are boundary and privacy considerations.

A Disappearing Act

The last three points above cannot be overemphasized. To be consistently successful with approaching animals and Humans, as well as maintaining respect toward them, we need to be free of passion, expectation, and surprise reaction.

Animals have ways of picking up on our expectations, even when we make an effort not to focus on them. It's best to hold off on clarifying our intention, along with waiting until the last possible moment to move or act, after we have gathered all of the available information. Otherwise the animal could suddenly bound away for no apparent reason, as happened in the following story.

Mind-Reading Deer

"I was out scouting for Deer," Tom said to me, "and I came across a buck grazing up ahead a ways. 'I think I'd like to take that one,' I thought to myself, and right away he raised his head and bolted. It's like he read my thoughts. Is that possible?"

"It's possible," I replied, "but he may not have done it directly. Your thought was reflected in the energy you radiated, which set up a disturbance pattern. It may have been transmitted through your posture or your gaze, which made you conspicuous. At that moment, your focus pulled you out of attunement and you quit Shadowing the movement around you. That may have caused the Blue Jay above you to nervously twitch, which triggered a Red Squirrel to flick her tail, which is what the Deer picked up. Or it could have been the opposite: the pocket of silence you created by dropping out of attunement became conspicuous."

"What could I have done differently?" he asked.

"Approach the hunt as a Native would," I suggested. "Rather than I want to hunt that Deer, think I might like to hunt that Deer, if it is so intended. It's the difference between putting oneself in the center of the experience and being in balance with the Hoop of Life. Rather than a simple cause-and-effect relationship, stepping back allows us to recognize the interrelationship that exists between the animals and ourselves. Young predator animals learn this very quickly, as it's the only way they can keep themselves fed."

A Game of Deception

Following are the evasive techniques I learned from Wolves, and—not so coincidentally—from playing tag as a kid. Similar to canine pups, feline kittens, and the young of many other animals, Human children worldwide play tag. It is no more than a game of Counting Coup, which is played instinctively as training for the hunt and Guardian missions.

With these techniques it's possible to get close to an animal and even Count Coup, all while remaining visible. A prey animal, accustomed to the endless flow of life before him, feels threatened only when he perceives attention being directed at him. When Prairie Wolves aren't hunting, they can stay within sight of a herd of Buffalo and be ignored.

To Delude an Animal

- **Approach conspicuously,** yet indirectly.
- **Be about some other business.** Don't just pretend, but have another goal in mind.
- **Don't be concerned about creating a disturbance,** which will allow our disturbance to be a voice in the chorus.
- **Transition in an instant** from casual, passing interloper to keened, tensed predator. If we hesitate, all we'll see is the animal's track.

Anywhere Training

The beauty of learning to Count Coup is that it can be practiced anytime and anyplace. It requires no equipment, it's always open season, and everything is fair game, whether it's people, pets, or Squirrels in the park.

Let the Animals Come to Us

I'm writing this while sitting under a Maple Tree overlooking a small woodland pond. A short while ago a Squirrel made her way silently down the trunk of the nearby Tree and peered around at me. I doubt that she knew I was aware of her. Now a Raccoon comes up to me and sniffs my shoulder. We engage in a brief, wordless communication, and he ambles on.

Letting animals come to us could appear to be the reverse of stalking, yet the two approaches require the same indifference and nonchalance. When Raccoon sniffed me, neither of us made a big deal of it. I continued with my writing as though I was unaware of his approach, so he wasn't threatened. He calmly left the same way he came.

This letting-them-approach method works because foraging animals generally have a curiosity for any disruption from the norm. They make a portion of their livings by noticing and exploiting whatever foodstuffs are kicked up by disturbances, and we can take advantage of this survival trait to lure animals to us.

To Attract Animals

- **Stir up silt in the shallows of a pond or lake** to attract small Fish that feed on the minute life-forms that reside in the pond muck. The small Fish will attract predators.
- **Use shiny objects and swatches of bright cloth,** which are irresistible to some creatures.
- **Create a brush pile, upturn a log, or mound dirt,** all of which will draw attention.
- **Plant a scent,** such as an open can of sardines or a ripening piece of flesh.
- **Act silly or out of character.** The more clever Wolves are great at hamming it up to mesmerize small prey animals.

What about Attracting Animals with Food?

When we feed animals—especially regularly—we disrupt their movement and migration patterns, create and sustain artificially high populations (which harm unrelated species), and cause animals to lose some of their survival savvy.

The Ultimate Test: The Backstalk

One reason that Counting Coup could appeal to some of us is that we come from a goal-oriented culture. When Counting Coup becomes our primary goal, our forays into Nature will amount to little more than games of Ring and Run, where children ring a neighbor's doorbell then run and hide before it is answered. Like the irritated neighbor, an animal may become stressed, and we will lose out because of our goal orientation.

As with many of the adventures I've shared in this book, I usually choose to have close-up experiences with animals in ways other than directly touching them. Along with the reasons I've already mentioned, I gain a deep sense of satisfaction from counting Stealth Coup. The reason is that I need to meet the supreme challenge: exiting without being detected. This takes proficiency in backstalking, which is retracing the steps taken to stalk into range for Counting Coup.

As tremendously challenging as Counting Coup can be, backstalking adds not just another layer of difficulty, but a whole new dimension. When moving in to Count Coup we are focused mainly in one direction: toward the animal. However, if we want to stay undetected and backstalk, we must remain attuned to the animal *as well as* to our departure route in the opposite direction.

Along with the degree of difficulty that makes backstalking so rewarding for me, I consider it a necessary skill. If I spooked Deer when Counting Coup, they'd grow all the more wary of me and I'd have trouble approaching them in the future. Due to the risk of damaging my relationships with animals, I typically backstalk only when I have a reasonable chance of success.

To learn the skill of backstalking, we start by realizing that Counting Coup is no longer our goal, but just one part of the circular flow that takes us past the animal and back to our starting point. Without this awareness it's hard to maintain attunement, as once we reach our goal of Counting Coup we typically lose our edge and relax. That does not bode well for us with backstalking, where we need to be *more* attuned than on the approach stalk.

As we are often moving backward on the backstalk and not able to see where we are going, it is akin to the blindfold exercise in step 7. Practicing that exercise will help evolve our backstalking skills.

In preparing to backstalk, take inventory of the landscape. Note any obstructions and variations in terrain that will have to be negotiated. The tips found under "Natural Walking" and "Deerstepping" in step 8 will prove helpful here. The rest is practice.

WHEN NOBLE FARE IS FAR AWAY

Many of us live in areas where the likes of Otter, Deer, and Snapping Turtle are no longer found. Yet if there is shallow water of any kind, whether it is a park pond, a forgotten patch of wetland, a roadside ditch, or even a vacant lot, there is probably wildlife. Even amid the bustle of major metropolitan areas, the residents of these tiny wild patches carry on their lives as oblivious to our existence as most of us are to theirs. I've found Turtles in ponds barely bigger than my living room, and many Frogs are happy with bathtub-size puddles.

From my earliest years, Frogs have captured my imagination. Sitting completely still while sunning themselves, they are perfectly attuned to their surroundings. That is, their immediate surroundings. With eyes designed to detect close-up prey, anything at a distance is just a blur. Yet they are aces at picking up movement: when it comes too close for comfort, they respond quickly by leaping to safety.

However, they find it difficult to detect slow movement. A predator either has to be very fast to get the jump on them, or very slow to sneak in under their radar. Snakes and Herons have become masters of the slow stalk, with a rapid strike right at the end. My brothers and I learned to do the same when we were kids catching Leopard Frogs in the tall Grass behind the neighborhood school. Nabbing them was a challenge, as they knew to jump just as we pounced. Leopard Frogs are masters of the Great Leap, which must have made us look pretty ridiculous leaping after them.

Sixty years later, I'm still after Frogs, only now it's mostly to join their world and enjoy seeing life through their eyes. I use some of the tricks I learned in childhood, such as how to get close and pass by without disturbing them. Occasionally I'll Count Coup, which I consider especially successful when I can pull off a Stealth Coup.

As with all animals, my first consideration is for the Frogs. I make sure they are mature, nonbreeding adults and that there is a sustainable population. Some species are protected, and in many areas Frog populations are declining, for reasons currently unknown.

The stalking method I use most often was taught to me by those master froggers, the Herons. They have the patience of a Tree stump and move just as quietly. They know that Frogs are designed to jump forward and are not as adept at escaping to the side or back (which is one reason they stick close to water and nearly always face it).

To Count Coup on a Frog on Land

1. **Approach to within two arm lengths,** which can usually be done without precaution. The warmer the weather, the more skittish the Frog.
2. **Stoop low** so that from the Frog's perspective your silhouette blends with the immediate background.
3. **Move slowly** to within coup-counting distance, while looking beyond the Frog and appearing as though you are going to pass him by.
4. **Extend your hand** very, very slowly toward the Frog.
5. **Touch the Frog.**
6. **Backstalk** by taking steps 1–4 in reverse, only more conscientiously.

To catch the Frog (which I still occasionally do when in need of food), bring your hand in, with fingers spread, toward her face. Just before she reaches her panic point (which you will learn by trial and error), strike quickly, pinning her to the ground. If she jumps before you pin her, it will likely be right into your hand.

When Frogs are in the water they can't be easily pinned down; however, they are easier to catch and Count Coup on than when they are on land.

 ## To Count Coup on a Frog in Water

1. **Take steps 1 and 2 above,** either on foot or by boat (see the canoe-stalking guidelines in step 8).
2. **Slip your hand beneath the Frog** by submerging your hand and ever so slowly working it into position.
3. **Gradually raise your hand,** palm up, and the Frog will sit contentedly upon it as you break water. This impresses the bejesus out of people when they first see it done.

Let's keep in mind that we can stop at any step and just enjoy being immersed in the Frogs' world. Some of us may simply want to Become the Frog, as shown in step 11. Something else to note is that whether it's a Frog or another animal, Counting Coup requires the same awareness and attunement skills. Each animal offers unique challenges and gives us a special opportunity for learning.

Above all, let's remember that we are still kids—children of Nature. It'll help us not be so self-conscious about crawling around the Lily pond in the middle of the park or the ditch along the bike trail. We might end up being an inspiration for someone passing by to join us. Other than experiencing amphibian consciousness, what better outcome could there be than helping others discover their nature by Becoming Nature themselves?

TO TOUCH THE SOUL

It's inevitable: some of us have found the process of Becoming Nature to be overwhelming, at least at times. That's beautiful, as I can think of nothing better than being overwhelmed by rejoining the Trees of the forest, the Birds of the air, and every other living thing in the splendid community of Nature. I assure you that once you reawaken to what it is to be fully Human, you will find Becoming Nature as easy as breathing. And the discoveries—the endless kaleidoscope of discoveries that await you!

What I most want everyone to appreciate and revel in is the deep relationships with our nonhuman kin that we may have never before thought possible. When we can truly step over the artificial Human-Nature boundary and embrace all of life—not just visually or poetically, but literally—we have restored heaven on Earth. It is kinship that engenders honor and respect, and it is renewed kinship that will save not only our own species, but all of life as we know it.

It is for these reasons that I have shared with you what I know about re-Becoming our world. For me, the richness of our Nature relationships comes alive all over again when we tell our stories around the evening campfire. I'd like to leave our journey together by sharing one more story that echoes what Nature has gifted me. Perhaps someday you and I will sit together around the fire and I'll get to hear some of your stories.

A Hunger for Counting Coup

The sun has reached its zenith, and I am hungry. It's been two days since my last meal, yet I'm feeling sharper than ever. I learned from the Native Elders that if you want to find something, go without it. Anyone who has been around hunting Dogs knows that a hungry Dog hunts best. The same is true with Humans: hunger sharpens the senses and hones us to peak alertness.

That's the primary reason I am going hungry. I could have equipped myself well, and there's food all around me here in the wilderness. Yet I'm most in my bliss here when I'm traveling light and fully attuned, as opposed to lazing along with a full belly and a load of supplies.

While I'm paddling along and reflecting on such matters, I glance down and there swimming by is a meal-size Turtle. She seems oblivious to me hovering over her. I'm probably just another log in the stream to her, as I'm stalk-paddling (see step 8) and creating very little disturbance. I move in rhythm with the current and the breeze, and I avoid looking directly at her.

My hand dangles in the water like a side branch of the log, with the tips of my fingers barely skimming her smooth shell. She swims on, oblivious to my existence.*

A couple of paddle strokes after the Turtle, the shadow of my canoe drifts over a large Suckerfish resting on the streambed. I pass my hand over him as though it were a wayward branch drifting in the current, while simultaneously imagining how I'd lock my thumb and forefinger into his gills if I needed him for food. I drift on by and he doesn't move.

Glancing up from the water, I quickly realize that even though I'm sculling slowly with only one hand gripping the paddle, I'm traveling faster than the unfolding situation warrants—that being my imminent collision with the broadside of a Deer. To escape the biting Flies, she's standing in the middle of the stream, where the water is deepest. I consider drawing my knife and barely touching it to her belly, both to Count Coup and practice my hunting skills.

---

*For another Turtle coup story, see pages 79–82 of *Entering the Mind the Tracker,* Rochester, Vt.: Bear & Company, 2013.

Instead, I whistle the Red-winged Blackbird's tew-tew *predator alert.*
The Deer perks up and looks around, with her gaze seeming to shoot right
over me. Does she not see me, or is she so shocked at how close I am that
she decides it's safest to play it cool? She flits up the bank and stands there
with ears perked and tail nervously twitching, which is typical behavior for
Deer who are alerted to danger but don't know what or where it is. They
are reluctant to flee, for fear of running directly into the threat.

As I paddle by, she looks down at me over her shoulder. Our eyes
meet fleetingly, which is enough for me, as I don't want to startle her any
further. I'm content to keep my smile and nod of recognition to myself.

Acknowledgments

It's unfortunate that my name is the only one to appear on the cover of this book, as it has been a collective project. "It takes all of us working together in dedication to the greater purpose that this book serves," I stated to the staff when we began. From the onset, they got behind the book, and it has been a sheer joy to work with them.

Without the eight months of effort that project editor Julie Plumitis put into shaping my rough draft into something coherent, along with working on all other aspects of production, I'd still have . . . well, a rough draft. Editor Margaret Traylor gave the manuscript a critical read-through early on that caught inconsistencies and helped structure the book. "Be heartless," I implored final editor Rebecca Lill. "Don't worry about bruising my ego—I want this book to be the best it can possibly be." I have no comment on the state of my ego, yet I will say that she was anything but heartless, as you can see by the honey-smooth flow of the text.

I didn't envision this to be a visually appealing book, yet here it is, bedecked with artwork of a caliber that you'd expect to see framed. This is thanks to the gifted hands of Jennine Elberth and Kristine Scheiner.

Yes, agents place books and negotiate contracts—which are indeed valuable services—yet the checking in, encouragement, sage feedback, and career consulting they do is equally as valuable. If it were not for Rita Rosenkranz, my agent, this book could still be sitting on the unfinished projects shelf.

To call Bear & Company a publishing house is a misnomer, as the staff works together more as an extended family. Right away they made me feel at home with them, and the quality of their book crafting—the proof of which you hold in your hand—speaks family pride.

With all of the good people who have come together to help birth this book, there is one who was there for every moment, from conception on: my mate, Lety Seibel. The range of her knowledge and ability, along with the comfort and inspiration that only she could provide, gave this project both substance and soul.

To the donors who support my writing through the Old Way Foundation, and to you, the reader, for completing the circle, I convey my deepest gratitude.

APPENDIX 1

List of Stories

APPENDIX 2

List of Exercises

Notes

IN HONOR OF MY TEACHERS

1. Paytiamo, "James Paytiamo—Acoma Pueblo," *First People.* www.firstpeo ple.us/FP-Html-Wisdom/JamesPaytiamo.html.
2. Luther Standing Bear, *Land of the Spotted Eagle,* 193.

TO KNOW NATURE IS TO BECOME NATURE

1. Horvath, Farkas, Boncz, Blaho, and Kriska, "Cavemen Were Better at Depicting Quadruped Walking than Modern Artists: Erroneous Walking Illustrations in the Fine Arts from Prehistory to Today."
2. Einstein, *Cosmic Religion,* 97.

STEP 1. REMEMBERING NATURE SPEAK, THE FIRST LANGUAGE

1. Boone, *The Language of Silence,* 96–97.

STEP 2. LEARN THE SILENT LANGUAGE OF BIRDS

1. Westneat and Sherman, "Density and Extra-Pair Fertilizations in Birds: A Comparative Analysis," 205–15.
2. Hasselquist and Sherman, "Social Mating Systems and Extrapair Fertilizations in Passerine Birds," 456–57.
3. Westneat, "Polygyny and Extrapair Fertilizations in Eastern Red-winged Blackbirds *(Agelaius phoeniceus),*" 49–60.
4. Bouwman, van Kijk, Wijmenga, and Komdeur, "Older Male Reed Buntings Are More Successful at Gaining Extrapair Fertilizations," 15–27.

STEP 3.
AWAKENING THE ANIMAL MIND

1. Vine, *God Is Red: A Native View of Religion,* 81.
2. Goleman, et al, *Measuring the Immeasurable,* 192.
3. Song, *Song of Trusting the Heart,* 14.
4. Ibid., 7.
5. Ibid., 23.
6. Boone, *The Language of Silence.*

STEP 4. THE TIME-MEDIA TRAP

1. Oulasvirta, Rattenbury, Linqyi, and Eeva, "Habits Make Smartphone Use More Pervasive," 105–14.
2. McLuhan, *The Gutenberg Galaxy,* 18.
3. Peter Bongiorno, "Your Unhappy Brain on Television," www.psychologyto day.com/blog/inner-source/201110/your-unhappy-brain-television.
4. Wu, "Goal Structures of Materialists vs. Non-Materialists."
5. Jeffres and Dobos, "Separating People's Satisfaction with Life and Public Perceptions of the Quality of Life in the Environment," 181–211.
6. Kantra, "Lost in the Tube," http://psychdigest.com/is-television-harmful.
7. Goines and Hagler, "Noise Pollution: A Modern Plague," 287–94.
8. Rugg and Andrews, "How Does Background Noise Affect Our Concentration?" www.scientificamerican.com/article/ask-the-brains-background-noise.
9. Carothers, "Culture, Psychiatry and the Written Word," 308, 310–11.
10. Begley, "Your Child's Brain," www.newsweek.com/your-childs-brain-179930.
11. Ware, "Neurons that Fire Together Wire Together," www.dailyshoring .com/neurons-that-fire-together-wire-together.
12. Ibid.
13. Bartels, "Neuroplasticity and the Brain that Changes Itself," http://sharp brains.com/blog/2008/11/12/neuroplasticity-and-the-brain-that-changes-itself.
14. Michelon, "Brain Plasticity: How Learning Changes Your Brain," http:// sharpbrains.com/blog/2008/02/26/brain-plasticity-how-learning-changes-your-brain.
15. Kuszewski, "You Can Increase Your Emotional Intelligence." http://blogs .scientificamerican.com/guest-blog/2011/03/07/you-can-increase-your-intelligence-5-ways-to-maximize-your-cognitive-potential.
16. Bartels, "Neuroplasticity and the Brain that Changes Itself," http://sharp

brains.com/blog/2008/11/12/neuroplasticity-and-the-brain-that-changes-itself.

17. Ivins, *Art and Geometry,* 5.

18. Plato, *The Republic,* 603.

19. Ivins, *Art and Geometry,* 52, 58.

20. Ong, *Orality and Literacy,* 32.

21. Ibid., 39, 43.

22. Ibid., 49

23. Ivins, *Prints and Visual Communication,* 160.

24. Innis, *The Bias of Communication,* 4, 9.

25. Ong, *Orality and Literacy,* 77.

26. Luther Standing Bear, *My Indian Boyhood,* 69.

27. Palahniuk, *Diary: A Novel,* 9.

STEP 5.
BE WHERE THE MAGIC HAPPENS

1. Luther Standing Bear, *My Indian Boyhood,* 69.

2. Thoreau, *Walden, and on the Duty of Civil Disobedience,* www.gutenberg
.org/files/205/205-h/205-h.htm.

3. Barks, *The Essential Rumi,* 36.

4. Schur, *Birds of the Different Feather.*

5. Bliss and Hasher, "Happy as a Lark," 437–41.

6. Ibid.

7. Luther Standing Bear, *My Indian Boyhood,* 7–8.

8. "Reset Your Brain for Better Sleep," www.helpguide.org/harvard/how-your-body-clock-affects-your-sleep.htm.

9. Dement, "The Effect of Dream Deprivation," 1705–7; Fisher, "Psycho-analytic Implications of Recent Research on Sleep and Dreaming, Part I: Empirical Findings," 197–270; "Part II: Implications for Psychoanalytic Theory," 271–303.

10. Sampson, "Psychological Effects of Deprivation of Dreaming Sleep," 305–17.

11. Mednick, et al., "The Restorative Effect of Naps on Perceptual Deterioration," 677–81.

12. "Napping May Not Be Such a No-No," www.health.harvard.edu/newsletters/Harvard_Health_Letter/2009/November/napping-may-not-be-such-a-no-no.

13. Price, "The Risks of Night Work," 38. Found online at www.apa.org/monitor/2011/01/night-work.aspx.

14. Ibid.

STEP 6. ENTER THE SILENCE, LISTEN, AND YOU WILL SEE

1. Jones, *Simply Living*, 35.
2. Eastman, *The Soul of an Indian*, 7–8.
3. Jones, *Simply Living*, 56.
4. Farrer, *Living Life's Circle*, 7.
5. Jones, *Simply Living*, 102.
6. Eastman, *Indian Scout Craft and Lore*, 152.
7. Ibid., 25.
8. Reynolds and Fletcher-Janzen, *Concise Encyclopedia of Special Education*, 428–29.
9. *Webster's Third New International Dictionary of the English Language*, s.v. "Look."
10. Ibid., s.v. "See."

STEP 7. ENERGIZE AND ATTUNE YOUR SENSES

1. Calaprice, *The Expanded Quotable Einstein*. Found online at http://press .princeton.edu/chapters/s6908.html.
2. Krishnamurti, "Jiddu Krishnamurti: Biography," www.egs.edu/library/ jiddu-krishnamurti/biography.

STEP 9. TURN INVISIBLE AND INSTILL NO FEAR

1. Robert Wolff (author of *Original Wisdom: Stories of an Ancient Way of Knowing*, Rochester, Vt.: Inner Traditions, 2001) in discussion with the author, June 28, 2010.
2. Eliot, *The Complete Poems and Plays*, 129.

STEP 10. THE BEST TRICKS FOR SEEING ANIMALS

1. Eastman, *Indian Scout Craft and Lore*, 20.

STEP 11. BECOME THE ANIMAL

1. Alan Howell (African conservation officer) in discussion with the author, November 2010.
2. Tony Kemnitz (special investigations tracker) in discussion with the author, March 2010.

STEP 12. TO TOUCH AN ANIMAL

1. Luther Standing Bear, *My Indian Boyhood*, 153.

Glossary

Aborigine: See **Native.**

ancestral memories: The practices and behaviors of our distant Ancestors that proved so beneficial to their well-being that they became genetically imprinted and transmitted to descendants. Also known as *genetic memory.*

Animal Mind: The brain's limbic system, which is the seat of consciousness and governs social processing, long-term memory, pain, pleasure, motivation, and the fight-or-flight response. When centered in the Animal Mind, one can think without thoughts and act without judgment.

Animal Mind consciousness: See **one/Oneness.**

at-one: See **one/Oneness.**

attunement: The sensory acuity and psycho-emotional presence that allows us to engage with what we perceive.

awareness: Cognizance of the Web of relationship that is intrinsic to our surroundings.

backstalk: The reverse of **stalk** (see definition).

Bearwalking: A method of **natural walking** (see definition) that is slow and flat-footed.

Become: To assume another identity for the purpose of gaining ıtimate knowledge of the feelings, thoughts, motivations, and circumstances of the entity.

ırcadian rhythm: The body's biological clock that regulates daily activity-rest-sleep cycles. It is made up of clusters of nerve cells in the hypothalamus, a specialized area at the base of the brain that links the nervous system to the glandular system.

clan knowledge: A group's collective intelligence, which is demonstrated when individuals pool their skills, memories, and reasoning abilities. It enables a group to function better than any member individually.

Count Coup: To stealthily **stalk** (see definition) in to touch an animal or Human without being noticed or apprehended. As practiced by Native Americans, one would gain honor by either plucking an adversary's conspicuously worn feather or cutting off his scalp lock.

Deerstepping: A method of forefoot-based **natural walking** (see definition) that allows for quick and agile movement.

dovecote: A birdhouse for Doves or Pigeons, which can range in size from accommodating several birds to hundreds.

ego: The aspect of personality that creates self-consciousness and individual identity. Ego dominance can inhibit development of relationship with other entities.

Envision: To mentally create a scenario for the purpose of discovering its characteristics or outcome without needing to directly observe or experience it.

Hoop of Life: The interrelatedness of an area's plants, animals, and geographical features. An inhabitant's immediate environmental support community. Natives live by the premise that all their needs, whether physical, relational, or spiritual, can be met within their Hoop of Life; that is, within walking distance. Also known as *Circle of Life*.

hunter-gatherer: See **Native**.

innate ability: Aptitude that is intrinsic to one's being.

invisible: Not seen, whether disguised from sight or exposed.

Native: A plant or animal living a **natural** (see definition) life in her natural habitat. Also known as *hunter-gatherer* and *aborigine*.

natural: Intrinsic to a species or system.

Nature consciousness: See **one/Oneness.**

natural walking: The method of locomotion used by Humans and animals in natural environments that allows for continual adaptation to changing terrain. Characterized by ever-changing posture and foot placement. Includes methods such as **Wolfwalking, Deerstepping,** and **Bearwalking** (see definitions). Also known as *Native walking* or *Indian walking*.

Nature Speak: The mother tongue of all life and the foundation of interspecies communication. It is the operating system for our minds and the basic lens through which we perceive our world. It is the root from which our spoken and written languages grew.

one/Oneness: A state of being where one is both deeply relaxed and keenly attuned to her surroundings. The normal functioning state for sentient creatures.

Old Way: The lifestyle and practices intrinsic to hunter-gatherers.

Shadowing: The practice of following someone and becoming her mirror image by moving, thinking, and feeling as she does.

sign: The clues of an animal's passage and activities that are read when **tracking** (see definition). Primary sign includes footprints, scat, fur, scrapes, and chews; secondary sign (also called *environmental imprint*) includes disturbed spiderwebs, altered vegetation, and waves in the water; invisible sign includes the calls and behavioral patterns of animals affected by the tracked animal's passage.

Silence: The state of active listening that is free of focused attention, thought-based thinking, and dominant voices.

song of the track: The greater voice of an animal's imprint that is comprised of **sign** (see definition), **ancestral memories** (see definition), intuitive and instinctive guidance, prior knowledge and experience, and continual questioning.

stalk: To approach or track an animal using stealth techniques and **natural walking** (see definition) so as to avoid detection.

rational mind: The seat of deliberate thought and the **ego** (see definition), it governs language and spatial sense. Found only in mammals, it evolved as an adjunct to the **Animal Mind** (see definition) to give it additional range and scope for the complexities of survival and the hunt. Also called the *neocortex* or *new brain.*

tracking: The practice of following an animal or person who is no longer in sight by reading **sign** (see definition) and listening to the **song of the track** (see definition).

Wolfwalking: A method of group travel where a leader breaks trail and the others follow in her footsteps. The leader drops back when she tires, to be replaced by a new leader. Used to conserve energy in deep snow conditions, to minimize disturbance in environmentally sensitive areas, and to disguise the number of people in a group.

Bibliography

Barks, Coleman. *The Essential Rumi.* New York: HarperCollins, 2010.

Bartels, Laurie. "Neuroplasticity and the Brain that Changes Itself." *Sharp Brains: Tracking Health and Wellness Applications of Brain Science.* Nov. 12, 2008. http://sharpbrains.com/blog/2008/11/12/neuroplasticity-and-the-brain-that-changes-itself.

Begley, Sharon. "Your Child's Brain." *Newsweek,* Feb. 18, 1996. www.newsweek.com/your-childs-brain-179930.

Biss, Renee, and Lynn Hasher. "Happy as a Lark: Morning-Type Younger and Older Adults are Higher in Positive Affect." *Emotion* 12, no. 3 (June 2012): 437–41.

Bongiorno, Peter. "Your Unhappy Brain on Television." *Psychology Today: Inner Source,* Oct. 6, 2011. www.psychologytoday.com/blog/inner-source/201110/your-unhappy-brain-television.

Boone, J. Allen. *The Language of Silence.* Edited by Paul Leonard and Blanche Leonard. New York: Harper & Row Publishers, 1970.

Bouwman, Karen, René van Dijk, Jan Wijmenga, and Jan Komdeur. "Older Male Reed Buntings Are More Successful at Gaining Extrapair Fertilizations." *Animal Behaviour* 73, no. 1 (January 2007): 15–27.

Calaprice, Alice, ed., *The Expanded Quotable Einstein.* Princeton: Princeton University Press, 2002. Found online at http://press.princeton.edu/chapters/s6908.html.

Carothers, John Colin. "Culture, Psychiatry and the Written Word." *Psychiatry* (Nov. 1959): 308, 310–11.

Cornell, Joseph B. *The Sky and Earth Touched Me.* Nevada City: Crystal Clarity Publishers, 2014.

Dement, William. "The Effect of Dream Deprivation." *Science* 131, no. 3415 (June 10, 1960): 1705–7.

Eastman, Charles Alexander. *Indian Scout Craft and Lore.* New York: Dover, 1974.

———. *The Soul of an Indian: And Other Writings from Ohiyesa.* Edited by Kent Nerburn. Toronto: Publishers Group West, 2001, 7–8.

Einstein, Albert. *Cosmic Religion: With Other Opinions and Aphorisms* (New York: Covici-Friede, 1931), 97.

Eliot, T. S. *The Complete Poems and Plays.* New York: Harcourt, Brace, and Company, 1952.

Farrer, Claire R. *Living Life's Circle: Mescalero Apache Cosmo Vision.* Albuquerque: University of New Mexico Press, 1991.

Fisher, C. "Psychoanalytic Implications of Recent Research on Sleep and Dreaming, I: Empirical Findings." *Journal of the American Psychoanalytic Association* 13, (1965): 197–270.

Goines, Lisa, and Louis Hagler. "Noise Pollution: A Modern Plague." *Southern Medical Journal* 100 (March 2007): 287–94.

Goleman, Daniel, Greg Braden, Bruce H. Lipton, Candace Pert, and Gary Small. *Measuring the Immeasurable: the Scientific Case for Spirituality.* Boulder: Sounds True, 2008.

Hasselquist, Dennis, and Paul Sherman. "Social Mating Systems and Extrapair Fertilizations in Passerine Birds." *Behavioral Ecology* 12, no. 4 (2001): 457–56.

Horvath, Gabor, Etelka Farkas, Ildiko Boncz, Miklos Blaho, and Gyorgy Kriska. "Cavemen Were Better at Depicting Quadruped Walking than Modern Artists: Erroneous Walking Illustrations in the Fine Arts from Prehistory to Today." *Public Library of Science ONE* 7, no. 12 (2012).

Innis, Harold A. *The Bias of Communication*, 2nd ed. Toronto: University of Toronto Press, 2008.

Ivins, William M. Jr. *Art and Geometry: A Study in Space Intuitions.* New York: Dover Publications Inc., 1964.

———. *Prints and Visual Communication.* Cambridge: The MIT Press, 1969.

Jeffres, Leo, and Jean Dobos. "Separating People's Satisfaction with Life and Public Perceptions of the Quality of Life in the Environment." *Social Indicators Research* 34, no. 2 (1995): 181–211.

Jones, Shirley Ann, ed., *Simply Living: The Spirit of the Indigenous People.* Winnipeg: New World Library, 1999.

Kantra, David S. "Lost in the Tube." *Psych Digest,* Jan. 2010. http://psychdigest.com/is-television-harmful.

Krishnamurti, Jiddu. "Jiddu Krishnamurti: Biography." *The European Graduate School: Graduate & Postgraduate Studies,* 2012. www.egs.edu/library/jiddu-krishnamurti/biography.

Kuszewski, Andrea. "You Can Increase Your Emotional Intelligence: 5 Ways to Maximize Your Cognitive Potential." *Scientific American,* March 7, 2011. http://blogs.scientificamerican.com/guest-blog/2011/03/07/you-can-increase-your-intelligence-5-ways-to-maximize-your-cognitive-potential.

Luther Standing Bear. *Land of the Spotted Eagle.* Lincoln: University of Nebraska Press, 2006.

———. *My Indian Boyhood.* Lincoln: University of Nebraska Press, 1988.

McLuhan, Marshall. *The Gutenberg Galaxy.* Toronto: University of Toronto Press, 1988.

Mednick, Sara, Ken Nakayama, Jose Cantero, Mercedes Atienza, Alicia Levin, Neha Pathak, and Robert Stickgold. "The Restorative Effect of Naps on Perceptual Deterioration." *Nature Neuroscience* 5 (May 28, 2002): 677–81.

Michelon, Pascale. "Brain Plasticity: How Learning Changes Your Brain." *Sharp Brains: Tracking Health and Wellness Applications of Brain Science,* Feb. 26, 2008. http://sharpbrains.com/blog/2008/02/26/brain-plasticity-how-learning-changes-your-brain.

"Napping May Not Be Such a No-No." Harvard Health Letter, *Harvard Health Publications,* Nov. 2009. www.health.harvard.edu/newsletters/Harvard_Health_Letter/2009/November/napping-may-not-be-such-a-no-no.

Ong, Walter J. *Orality and Literacy.* New York: Routledge, 2012.

Oulasvirta, Antti, Tye Rattenbury, Ma Linqyi, and Raila Eeva. "Habits Make Smartphone Use More Pervasive." *Personal and Ubiquitous Computing* 16, no. 1 (2012): 105–14.

Palahniuk, Chuck. *Diary: A Novel.* New York: Anchor Books, 2004.

Paytiamo, James. "James Paytiamo—Acoma Pueblo." *First People.* www.first-people.us/FP-Html-Wisdom/JamesPaytiamo.html.

Plato. *The Republic.* Translated by Davies and Vaughan. London: Macmillan & Co., 1891.

Price, Michael. "The Risks of Night Work." *Monitor on Psychology* 42, no. 1, (Jan. 2011): 38. See www.apa.org/monitor/2011/01/night-work.aspx.

Reynolds, Cecil R., and Elaine Fletcher-Janzen, eds. *Concise Encyclopedia of Special Education: A Reference for the Education of The Handicapped and Other Exceptional Children and Adults,* 2nd rev. Hoboken: John Wiley & Sons Inc., 2004.

"Reset Your Brain for Better Sleep: How Your Body Clock Affects Sleep."

Helpguide.Org, accessed Dec. 18, 2014. www.helpguide.org/har vard/how-your-body-clock-affects-your-sleep.htm.

Rugg, Michael, and Mark A. W. Andrews. "How Does Background Noise Affect Our Concentration?" *Scientific American,* Jan. 8, 2009. www.scien tificamerican.com/article/ask-the-brains-background-noise.

Sampson, Harold. "Psychological Effects of Deprivation of Dreaming Sleep." *Journal of Nervous & Mental Disease* 143, no. 4 (1966): 305–17.

Schur, Carolyn. *Birds of the Different Feather: Early Birds and Night Owls Talk about Their Characteristic Behaviors.* Saskatoon: Schur Goode Associates, 2013.

Song, Tamarack. Preface to *The Sky and Earth Touched Me* by Joseph B. Cornell. Nevada City: Crystal Clarity Publishers, 2014.

——. *Song of Trusting the Heart: A Classic Zen Poem for Daily Meditation* Boulder: Sentient Publications, 2011.

Thoreau, Henry David. *Walden, and on the Duty of Civil Disobedience.* Project Gutenberg, last modified 2013. HTML e-book, www.gutenberg.org/files/205/205-h/205-h.htm.

Ullrich, Jan F. *New Lakota Dictionary.* Bloomington: Lakota Language Consortium, 2011.

Vine, Deloria Jr. *God Is Red: A Native View of Religion.* Golden: Fulcrum Publishing, 1994.

Ware, Deann. "Neurons that Fire Together Wire Together." *Psychologists Guide to Emotional Wellbeing,* Oct. 8, 2013. www.dailyshoring.com/neurons-that-fire-together-wire-together.

Webster's Third New International Dictionary of the English Language, Unabridged, vol. 2. Edited by Philip Babcock Gove. Chicago: Merriam Webster, 1993.

Westneat, David. "Polygyny and Extrapair Fertilizations in Eastern Red-winged Blackbirds *(Agelaius phoeniceus)." Behavioral Ecology* 4, no. 1 (1993): 49-60.

Westneat, David, and Paul Sherman. "Density and Extra-Pair Fertilizations in Birds: A Comparative Analysis." *Behavioral Ecology and Sociobiology* 41 (1997): 205–15.

Wu, Ping. "Goal Structures of Materialists vs. Non-materialists." Ph.D. diss. Ann Arbor: University of Michigan, 1998.

Wolff, Robert. *Original Wisdom: Stories of an Ancient Way of Knowing.* Rochester, Vt.: Inner Traditions, 2001.

Index

About the Author

Tamarack Song

Tamarack Song spent most of his childhood running with wild animals, and as a young adult he lived with a pack of Wolves. There are times during those years when he talked more with animals than with people.

Now living in the Nicolet National Forest in northern Wisconsin, his yard is a certified wildlife habitat, and he manages a nature preserve. He helped pioneer the natural landscaping movement by being the first person in his state to win the legal right to convert his lawn into native prairie and woodland. Out in the woods for at least a short time every day, he says it's possible for nearly everyone to do so, either by converting a part of their yard into natural habitat or making an apartment balcony attractive to birds and butterflies.

His goal is to help everyone learn animal language who wishes to, so that they too can look into the eyes of a Wolf or just talk with the Birds and Squirrels outside their windows.

Tamarack is the director of the Teaching Drum Outdoor School and the author of several other books on nature. He can be reached at **tamarack@teachingdrum.org**, and you'll find his outdoor blog at **www.trackersjournal.org**.

About the Artists

JENNINE ELBERTH

The chapter-opening artwork was rendered by Jennine Elberth, a Michigan artist who has evolved a personal style rich in detail and symbolism. She revels in making the natural world more accessible to others with her interpretive watercolors and pen-and-ink renderings. Coming from a family of educators, Jennine also inspires through teaching.

KRISTINE SCHEINER

The instructional illustrations were created by Kristine Scheiner, a Brooklyn-based writer and artist. Her work includes book covers, coloring books, and comics. With a keen interest in biology and entomology, she writes articles on urban Insect life. As well, she appreciates the macabre and absurd. View her work at
https://www.flickr.com/photos/18279334@N08.